THE FUTURE OF CHINESE MANAGEMENT

STUDIES IN ASIA PACIFIC BUSINESS
1369-7153

General Editors: Chris Rowley, Paul Stewart and Malcolm Warner

Greater China: Political Economy, Inward Investment and Business Culture
Edited by Chris Rowley and Mark Lewis

Beyond Japanese Management: The End of Modern Times?
Edited by Paul Stewart

Management in China: The Experience of Foreign Businesses
Edited by Roger Strange

Human Resource Management in the Asia Pacific Region:
Convergence Questioned
Edited by Chris Rowley

Korean Businesses: Internal and External Industrialization
Edited by Chris Rowley and Johngseok Bae

China's Managerial Revolution
Edited by Malcolm Warner

Managed in Hong Kong:
Adaptive Systems, Entrepreneurship and Human Resources
Edited by Chris Rowley and Robert Fitzgerald

Globalization and Labour in the Asia Pacific
Edited by Chris Rowley and John Benson

Work and Employment in a Globalized Era: An Asia Pacific Focus
Edited by Yaw A. Debrah and Ian G. Smith

Managing Korean Business: Organization, Culture, Human Resources and Change
Edited by Chris Rowley, Tae-Won Sohn and Johngseok Bae

ASEAN Business in Crisis
Edited by Mhinder Bhopal and Michael Hitchcock

Migrant Workers in Pacific Asia
Edited by Yaw A. Debrah

THE FUTURE

OF

CHINESE
MANAGEMENT

Editor

Malcolm Warner

FRANK CASS
LONDON • PORTLAND, OR.

First published in 2002 in Great Britain by
FRANK CASS PUBLISHERS
Crown House, 47 Chase Side, Southgate, London N14 5BP

and in the United States of America by
FRANK CASS PUBLISHERS
c/o ISBS, 920 NE 58th Street, Suite 300
Portland, Oregon 97213-3786

Website www.frankcass.com

British Library Cataloguing in Publication Data

The future of Chinese management – (Studies in Asia
    Pacific business
    1. Management – China.
    I. Warner, Malcolm. .
    658′.00951

ISBN 0 7146 5550 3 (cloth)
ISBN 0 7146 8433 3 (paper)
ISSN 1369-7153

Library of Congress Cataloging-in-Publication Data

The future of Chinese management / editor Malcolm Warner.
    p. cm. – (Studies in Asia Pacific business, ISSN 1369-7153)
Includes bibliographical references and index.
    ISBN 0-7146-5550-3 (cloth) – ISBN 0-7146-8433-3 (pbk.)
    1. Management–China. I. Warner, Malcolm. II. Series.
    HD70.C5F88 2003
    658′.00951–dc21

                                                    2003007390

This group of studies first appeared in a special issue of
Asia Pacific Business Review [ISSN 1360-2381], Vol.9, No.2 (Winter 2002)
published by Frank Cass and Co. Ltd.

Printed in Great Britain by Antony Rowe Ltd., Chippenham, Wilts.

Contents

Notes on Contributors

Malcolm Warner is Professor and Fellow, Wolfson College, Cambridge and the Judge Institute of Management, University of Cambridge. He is the Editor-in-Chief of the *International Encyclopedia of Business and Management*, the author of a number of books on Asian management, and Co-Editor of *Asia Pacific Business Review*.

Ying Zhu is Senior Lecturer in the Department of Management, University of Melbourne. He has published extensively on Chinese industrial relations and HRM.

Ingmar Björkman is Professor in the Department of Management and Organization, Swedish School of Economics, Helsinki, and affiliated with INSEAD Euro-Asia Centre, France.

Simon Clarke is Professor of Sociology in the Centre for Comparative Labour Studies at the University of Warwick, and Scientific Director of the Institute for Comparative Labour Relations Research (ISITO) in Moscow. He has researched and published extensively on labour and employment, the workers' movement and trade unions in Russia.

Chang-Hee Lee is a specialist in East Asian industrial relations. He was active in the democratic movement in Korea, before joining the International Labour Organisation in Geneva. He now leads the industrial relations team in the ILO Regional Office for Asia and the Pacific.

Dominique Jolly is Professor of Strategy at Ceram Sophia Antipolis (France). His works on inter-firm alliances and technology management have been published by *The International Journal of Technology Management*, *The European Management Journal*, *Management Decision*, the *European Business Forum*, and *Revue Française de Gestion*.

Jan Selmer is Professor of Management at Hong Kong Baptist University. Having lived and worked in Asia for the last fifteen years, his research interest lies in cross-cultural management with a special focus on the region, and he has published extensively on these issues.

Jay Dahya is an Assistant Professor at City University of New York (CUNY). His teaching and research interests include corporate finance and international finance, and he has researched and published widely in leading journals such as the *Journal of Finance*.

Yusuf Karbhari is a Lecturer in Accounting and Director of the Asian Accounting, Finance and Business Research Unit at Cardiff Business School. He was a Visiting Professor in 2000–2001 at King Fahd University of Petroleum and Minerals, Saudi Arabia. He researches and publishes in the areas of international public sector accounting, international accounting and auditing, and Middle East accounting and finance.

Jason Zezhong Xiao is a Senior Lecturer and Joint Director of the Chinese Accounting, Finance and Business Research Unit at Cardiff Business School, and an Adjunct Associate Professor at Beijing Technology and Business University. He researches into accounting and corporate governance issues in China and accounting information systems with special reference to Internet-based corporate reporting.

Yuan Wang is a Lecturer in management at the Faculty of Business, University of Technology, Sydney. Her research examines the processes by which social values and beliefs influence managerial practice, such as trust, organizational justice, decision making and leadership styles, from a perspective of cross-cultural psychology. She has published a book on the development of business in the context of Chinese culture, *Business Culture in China* (1998).

Godfrey Yeung is a Lecturer in the School of Social Sciences at the University of Sussex. His research focuses on the socio-economic effects of globalization and liberalization in China.

Vincent Mok is an Assistant Professor in the Department of Business Studies at the Hong Kong Polytechnic University. His research focuses on industrial reform and productive efficiency analysis in relation to China.

Man-Kwong Leung is an Associate Professor in the Department of Business Studies at the Hong Kong Polytechnic University, PRC. His teaching and research interests include banking and finance in the Chinese Mainland and Hong Kong, and he has published in international business and economics journals.

Trevor Young is Professor and Head of School of Economic Studies at the University of Manchester. Much of his research has focused on the quantitative analysis of commodity and other markets, and he has published widely in international academic journals.

Introduction:
Chinese Management in Perspective

MALCOLM WARNER

Whither Chinese management? In this introductory contribution, we attempt to put the topic in perspective and then ask to what extent has management in the People's Republic of China (PRC) changed since the economic reforms were launched by Deng Xiaoping in 1978, how it has developed over the last two decades and where it now appears to be going as China enters the World Trade Organization (WTO). 'The Future of Chinese Management', the title of this collection, very much depends on both the past and the present state of practice in the field. We therefore first survey the economic background of the last two decades; we then examine the reforms that have taken place over the period; after this, we describe the various studies other contributors of these essays have set out the past, present and possible future trends of Chinese management; last, we sum up.

ECONOMIC BACKGROUND

China has experienced two decades of impressive economic growth since Deng launched the 'Open Door' policy in 1978, as the road to 'socialist modernization'. It was a bold step into the unknown but one that has paid off handsomely. Whether or not there was a well thought out strategy rather than a *pragmatic* sequence of 'feeling the stones in the water, while crossing the river', is a moot question (Naughton, 1995). Its achievements have, however, been ultimately quite remarkable, over the period as a whole. Few could have expected such an outcome in the mid-1970s, with Mao Zedong's demise in 1976, following a decade or more of turmoil (see Cheek, 2002). The economy has, for example, seen faster growth per annum than occurred in the former Soviet Union (see Nolan, 1995). While the early period of Mao's rule saw the institutionalization of the economy on Soviet lines in the 1950s (for details see Schurmann, 1966; Kaple,

1994), followed by the upheavals of the 'cultural revolution' in the 1960s, Deng's legacy has been one of reform and consolidation in the late 1970s and after. He explicitly promoted the building of market socialism 'with Chinese characteristics', an economic leap forward but within recognizable, older (often traditional) cultural parameters (see Yao, 2002). It was a further step towards Westernization (Gregory, 2003) and its 'search for modernity' (see He, 2002) but still holding on to 'Chineseness'. In embarking on this, China was to evolve new *institutional norms*, ones that enabled it more or less successfully to effect *systemic* change, particularly in its economy and management (see Scott, 2002).

The outcome has far exceeded even the expectations of China's leaders since reform became the order of the day, as well as those of Western observers, in this regard. Some economists now see the country as a potential 'economic superpower', such as those in international bodies like the World Bank. By the year 2020, its economy may rank *second* in the world, after the US (see Newton and Subbaraman, 2002).[1]

The Chinese man and woman 'in the street' have clearly benefited, some probably much more than others. Living standards for most of them have improved greatly in recent years but the distribution of wealth and well-being has been uneven and many as we shall see have lost their jobs. Those in urban areas have done better than those in rural ones; most urban workers have benefited vis-à-vis most peasants. But 'relative deprivation' is now the operative concept in analysing the uneven welfare outcome. A 'new middle class' of consumers, possibly over 150 million, those enjoying the fruits of the past two decades, is now visible in this scenario, particularly in Beijing and Shanghai as well as in many of the big Eastern coastal towns and cities. Even within the cities, there are more gains for some than others. Indeed, income inequality has been stretched and the 'Gini coefficient' (measuring income-distribution) is now bigger (around 0.4, some say even higher[2]) than it was under Mao (around 0.2) and apparently converging with that of other East Asian countries (see World Bank, 2000).

The heady days of growth at very fast rates of economic expansion per annum, at least on paper, one might have thought, have now passed. But China has seen further relatively impressive economic growth since the mid-1990s under the leadership of the former Prime Minister, Zhu Rongji and now retired President, Jiang Zemin.[3] The growth rate has stayed high but a little weaker than in the previous decade (it grew at nearly 10 per cent per annum on average over the last two decades). Whilst the management of the economy has seen its ups and downs, with continued indebtedness especially in the state sector and deflation in the marketplace, China has continued to grow faster than most of its Asian neighbours, many of which have not fully recovered from the 1997 economic and financial crisis (see Ip *et al.*, 2000).

The Hong Kong Special Administrative Region (HKSAR) handed over to the 'Mainland' by the British in 1997 has seen few better days since, with a depressed stock market, negative equity and rising unemployment. Singapore is also in the doldrums economically and Taiwan is not doing much better.

China's economic record has been questioned by those sceptical of its official figures. But in terms of the official statistics, Gross Domestic Product (GDP) per capita is now much larger than half a decade ago, if we take the five years from 1998 onwards (see Table 1). In this half-decade, the economy grew impressively. Between 1998 and the end of 2002, GDP per capita went up from just over US$750 to just under US$1000. Spending power of its citizens was boosted impressively. If in 2002, in nominal terms, it was somewhat under US$1,000, it was much higher than this in *purchasing power*, possibly three to four times so, according to World Bank estimates (see World Bank, 2000). Deflation has led to price cuts in the shopping malls and street markets; 'black money' changes hands extensively. Taxes are low or even flouted. 'Conspicuous consumption' is even more noteworthy in

TABLE 1
CHINESE MACROECONOMIC STATISTICS 1998–2003

GDP(US$bn)	1998	946.3
	1999	991.4
	2000	1080.0
	2001	1157.3
	2002	1236.0 (f)
	2003	1331.6 (f)
GDP per capita (US$)	1998	758.2
	1999	787.4
	2000	853.2
	2001	907.1
	2002	961.7 (f)
	2003	1029.0 (f)
Population (mn)	1998	1248.1
	1999	1259.1
	2000	1265.8
	2001	1275.8
	2002	1285.2 (f)
	2003	1294.1 (f)

Sources: Miscellaneous
f = forecast

its scale in cities, like Shanghai. But even elsewhere, living standards have also risen in real terms for most people, if relatively more slowly over the period.

MANAGEMENT REFORMS

Over the past two decades, Chinese management has undergone a number of major transformations. While Mao was still leader, the system was based on the *Soviet model* as they understood it (see Kaple, 1994) with a 'cadre management' policy firmly in place.[4] After 1979, when Deng introduced the fore-mentioned 'Open-Door' strategy and 'Four Modernizations' (of Agriculture, Industry, Science and Technology, and Defence) policy, a new kind of management was evidently required to implement these changes. The former policy of opening the door was predicated on greater trade with the outside world, then leading on to the latter reforming the four main sectors of the Chinese economy, noted above. It may have been designed as a major attempt to transform the China's strategy and structure but as we have suggested it was 'pragmatic' and even piecemeal. The 'Four Modernizations' had originally been set envisaged by the earlier Prime Minister, Zhou Enlai, who like Mao Zedong, died in 1976 but whose project had not yet been launched. In order to best bring about these at best pragmatic 'strategic choices' (see Child, 1994) specific enterprise and management decentralization policies were implemented in the mid-1980s. The economy thus gradually evolved from a centrally planned model to one based on market socialism (Naughton, 1995).

Over the same period, Chinese industry and its management has, on the face of it, been dramatically reformed. State-owned enterprises ('owned by the whole people', in the official jargon) had formerly been the supporting arch of Chinese industry since the 1950s (see Walder, 1986). They had been built on what they Chinese thought were Soviet lines (see Kaple, 1994), if adapted to Chinese circumstances. The state firms – state-owned entreprises (SOEs) – were and are still mainly found in major industrial cities like Beijing, Dalian, Guangzhou, Shanghai, Shenyang, Wuhan, and so on. They were, and still are in many cases, big employers of labour and therefore provided a livelihood for millions of Chinese urban workers (Lu and Perry, 1997). They once contributed the lion's share of China's industrial production. Large and medium-sized SOEs in this sector accounted for nearly 80 per cent of the bulk of total gross value of industrial output in 1978 but their total is now down to around 20 per cent (and possibly even less) of this, although it had been growing in absolute terms. Employing over 100 million workers in all by the late 1990s, state firms were regarded by some Chinese and most Western economists as a drag on the economy as they were deemed both *inefficient* and *over-manned* (see Warner, 1995). At least 40 per cent or possibly more were said to be 'in the red' by the end of the 1990s and many are now to be sold off or made bankrupt. In these firms were to be found the mainstay of Chinese labour–management relations involving the 'iron rice bowl' (*tie fan wan*) system – providing jobs for life and 'cradle-to-the-grave' welfare – but this arrangement is now in question (see Ng and Warner, 1998; Warner and Ng, 1999; Ding *et al.*, 2000; 2001; 2002). 'Downsizing' is now the order of the day (O'Neill, 2002).[5]

The so-called 'lifetime' employment system was generally seen, by most Western observers at least, to be associated with weak management and in order to remove factor-immobility and inefficiency, many said that it had to go (see Warner, 1992; 1993; 1995). The general view of such experts working on China as an academic field of study was that the entrenched form of management was often highly wasteful and thus was holding back economic development.

Deng then set in train a major reform of the managerial status quo in 1984 for example, followed by the 1992 personnel reforms. Managers were now allowed more autonomy, particularly in SOEs to hire and fire; decision-making was to become more decentralized, in not only personnel but also marketing and purchasing domains. The role of the Party in enterprise decision making was reduced. The most important reforms were certainly designed with factor-rigidities in human resources allocation in mind. This set of changes has now become the new orthodoxy in Chinese enterprises with different ownership forms, although less so in many of the remaining SOEs.

Some state firms have become very successful businesses and 'brand-leaders', like *Haier* or *Legend*; a minority of 'star players' such as these have been corporatized and even been floated on the stockmarkets as 'red chips', both at home and/or abroad. Western-style HRM is slowly being introduced into this kind of company, as it is already established in the larger International Joint Ventures (IJVs) like *Beijing Jeep* and Wholly Owned Foreign Enterprise (WOFEs) like *Motorola*. In the non-state sector, managers are more than likely to 'call the shots'; unions, there, are weak or non-existent.[6]

Since 1978, with the 'Open Door' policy, China has been regarded as a potentially lucrative target for foreign companies. Since 1993, it has consistently received inflows of Foreign Direct Investment (FDI) second only in value to America. A decade ago, this inflow of funds into China amounted to 18 per cent of all FDI going into Asia; but by the turn of the millennium, the proportion had increased to 60 per cent. There is little doubt that FDI has not only led to the transfer of 'hard' technology to China, but also to the importation of 'soft' managerial skills. But it has been an uphill struggle and many parts of China, their enterprises and their managers have seen limited benefits from this, particularly in the inland provinces and cities.

Until 1993, 'entry options' for foreign companies were limited by the State (but all this is now in process of changing with WTO entry) and the prime vehicle for such investment in China was the international joint venture (IJV). The number of such ventures in China peaked at over 54,000 in 1993, and by 1996 less than 25 per cent of this number was still functioning. A year later, the WOFE had become the dominant entry mode for foreign enterprises in China (see Chinese Statistical Yearbook, various). By the end of 2002, China had drawn in a total of over US$500 billion in capital investment from foreign direct investment since 1978. Despite the relatively large number of IJVs that have been formed in China, and their continuing use, this investment vehicle is less *de rigueur* and wholly-owned foreign firms are becoming more important.

The 'private firm' has now returned to China as a major economic phenomenon (Garnaut, 2002). The allegedly privately-owned part of the economy has now grown to be a significant producer and employer, with the state-owned enterprise sector shrinking *pari passu* by 2002, to well under 25 per cent of industrial output. There is today a wide range of firms with greatly contrasting ownership and governance structures, some indeed ambiguous.

For example, some firms claim to be 'collectively-owned' in order to be seen to be 'politically correct' – in the guise of the so-called red-hats – but are often essentially in private hands (see Ding *et al.*, 2001; 2002). Urban and rural collective enterprises now run to just under 40 per cent of industrial output, firms with foreign investment such as joint ventures produce over 15 per cent, and ostensibly private firms over 20 per cent. Except for a few SOEs, all these firms gain resources and sell outputs through markets (see Warner, 1999).

Thus, it is evident that much has changed in terms of both the economy and management since the dire uncertainties of Mao's death and the early, pragmatic reforms of Deng. The post-1978 'Long March' from command economy (see Schurmann, 1966) to market socialism (see Naughton, 1995) in just over two decades has been a 'sea-change' of major proportions.

CONTRIBUTIONS TO THE DEBATE

In this collection of essays, we cover a wide range of topics including human resource management, industrial relations (IR), joint ventures, corporate governance, WTO entry and so on, highlighting the two decades of change referred to above. The contributors hail respectively from Australia, Britain, China, Finland, France, Hong Kong, Sweden and the USA, amongst others. They are an interdisciplinary group of management scholars, some in economics departments and others in business schools. We present the essays on these 'cutting-edge' themes as possible pointers to *future* trends in Chinese management. We do, nonetheless, at this juncture, offer a disclaimer against over-simplistic extrapolation of past and present trends forward. We hope to show in our concluding essay how we think the various strands of research tie together into a meaningful *gestalt*.

Starting off the sequence, the study by Malcolm Warner and Ying Zhu examines the management of human resources in two Chinese cultural settings, namely mainland China and Taiwan. Based on the illustration of the relationships between cultural tradition, and other social norms such as political, economic and historical factors on the one hand and formation and transformation of HRM on the other hand, they compare and contrast the similarities and differences of HRM policies and practices in mainland China and Taiwan. A number of characteristics that are clearly 'Chinese', such as collectivism, harmony, loyalty, quality of leadership and hierarchy, and strategic thinking can, for instance, be found in both management systems. Those characteristics are reflected in their HRM, such as group-oriented production activity (teamwork), group-based performance evaluation and incentives, relatively close salary gap between management and employees, co-operative and harmonized labour management relations, and seniority-based wage system (in particular during the pre-reform systems).

However, though the two economies respectively enjoy greater 'labour market flexibility' in admittedly varying degrees, the authors concede, this may vary between the economies with stronger state support and those with less, and with different political, economic and social environments, the authors argue. In China, the 'iron rice bowl' system is being phased out, more or less, as the economy enters an era of greater openness in its product and factor markets, with WTO entry and accompanying a flood of foreign direct investment. Many performance-driven rewards systems were adopted, in the 1980s and 1990s, by the nominally socialist mainland state. Social security has also been diluted – with the demise of the 'iron rice bowl' – and is now dependent on individual workers' contributions added to by the employers. Collective contracts offer the prospect of a nascent collective bargaining system. More multinationals will establish their business operations in China and the so-called 'international standardized HRM' policies and practices will be implemented in their Chinese ventures with certain modifications now and in the future, they argue. On the other hand, increasing unemployment and redundancy (the so-called off-post *xiagang*), floating population (*mangliu*) and disparity among its population and between different regions has raised more difficulties for its reform agenda (see Warner, 1999; 2000; 2002).

In Taiwan, although its economy has enjoyed a better outcome in terms of coping with the negative influence of the Asian crisis of 1997 and the latest global economic slow-down compared with other 'Asian Tigers', high unemployment and low economic growth have also been common in recent years since that date. A number of firms have relocated their major business operations across to mainland China. Lack of confidence in Taiwanese Democratic Progress Party (DPP) government did not help improve the economic situation and efforts to keep good relationship with the mainland has led to greater capital outflows from Taiwan and less foreign direct investment inflow into its economy. Insecurity in Taiwan also puts at risk the opportunities for further SOE reform and restructuring of family-based Small and Medium-sized Enterprises (SMEs). In this regard, HRM policies and practices are also under pressure.

The above are the main comparisons and contrasts that have affected the respective paths of HRM development in the two economies, Warner and Zhu argue. New political environment, reformed legal frameworks and economic pressure have added new dimensions of HRM and offer pointers as to future trends. However, the evidence shows that traditional Chinese culture (see Warner, 2000) has had a profound influence on HRM policies and practices, as well as political, economic and historical factors. The argument from 'culture' would point to greater 'family resemblances' (see Warner, 2002). Hence, an ongoing and increasing 'relative convergence' or even possibly 'cross-vergence' (values overlapping between cultures) with 'Chinese characteristics', is to be found in this study that is different from the main streams of current debates on both sides: the convergence approach based on globalization/universalism and institutional theory versus the divergence approach based on diversity (for the details of these two positions, see Braun and Warner, 2002).

After this, Ingmar Björkman sets out his study of HRM in foreign firms in China and how this influences wider management behaviour. There is a long-standing debate about the impact of multinational corporations (MNCs) on the host country. Most of this discussion has been on the direct economic implications of multinational firms. In spite of calls for research into the influence of the organizational patterns of multinational enterprises on host countries, there has been much less work on the impact of foreign firms' operations on non-economic aspects of the local society. The question addressed in this study is how Western corporations through the HRM practices that they introduce in China more and more influence the practices adopted by Chinese firms.

Already several decades ago, it was proposed that the process of industrialization and the spread of modern technologies would lead to a convergence of economic systems and across countries. The 'convergence' hypothesis has fuelled extensive debate also within the field of HRM, argues the author. Proponents of the convergence hypothesis propose that there is a tendency for countries to become more alike in terms of HRM policies and practices under the impact of globalization and the emergence of international 'best practices'. Although numerous studies have shown that considerable differences in HRM remain across countries due to cultural and institutional factors, also within Asia, there are clear indications of some degree of convergence taking place. In this contribution, the author argues that MNCs through their activities in Asia significantly contribute to the diffusion of Western-style HRM practices among local corporations and that this is a trend that is likely to progress further.

Knowledge about the factors contributing to the introduction of Western-style HRM in China is still limited. Although several foreign scholars have described and analysed some of the changes taking place in Chinese HRM (or 'personnel management') during recent years, there is a paucity of research on the way in which Western corporations through their practices have induced changes in the Chinese society, according to this contributor. Notably, Western companies are likely to contribute to the diffusion of Western-style HRM practices and policies among local Chinese organizations. In his paper, Björkman uses two selected HRM practices, performance appraisal (or 'management') systems and performance-based compensation, to illustrate the effects that Western multinational corporations may have on local business practices in future.

In doing this, the author hopes to develop testable propositions that can be used as a foundation for future empirical research. He first reviews research on Chinese performance appraisal and compensation systems and how these systems tend to differ from Western HRM practices. The subsequent section examines research into the HRM practices in Western-owned units in China. He then argues that the institutionalization perspective provides a useful theoretical lens for understanding the diffusion of business practices. Drawing on the institutionalization perspective, he develops a range of propositions concerning factors influencing the spread of Western-style HRM practices among Chinese firms. To conclude, he suggests possible avenues for future research, including the potential impact of Western-style HRM practices on changes in local values.

In their contribution, Simon Clarke and Chang-Hee Lee review the first stages of the implementation of the new system of 'tripartite consultation', introduced into China in August 2001. Previous commentators have suggested that the subordination of trade unions and employers' associations to Party-state control is a fundamental barrier to the development of effective tripartite institutions and real social dialogue. The hypothesis, to be explored in the study, is that it may turn out to be precisely the requirements of 'true social dialogue' that provide the lever that will induce the Chinese government to concede greater freedom of representation to employers and employees, so that China is able to develop industrial relations institutions similar to those of developed capitalist societies. On the basis of an analysis of the practice of tripartite consultation, both at national and municipal levels in the period of its introduction, the authors identify three principal barriers to the achievement of 'real social dialogue'. First, they examine the limited terms of reference of tripartite consultation, which is confined to the areas of responsibility of the Ministry of Labour and Social Security and so is not able to address broader policy issues, particularly those with financial implications. Second, they look at the potential duplication of the established methods of dispute resolution, with the risk of undermining the latter. Third, they review the limited representative base of the three parties. The China Enterprise Confederation (CEC) and the All-China Federation of Trade Unions (ACFTU) have not developed representative structures, have limited penetration of the non-state sector and remain subject to the direction of the Party-state. Nevertheless, there is clear evidence, according to the authors, that both organizations are making a concerted effort to enhance their status as representatives of the employers and employees and to broaden their representation from the state sector to embrace all sectors of the national economy. The issue of the degree of independence of both of the parties remains a matter of intense internal debate, the eventual outcome of which it would be too early to judge.

The review of this important development concludes that it is premature to characterize tripartite consultation as a developed system of social dialogue but identifies the main barrier to the achievement of such a system, not as the control of the Party-state, so much as the dependence of the trade union on management in the workplace. This is a barrier to the ability of the trade unions to articulate the interests of the members, in the absence of which management has no incentive to represent its interest as an employer in opposition to the trade unions. This is by no means a problem unique to China, or even to those countries in which government is under the control of a single party. For this reason, China has much to gain from the international experience of the International Labour Organization (ILO) and the ACFTU from international trade union co-operation vis-à-vis present and future developments.

Next, in his empirical study on Sino–foreign joint ventures, Dominique Jolly argues that knowledge sharing and decision-making have become topical areas of research in the past few years. Two issues related to such processes are raised in the paper. The first is to examine how the power of decision making is shared. Contrary to wholly foreign owned enterprises, equity joint ventures have at least two partners. Research has shown that partners want to exert management control on the joint venture's strategy so as to ensure the most effective use of the resources pooled into the joint venture. This research is based on the distinction between three types of decision: strategic, functional and operational. Jolly argues that the higher the decision level in the hierarchy, the more the power of decision is shared by the two partners. The second issue relates to resources pooled by the main players. Research has shown that partners of Sino–foreign joint ventures pool resources of different kinds, he argues: the Chinese one brings locally available resources such as physical assets, human resources, local connections, etc., while the foreign one contributes resources that can be more easily transferred from one place to another, such as technological resources (hard and soft), managerial abilities and brand image. This situation means that these joint ventures are 'exogamic' partnerships. It has also been demonstrated that there are significant inside and outside flows of knowledge between the partners' organizations and the joint venture. Each partner is trying to capture knowledge from the other. The objective of Jolly's contribution is to explore the barriers and incentives to these flows of knowledge. He hypothesizes that knowledge transfers are hampered by *exogamic* barriers but are stimulated by business incentives.

Data was collected by Jolly in 67 equity joint ventures mostly in the Shanghai area. Foreign partners originated mainly from the USA and Europe. Semi-structured face-to-face interviews were conducted with a majority of Chinese managers. Bias was eliminated from the issues raised in this study by the use of open questions. The data collected showed that the distribution of roles for decision-making observable in Sino–foreign joint ventures is no different from the traditional pattern existing in the West: the board of directors deals with strategic decisions, company general managers with functional decisions and department heads with operational decisions. Interestingly, and contrary to the hypothesis, strategic decisions are not taken jointly, but are dominated by the foreign partner. Examination of barriers and incentives to knowledge exchange showed that exogamic differences between Chinese and foreign partners tended act as barriers. These differences encompass cultural and language differences, different approaches to management as well as unwillingness to share technology. By contrast, Jolly concludes, business perspectives act as incentives in this dynamic of knowledge transfer that can be a pointer to the future.

In a contribution by Jan Selmer on 'expatriate managers' in China, he argues that many firms prefer parent country nationals to manage their overseas operations but typically face a shortage of such employees with the required international skills and knowledge for international operations. Difficult to explain why, the literature on third-country nationals has mostly focused on aspects of compensation and benefits of such employees while staffing issues have been largely neglected. One reason for making use of third-country nationals is their supposed superior cross-cultural effectiveness, but no study is known to have compared how third country and parent country nationals adjust to a foreign cultural context. Accordingly, the purpose of his study is to compare the degree of adjustment of these two groups of expatriates in the same host location, China. Since third-country nationals are often 'regionalists', that is, thought of as being the most suitable candidates to fill higher positions in countries in the same region, the study makes a distinction between Asian and Western third-country nationals. Hence, three expatriate groups in China are compared: Asian, Western third-country nationals, and Western parent-country nationals.

This is an important investigation for several reasons. First, a crucial assumption in using third-country nationals is examined by this investigation. Do they really have superior cross-cultural skills compared with parent country nationals? Second, the reason for the regional character of third-country national assignments is examined. Are regional third-country nationals better adjusted than their non-regional counterparts? China, as the place of investigation, is an important current and potential market for Western and other international business firms, further accentuated by China's entry into the World Trade Organization. China has a huge need for foreign investment. However, establishing operations in China may constitute more than a financial challenge to foreign firms. China is distinctly different from most other countries. From a Western perspective, China is frequently regarded as the most foreign of all foreign places. Chinese culture, institutions, and people may appear completely baffling. This makes China a challenging destination for Western business expatriates, and their need for effective cross-cultural skills appears to be substantial. Hence, China is a suitable host location for comparing the extent of adjustment among different groups of business expatriates. Data on the adjustment of Asian and Western third-country nationals as well as Western parent-country nationals were extracted from mail surveys directed to business expatriates assigned to China. Answering the two initial questions, the results show that third-country nationals do not necessarily have superior cross-cultural skills compared with parent-country nationals. Selmer argues that the reverse may be true for regional third-country nationals in terms of work adjustment. Second, regional third-country nationals may not be better adjusted than their non-regional counterparts, or even parent-country nationals. In fact, regional third-country nationals may be even less well adjusted to their work than both the other groups of expatriates. Although primarily concerning foreign companies in China, Selmer concludes that these insights may also comprise a powerful message for the future to globalizing firms in general not to take anything for granted when composing their international workforce in the future.

Next, the study by Xiao *et al.* dealing with company law in China, notes the requirement that Chinese listed companies have to adopt a two-tier board structure, consisting of a Board of Directors (BoD) and a Supervisory Board (SB). Both the BoD and the SB are appointed by, and report to, shareholders. This corporate governance system is markedly different from the Anglo–American unitary board model. It is not the same as the Germanic two-tier boards either. Unlike German supervisors, Chinese supervisors are not empowered to appoint and dismiss directors and executives. So far, the Chinese Supervisory Board has attracted little research attention partly because the SB is regarded as being ineffective. However, if the Chinese Supervisory Board is deemed to be ineffective, there is then a strong case to subject it to rigorous examination. Such research could uncover the reasons why this is the case and point to ways to improve the functioning of corporate governance in general and the SB in particular.

The team examined the function of the SB in Chinese listed companies. The focus is on the main problems facing the SB as well as the likely causes and consequences of these problems. The study also seeks to find possible remedies. The transitional nature of the Chinese economy implies that market-oriented institutions are emerging and the influence of the traditional planned economic system continues. Therefore, the study hypothesizes that, due to the transitional nature of the Chinese corporate sector, problems and difficulties exist which inhibit the effectiveness of the Supervisory Board in Chinese listed companies. To assess this hypothesis, they undertook face-to-face semi-structured interviews with directors, supervisors, and senior executives in 16 Chinese listed companies. They also interviewed four separate expert panels comprising financial analysts, academics and securities regulatory officials in Beijing, Shanghai and Shenzhen.

Consistent with the hypothesis, the study finds that lack of legal power, lack of independence, lack of technical expertise, perceived low status, information shortage, and poor incentives are the major problems facing Chinese SBs. Some of these problems arise from imperfections in the corporate law while others exist because of the continued influence of traditional governance mechanisms such as government control over, and intervention into, corporate affairs.

The research argues that the Supervisory Board should be an important governance mechanism in China in the future because of the contradiction between government direct interventions into corporate affairs and the spirit of economic reform, because of the need for balancing the power of insiders who control most listed companies, because of the lack of a market for corporate control, and because of the young audit profession which is perceived to lack independence. The authors propose that SBs be given additional powers as well as granting greater independence by amending company law in future. The legal responsibilities of the SB should be clearly prescribed. They also argue that further economic and political reforms are needed to reduce government control over corporate affairs. In addition, China may consider replacing the two-tier board with a unitary board or incorporate some of its elements into the two-tier board structure.

Following this, Yuan Wang looks at building 'trust' in specific ownership contexts in her contribution to the debate on Chinese management, in the context of the economy being one of the world's fastest growing economies during the 1990s. China's entrance into the World Trade Organization, she continues, is accelerating this phenomenon. More and more multinational companies seek strategic alliances among Chinese enterprises. A major challenge for them is to understand changing and complicated operating systems that have been introduced by China's economy reforms. Currently, state-owned, collectively owned, privately owned and international joint venture forms coexist in China. There is an increasing necessity for foreign investors to comprehend Chinese staff at management level in specific ownership contexts, as localization of foreign-invested companies have become a crucial issue.

Building trust, Wang argues, involves the trustor in multiple processes of calculation, predication and perception about the trustee's intentions and capacity. This research tests and compares the dimensions of managerial trust in employee dependability, predictability and good faith in the context of various ownership forms. These include collectively owned, privately owned and international joint venture forms in China. They are characterized by varying averages of employee quality and autonomy of human resource management, that in turn provide references to managers' trust-building strategies with respect to their employees.

Based on an investigation of 310 managers drawn from Northern China, this research study contributes empirical evidence to support the proposition that the trust placed by management in employees varies in divergent ownership models. Holding an autonomous right to recruit employees, managers in privately owned enterprises (POEs) develop the strongest sense of trust in the predictability of their subordinates, compared with managers in the other two types of ownership. This may indicate that although business conditions are extremely competitive in POEs, managers trust their employees as predictable, as long as they can influence recruitment. Managers in collectively owned enterprises (COEs) develop the lowest trust in employees. Historically, COEs have played a unique role in China's economic transformation since the early stages of China's economy reform. However the findings of this study may be an indication that they need to foster positive managerial beliefs of trust, which in turn favour effective motivation, so that increased long-term growth becomes sustainable over future years. The findings of the present study indicate that Chinese managers in IJVs are developing positive managerial beliefs and attitudes in operation; these are favourable to trust in employees and collectivism.

Managerial values have been identified by the author of the contribution as a useful tool for understanding people's perceptions and behaviour vis-à-vis 'trust' in the literature. The managerial values of 'power distance' and 'collectivism' are found in this study to have an effect on the development of trust by management in these forms of enterprises. The findings suggest that power distance has a negative effect on these managers' trust in employee predictability. They provide empirical evidence for a specific aspect of trust to support previous research that people placing a high value on allegiance to authority are likely to show low levels of trust with lower status. The findings of this study also suggest that the value of collectivism is positively related to trust in predictability, dependability and good faith. These findings support the proposition that collectivism promotes the aspect of trust in predictability. Collectivism, the author concludes, facilitates the development of managers' trust in employees in the context of China's current economic reforms, a possible lesson for future policy.

Entering the WTO will test the metal of China's managers over the coming years. Based on 31 case studies, the contribution by Godfrey Yeung and Vincent Mok argues that the skills of managers in Chinese manufacturing firms will be severely pressed in four specific areas, now that China has embarked on globalization. First, managers have to prepare for trade disputes with the importing countries like the United States which are still treating China as a 'non-market economy' during the 14-year transitional period. As a number of less developed countries (LDCs) are relying on low value-added exports, managers will have to develop contingency measures for trade disputes with competitor countries, both developed and less so. No matter how efficient the WTO resolution mechanism for trade disputes, the reality is that managers are either without the resources to fight allegations of dumping, or will have to divert valuable resources from product and market development, which will have significant implications for the long-term competitiveness of a firm. Second, managers are upgrading and localizing the value-added chain of their products and diversifying their markets to minimize the potential effects of trade disputes and improve the firms' competitiveness from the onslaught of competitive products manufactured or imported directly by MNCs and their subsidiaries. Managers of Sino–foreign IJVs will have to persuade their bosses at headquarters to transfer advanced manufacturing technology for the latest products to the IJVs, as China is not just a cost-effective manufacturing base for labour-intensive, low value-added products alone. Moreover, they have to guard the transferred technologies from piracy, and thus their competitive advantage over their competitors. Third, WTO accession not only accelerates the processes of management localization, but also highlights the importance of 'getting the strategy right' – to decide on the appropriate localization strategy and the pace of its implementation.

For general and human resources managers, the goals are to maintain a harmonious working relationship between expatriates and locals, and between overseas Chinese and mainland Chinese, and to retain the motivation and loyalty of the existing mid-ranking managers and prevent them from being headhunted by competitors. Due to wage inflation caused by the 'bidding war' for experienced local managers, they also have to be aware that localization will not necessarily lead to reductions in executive labour costs. Fourth, managers have to strike a balance between fulfilling international standards and maintaining a product's competitiveness. This not only involves the retraining of the workforce, but also requires the implementation of corresponding complementary policies by the government, for example regulations on migrant workers. Apart from the high costs of implementing international standards, some importing countries may use these standards as non-trade barriers to protect their local industries from 'hollowing out' by Chinese products. This is especially the case for the 'Technical Barriers to Trade' or 'Green Standards', where each importing country can have its own standards and pursue the 'necessary measures' in order to enforce them. The transaction costs for managers to comply with all these national standards will be even higher than for the international standards involved in the process. Finally, the authors argue, managers have to strike a delicate balance to deal with the above challenges in the future within the constraints of time available.

The contribution on another aspect of WTO entry, by Man-Kwong Leung and Trevor Young, goes on to investigate the decision of a foreign life insurer to enter the Chinese market and then to show that a foreign insurance company with certain attributes, such as large assets and special links to Hong Kong, is more likely to establish itself in this market. In a regression analysis, the availability of business opportunities and the improving political environment of the Chinese economy are found to be significant factors determining the growth of foreign life insurance companies. Turning to the present and future implications of China's entry to the WTO, it is argued that although the impact of entry on the domestic life insurance industry will be mixed, the prospects for foreign life insurers, albeit via joint ventures, are promising. This happens because the institutional constraints on demand, market competitiveness and the legal framework of the Chinese life insurance sector will become less binding, and foreign life insurance companies' access to the Chinese life insurance market will be much expanded. It is further argued that a foreign life insurer is more likely to be profitable if it is able to make sound managerial decisions in its choice of market niche and Chinese partner, its long-term planning, and its product and personnel management. As success in these areas is closely related to the attributes facilitating its entry, it is then important for foreign life insurance companies in future to examine whether they have the appropriate attributes before they enter the Chinese market, and, where they do, to build on these advantages in a bid to reduce costs and risks of their operations there. Moreover, investment expertise will become a critical determinant of profitability only when foreign life insurers are able to invest freely in the Chinese capital markets in the future.

Finally, this editor of the collection of studies attempts to sum up the thrust of the contributions and to offer final thoughts on the question of the future of Chinese management. He asks whether Chinese management will 'converge' with its Western (or for that matter, Japanese) counterparts and suggests that the path Chinese management takes may be no straightforward projection of present trends. Nonetheless, it is argued, there may be pointers in the evidence provided in this volume and the future trajectory may very well lay in the direction of 'relative convergence', or even 'cross-vergence'.

CONCLUSIONS

To sum up, the above set of studies seeks to ask and indeed answer, as far as it can feasibly do so, the main questions concerning the future of Chinese management. The authors cover a wide range of topics including Human Resource Management, Industrial Relations, Joint Ventures, WTO entry and so on, amongst others, highlighting the two decades of change discussed earlier.

Deng's legacy has been one of extensive macro- as well as micro-level reform; he explicitly promoted, as we have seen above, the building of 'market socialism with Chinese characteristics'. Clearly, China has evolved from a command economy (see Schurmann, 1966) to a market-driven one (see Naughton, 1995). *Pari passu*, its management has adapted to this change, if unevenly (see Tang and Ward, 2003).

We have pointed out earlier the degree to which Deng's change strategy was pragmatic and piecemeal, one of 'crossing the river by feeling the stones'. The result is that the patterns of management that have appeared have been difficult to categorize neatly; yet there have been some discernable shifts. How it handles people has been transformed most noticeably, for instance, as the contributions noted above on HRM and IR have suggested. Linking up with foreign firms, especially MNCs, has been a major source of new capital, techniques and innovations. Corporate governance has been transformed accordingly. Above all, entry into WTO has been a *grande finale*, at least as far as the last century has been concerned.

Given cultural affinities, Chinese management will most probably more or less 'converge', if only relatively and eclectically, with modules of Overseas Chinese, maybe more of Taiwanese, as well as

Japanese and Western practice. In the non-state sector above all, the greatest change has already taken place, as we have already seen. How fast and how far this will go, is hard to predict (see Nolan, 2001). But the way 'cutting-edge' Chinese firms have begun to resemble their overseas counterparts, in both strategy as well as performance, has give many informed observers much food for thought. What follows in the foregoing contributions points to 'interesting times' at least, as the Chinese phrase goes, the ultimate impact of Severe Accute Respiratory Syndrome (SARS) notwithstanding.

NOTES

1. We must be cautious here as this forecast is basically an extrapolation.
2. Pessimists may argue that it may now be as high as 0.5.
3. Zhu Rongji and Jiang Zemin retired formally in early 2003 but the latter retained the Chairmanship of the all-important Military Commission.
4. Kaple's view is that the Chinese took over a model that had not worked in the way it had been described in the Soviet Five Year Plans and one they did not fully understand anyway.
5. The reduction of payrolls in Chinese SOEs was part and parcel of the structural reforms advocated by outside bodies like the World Bank and has not seen its end yet.
6. In many smaller IJVs, especially those run by overseas Chinese investors, there are neither unions nor workers' representative bodies.

REFERENCES

Braun, W. and Warner, M. (2002), 'The "Culture-Free" versus "Culture Specific" Management Debate' in M. Warner and P. Joynt (eds.) *Managing Across Cultures: Issues and Perspectives*. London: Thomson Learning, pp.13–25.

Cheek, T. (2002), *Mao Zedong and China's Revolutions: A Brief History with Documents*. Boston and New York: Bedford/St Martin's.

Child, J. (1994), *Management in China During the Age of Reform*. Cambridge: Cambridge University Press.

Chinese Statistical Yearbook (various years), *Chinese Statistical Yearbook*. Beijing: State Statistical Bureau.

Ding, D.Z., Goodall, K. and Warner, M. (2000), 'Beyond the Iron Rice Bowl: Whither Chinese HRM?', *International Journal of Human Resource Management*, Vol.11, No.2, pp.217–36.

Ding, D.Z., Lan, G. and Warner, M. (2001), 'A New Form of Chinese Human Resource Management? Personnel and Labour–Management Relations in Chinese Township and Village Enterprises: A Case-study Approach', *Industrial Relations Journal*, Vol.32, No.4, pp.328–43.

Ding, D.Z., Lan, G. and Warner, M. (2002), 'Beyond the State Sector: A Study of HRM in Southern China', Working Paper, Cambridge: Judge Institute of Management, University of Cambridge.

Garnaut, R., Song, L., Yao, Y. and Wang, X. (2002), *Private Enterprise in China*. Canberra: Asia Pacific Press.

Gregory, J.S. (2003), *The West and China since 1500*. London: Palgrave and New York: St Martin's Press.

He P. (2002), *China's Search for Modernity: Cultural Discourse in the late 20th Century*. London: Palgrave and New York: St Martin's Press.

Ip, D., Lever-Tracey, C. and Tracey, N. (eds.) (2000), *Chinese Business and the Asian Crisis*. Aldershot: Gower.

Kaple, D. (1994), *Dream of a Red Factory: The Legacy of High Stalinism in China*. Oxford, Oxford University Press.

Lu, X. and Perry, E. (1997), *Danwei: The Changing Chinese Workplace in Historical and Comparative Perspective*. Armonk: New York and London, M.E. Sharpe.

Naughton, B. (1995), *Growing out of the Plan: Chinese Economic Reform 1978–93.* Cambridge: Cambridge University Press.

Newton, A. and Subbaraman, R. (2002), *China: Gigantic Possibilities, Present Realities.* London: Lehman Brothers.

Ng, S.-H. and Warner, M. (1998), *China's Trade Union and Management.* London: Macmillan and New York: St Martin's Press.

Nolan, P. (1995), *China's Rise, Russia's Fall.* London: Macmillan and New York: St Martin's Press.

Nolan, P. (2001), *China and the Global Business Revolution.* London: Palgrave and New York: St Martin's Press.

O'Neill, M. (2002), 'China warns of 20 million urban jobless', *South China Morning Post,* 30 April, p.1.

Schurmann, F. (1966), *Ideology and Organization in Communist China.* (Berkeley, CA: University of California Press).

Scott, W.R. (2002), 'The Changing World of Chinese Enterprise: An Institutional Perspective', in A.S. Tsui and C-M. Lau (eds.), *The Management of Enterprises in the People's Republic of China.* Boston, Dordrecht and London: Kluwer Academic, pp.59–78.

Tang, J. and Ward, A. (2003), *The Changing Face of Chinese Management.* London: Routledge.

Walder, A.G. (1986), *Communist Neo-Traditionalism: Work and Authority in Chinese Industry.* Berkeley, CA: University of California Press.

Warner, M. (1992), *How Chinese Managers Learn,* London: Macmillan and New York: St Martin's Press.

Warner, M. (1993), 'Human Resource Management "with Chinese Characteristics"', *International Journal of Human Resource Management,* Vol.4, No.1, pp.45–65.

Warner, M. (1995), *The Management of Human Resources in Chinese Industry.* London, Macmillan and New York: St Martin's Press.

Warner, M. (ed.) (1999), *China's Managerial Revolution.* London and Portland, OR: Frank Cass.

Warner, M. (ed.) (2000), *Changing Workplace Relations in the Chinese Economy.* London, Macmillan and New York: St Martin's Press.

Warner, M. (2002), 'Globalization, Labour Markets and Human Resources in Asia-Pacific Economies: An Overview', *International Journal of Human Resource Management,* Vol.13, No.3, pp.384–98.

Warner, M. and Ng, S.-H. (1999), 'Collective Contracts in Chinese Enterprises: A New Brand of Collective Bargaining under "Market Socialism"', *British Journal of Industrial Relations,* Vol.37, No.2, pp.295–314.

World Bank (2000), *Annual Report,* Washington DC: World Bank.

Yao, S. (2002), *Confucian Capitalism: Discourse, Practice and Myth of Chinese Enterprise.* London: RoutledgeCurzon.

Human Resource Management 'with Chinese Characteristics': A Comparative Study of the People's Republic of China and Taiwan

MALCOLM WARNER and YING ZHU

In the face of ever-encroaching globalization, both the People's Republic of China (henceforth to be referred to as 'China' in this study) and the Republic of China (henceforth to be referred to as 'Taiwan') have now joined the World Trade Organization (WTO); a more open market economy and closer integration with the global economic order appears to be inevitable for both states[1] (see Holbig and Ash, 2002; Magarinos *et al.*, 2002). The onset of the WTO membership and recent global economic recession beset both economies at the macro-level in their respective government policies and administrative systems on the one hand, and at the micro-level in terms of management and strategic responses at enterprise level towards such challenges, on the other. Human resource management (HRM) is one of the critical tools for improving productivity and competitiveness at the grass-roots level (see Warner, 1995; Poole, 1997). It may indeed be the key to survival vis-à-vis global competition. This study aims to identify and compare the current HRM systems and practices at different types of enterprises in both China and Taiwan, respectively (see Zhu and Warner, 2000; 2001), to evaluate their performance in this domain, as well as to illustrate the implications of the inter-relationship between social norms/environment and the transformation of HRM in both economies.

Why study China and Taiwan in terms of the above issues? The rationale for such a comparison is both subtle and relevant: both respectively have similarly deep roots (see Fairbank and Goldman, 1998; Gregory, 2003) as they are said to belong to the same 'family' historically, culturally and ethnically, although both have seen different political and historical changes in the past century; both claim to be the 'one representative' of Chinese people and the dominant *Han* affinity (the so-called the identity of 'Chinese-ness') but with a *realpolitik* of separation of political control between the mainland and Taiwan island; both to a degree depend on one another economically and learn from each other in terms of the pattern of economic modernization, and both push for modernization and competitiveness within the global economic system (see Nolan, 2001). It is thus most useful, we will argue in this account, to examine the two economies with a similar cultural and ethnic identity, with the so-called Chinese characteristics but very *prima facie* different political systems, historical influences and states of economic evolution, vis-a-vis specific present and future HRM strategies and practices.[2]

What may we learn from this approach? There are both theoretical and empirical implications. As for the theoretical implication, the outcome of this comparison may be 'meaningful' in terms of understanding the theoretical arguments about the trend of HRM development towards a 'convergent' or 'divergent' model within the global production and economic systems of our time (see Warner, 2000; 2002), or possibly a hybrid 'cross-vergent' phenomenon (where national cultural systems are blended with broader economic ideologies). The current theoretical debate on this issue can be divided into several streams:

1. Globalization causes convergence in HRM with the views based on universal-type theories (Appelbaum and Batt, 1994; Pfeffer, 1994; Delery and Doty, 1996). The central proposition is that a world-wide tendency for trends and forces (political, economic, social and technological) that tend to induce convergence of national systems, including HRM, towards uniformity (see Rowley and Bae, 2002: 523).
2. Reasons other than globalization for change and convergence are based on institutional theory. Certain practices are adopted not because of 'effectiveness', but other specific social constraining forces (McKinley *et al.*, 1995). Those changes then eventually gain legitimacy that reflects institutional environments.
3. In contrast to the convergence approach, the divergence approach questions the validity of such universal beliefs, by using case studies across the Asian economies (Rowley, 1997). Other research also found that divergence remains at national and international levels, as these forces are mediated by different institutions with their own traditions and cultures (Bamber and Lansbury, 1998: 32). Therefore, this comparative study may help us to gain further clarification of those debates.

As for the empirical implications, (this study may help the two economies to better come to terms with the current state of their evolving HRM systems and therefore enable them to 'improve' their practices and consequently to boost their levels of productivity and competitiveness. Furthermore, it promises useful insights for foreigners investing or about to invest in the two economies to adopt more effective strategies in terms of nurturing their human resources. It is thus clear that the HRM agenda is an important one for the future of the two economies.

* Such is the magnitude of the task ahead. In order to achieve our goal, this contribution reviews the traditional philosophical thinking and implications for HRM in both China and Taiwan; then provides information on the changing employment relations/HRM policies and deals with HRM strategies and practices and the relationship between the changing social environment and the adaptation of new HRM paradigms. There follows a discussion of the main findings and speculation on the causes of HRM transformation in the two economies. Finally, we conclude by highlighting the implications for both the state agencies and firms involved in the current process of globalization. In this context, we conceptualized the following hypotheses:

1. The more economic systems tend to have cultural affinities, the more likely their management systems will have 'family resemblances' in general, under the influence of globalization.
2. The more economic systems tend to have cultural affinities, the more likely their HRM systems will be likely to 'converge' in the future, under the influence of globalization.

In order to test the above propositions, we set out to present a systematic assessment of both the past traditions and current practices of the two societies in question. The data we have included in this study is both *comparative* and *qualitative*; thus it is not the conventional quantitative field study. On the one hand, the evidence we present may not be statistical in nature; however, on the other hand, we have mentioned a good number of quantitative empirical field studies previously carried out by ourselves and others. Even with these caveats, we believe that this type of approach can be insightful as well as useful in better understanding the art of Chinese management (see Tang and Ward, 2003).

TRADITIONAL INFLUENCES

What are the deep-rooted, traditional influences that are relevant to our discussion? Generally speaking, philosophical thinking relevant to the above societies may be traced back to ancient China thousands of years ago. During the period of Spring Autumn Warring States (770–221BC), a number of different philosophical schools made their imprint in an age when it has been suggested that long-standing social rules were collapsing (in the early Zhou dynasty, eleventh century–771BC) and the search was on for new ways of thinking to help to explain the apparently resulting chaos (McGreal, 1995: 62). It was to be seen as a momentous point in China's long history. This mould-breaking era was of great importance and has been tagged as the 'contention of a hundred schools of thought' (Chu, 1995). Four major streams, we suggest, dominated traditional thinking and are today most relevant to management thinking in contemporary Chinese society, namely Confucianism, Daoism, *Yi Jing* and War Strategies. We now consider each of these in turn.

We posit here that Chinese thought has a highly distinctive cast. One of the characteristics and indeed merits of Chinese thinking is that it does not set the search for knowledge into separate and rigid categories, with a separate set of principles governing each domain; it may be regarded as *holistic*. Different philosophies may benefit from influencing each other and efforts to merge different philosophical approaches are frequent. A good example of this process may be found in War Strategies and later neo-Confucianism (1130–1200AD) (Zhu and Warner, 2003).

Confucianism

We now turn to the major source of traditional thinking that had a far-sweeping impact not only on China but on much of east and south-east Asia. The 'master', Confucius (*Kongzi*, 551–479BC), developed a set of teachings based on a set of principles, among which was absolute respect for tradition (early Zhou dynasty) and based on a carefully ranked hierarchy founded on primary relationships not only between members of families but also between the people and their rulers. It has been seen as a guiding philosophy for people's everyday life, indeed one of the world's major sources of ethical inspiration, interestingly enough around the same time as Socratic thought was emerging in classical Greece. The major ideas of Confucius were three basic guides (that is, ruler guides subject, father guides son, and husband guides wife), five constant virtues (benevolence, righteousness, propriety, wisdom, and fidelity), and the doctrine of harmony. Confucius believed that *ren* or philanthropy/benevolence is the highest virtue an individual can attain and this is the ultimate goal of education (see McGreal, 1995). Putting it in context, *ren* may be perceived as a strictly natural and humanistic love, based upon spontaneous feelings cultivated through education.

How does Confucius see this primary virtue? He believed that the path to the attainment of *ren* is the practice of *li*, interpreted as rituals, rites or proprieties. In its broadest sense, the term covers all moral codes and social institutions. In its fundamental but narrow sense, it means socially acceptable forms of behaviour (McGreal, 1995). In addition, *li* involves the deliberate devices used by intellectuals to educate people and maintain social order (Zhu and Warner, 2003). Since *li* is related to moral codes and social institutions, people may be tempted to believe that the practice of *li* is to enforce conformity with social order at the cost of individuality (McGreal, 1995). However, in Confucianism, an individual is not an isolated entity. Confucius said, 'In order to establish oneself, one has to establish others. This is the way of a person of *ren*' (McGreal, 1995: 5). Therefore, individualization and socialization are two aspects of the same process.

The principle governing the adoption of *li* is *yi*, which means righteousness or good character and is a principle of rationality. *Yi* is the habitual practice of expressing one's cultivated feeling at the right times and in the right places. Confucius said: '*Junzi* (a perfect person or superior, a gentleman in English term) is conscious of, and receptive to *yi*, but *xiaoren* (a petty person, or a small man in English term) is conscious of, and receptive to gains' (McGreal, 1995: 6).

According to Confucius, the right method of governing is not by creating legislation or by law enforcement but through the moral education of the people (McGreal, 1995: 6). The ideal government for this thinker was a government of *wuwei* (non-action) through the solid groundwork of moral education. The reason given by Confucius is: 'If you lead the people with political force and restrict them with law and punishment, they can just avoid law violation, but will have no sense of honour and shame. If you lead them with morality and guide them with *li*, they will develop a sense of honour and shame, and will do good of their own accord.' (McGreal, 1995: 7). This doctrine of appealing to the human heart is central to the belief system proposed: self-realization toward world peace (harmony) and a peaceful world and orderly society are the ultimate goal of Confucianism (Zhu and Warner, 2003).

Daoism

Daoism is another highly influential school of thinking that has shaped Chinese culture. The philosopher Lao Zi (sixth century BC–?) inaugurated the idea of yielding to the fundamental paths of the universe (Whiteley *et al.*, 2000). Everything in the universe follows patterns and processes that escape precise definition and imprecisely this is called *dao*, the 'way' (McGreal, 1995: 9). In his work entitled

Daode Jing (Classic of the Way and its Power), Lao Zi argued that *de* (virtue) cannot be strived for, but emerges naturally. The best 'way' to act or think is *wuwei* (effortless activity), by following the natural cause rather than human intervention.

However, the most important element of Daoism is the 'oneness' and *yin-yang*. In Lao Zi's work, he indicated that 'Dao produces one. One produces two. Two produces three. And three produces ten thousand things (that is, everything). The ten thousand things carry *yin* and embrace *yang*. By combining these forces, harmony is created.' (*Daode Jing*, verse 42). These can be understood as the fundamental of the universe that contains polar complements of *yin* and *yang*. Yin represents the dark, recessive, soft, feminine, low, contractive, centripetal, short, hollow, empty, and so forth, and *yang* represents the light, dominant, hard, masculine, high, expansive, centrifugal, long, full, and solid. Nothing is ever purely one or the other; rather all things are in flux between one pole and its opposite (McGreal, 1995: 14).

De is another major theme within Daoism. *De*, usually translated as 'virtue' or 'power', is an object's personal stock of *dao*, or put another way, it is the natural potential or potency instilled within one. In contrast to Confucians who refer to *de* as a moral term, for Lao Zi, *de* signifies natural abilities that enable things to be their best spontaneously and effortlessly (McGreal, 1995: 13). Furthermore, Lao Zi argued that once ineffectual *ren* has regressed into rules, the conditions for conflict, rebellion, and repression have emerged. Since rules recommend doing something unnaturally, there will always be someone who will refuse to comply. For a rule to stay meaningful and not become an empty rule, compliance must be enforced (McGreal, 1995: 13).

For Lao Zi balance between the poles does not mean static parity, but a dynamic reversion that perpetually counterbalances all propensities toward one extreme or the other (Zhu and Warner, 2003). However, the world tends to privilege the *yang* while ignoring or denigrating the *yin*. Daoism aims to re-balance this by emphasizing *yin* over *yang*. In *Daode Jin*, Lao Zi claimed: 'Human beings are born 'soft and flexible'; when they die, they are 'hard and stiff'. Plants arise 'soft and delicate', when they die they are 'withered and dry'. Thus, the 'hard and stiff' may be seen as disciples of death; the 'soft and flexible' are disciples of life, later echoed in Goethe's 'green is the tree of life'. 'An inflexible army cannot be seen as victorious; an unbending tree will break.' (*Daode Jing*, verse 76). Thus, Daoism shows us the path of clear enlightenment and how to understand and follow the fundamental cycle of the universe, in order to attain the balance between the poles.

Yi Jing (Book of Changes)

Dao is the essence of oneness, and the *yi jing* is the ever-changingness of that oneness (Chu, 1995). According to tradition, the book was composed in several layers over many centuries and it was initially a manual of divination, but with the 'Ten Wings' appendices attached, the resultant *Yi Jing* may be considered a work of philosophy. As McGreal (1995: 60) claims that the *Book of Changes* has provided the stimulus for some of the most creative and useful thinking by Chinese seers and scholars, and in both its naive and its sophisticated uses the book has intrigued the Chinese mind and definitively affected the Chinese conception of the 'cosmos' and of the relations of human beings to the continuing changes that are the foreseeable outcome of the universal interplay of opposing natural forces.

The major ideas of *Yi Jing* include the following issues (McGreal, 1995: 60): hexagrams made up of *yin* and *yang* lines can be used as the basis of prognostications; the *yang* line denotes strength and movement, the *yin* line denotes pliancy and rest. There are eight basic trigrams: earth, mountain, water, thunder, heaven, lake, fire, and wood (or wind); change is of two different kinds: alternation (the reversal of polar opposites) and transformation (random change, or chance); the sequence of hexagrams is a model of the cosmos.

As these programmes of thought were debated in the intellectual centres of the various kingdoms, venerable texts such as the *Yi Jing* were reinterpreted. Confucian moralists concentrated on ethical issues reflected in the social content of the text. Daoists and *yin-yang* theorists were interested in cosmological issues suggested by the numerological and symbolic relations between the graphic matrices (McGreal, 1995: 63). Certainly, military strategists were interested in combining those elements into the formation of military strategies – so called *bing fa*.

Bing Fa (War Strategies)

Bing fa is a form of strategic thinking that was first developed for military purposes and has since been applied to almost all human interactions. One of the famous *bing fa* works was *Sun-zi Bing Fa*, written by Sun Zi in the fourth century BC (Chu, 1995). This book discussed the five elements that must be considered in formulating a strategy (Chu, 1995: 25–30):

1. The moral cause: the *dao* addresses the morality and righteousness of a battle;
2. Temporal conditions: heaven is signified by *yin* and *yang*,

manifested as summer and winter and the changing of the four seasons;

3. Geographical conditions: the earth contains far and near, danger and ease, open ground and narrow passes;
4. Leadership: the commander must be wise, trustful, benevolent, courageous, and strict;
5. Organization and discipline must be thoroughly understood. Delegation of authority and areas of responsibility within an organization must be absolutely clear (Zhu and Warner, 2003).

The harmony of the five elements is of great importance to success in any endeavour (Chu, 1995: 32). These elements are intangible, spiritual, as well as psychological, and are more related to people's mindsets.

Implications for the Development of HRM

From the above review, we can summarize the underlying elements that may be responsible for the development of modern HRM concepts in China and Taiwan. The following key issues can be identified as the fundamental, *relational* values that help to determine the formation of managerial knowledge based on a combination of Chinese traditional thinking. Even though this involves contradictions.

1. The establishment of the fundamental virtue of philanthropy/ benevolence within the organization. Under such influence, the concept of 'workplace is family' is widespread among Chinese organizations. It requires organization/management to look after the interests of fellow employees, while employees have a high commitment to the organization. The outcome of implementing this relational virtue can be reflected in management and individual behaviour, such as employment security, compensation and reward schemes, training (as part of educational function) and development (including promotion) systems from the management aspect, and high commitment, self-discipline, and individual sacrifice for the common goals and so on, from the employee's point of view. The eventual goal of such efforts is to achieve a peaceful and orderly workplace.
2. Collectivism and interdependent relational value: it is well-defined principle within Confucianism that an individual is not an isolated entity. Therefore, the concept of family life as the basic unit of society is emulated within the work setting and with it the broader societal values that ensure social harmony and behavioural ritual are preserved (Yau, 2002; Whiteley *et al.*, 2000). Teamwork,

sharing values and information, and group-oriented incentive schemes are based on the foundation of collectivism.

3. The doctrine of harmony and the balance between *yin* and *yang*: the effort to achieve harmonization in the workplace and maintain a dynamic reversion that perpetually counterbalances all propensities towards one extreme or another puts the organization in a stable and sustained position. The concept of *yin* and *yang* creates an attitude which copes with the environment in an adaptive and flexible way.

4. *Bing fa* and the philosophy of *yi jing* lead to strategic thinking and strategic management: the ever-changing nature of internal and external factors force human beings to adopt strategic thinking in order to survive not only in the short-term, but also in the long-term. The outcome of combining different philosophies such as *bing fa* provides the general guidance for strategic thinking which helps organizations to form business strategies.

5. The virtues and quality of leadership emphasized by Confucianism, it has been suggested, were later adopted by current management thinking in the area of leadership: managerial leadership requires the qualities of wisdom, trust, sincerity, benevolence, courage, and strictness to carry out policies (Chu, 1995: 29). If managers lack these qualities, it is argued, they will experience lack of support from employees, and the consequence will be low productivity and discontent (Zhu and Warner, 2003).

These implications show that traditional philosophies have a profound influence on the formation and practices of modern Chinese managerial approaches (see Child, 1994; Douw *et al.*, 2001; Noronha, 2002; Tang and Ward, 2002; Schlevogt, 2002). However, modification does exist in different societies in spite of their cultural affinities, in order to make their HRM approach more relevant to their social, political and economic environments.

CHANGING EMPLOYMENT RELATIONS AND HRM IN CHINA

As illustrated above, both economies had inherited the Confucian tradition and other philosophies, shaped in different ways by modernization over recent decades. In terms of political norms, neither case was 'democratic' in the Western sense; Taiwan was not a multi-party democracy until the 1990s but had not been a one-party state in the same rigid way as the mainland China had been. The Chinese system had been described as 'Confucian Leninism' (see Pye, 1985). Perhaps we should call the Taiwanese version 'Confucian

Capitalism'.[3] In economic terms, both economies experienced state-guided development for much of the time but Taiwan had been decidedly much more of a market economy than China for most of the period since 1949 to the present day.

China, for example, has a mixed ideological environment, which includes both traditional thinking, as well as 'Marxism–Leninism', 'Mao Zedong thought', and the 'Deng Xiaoping idea' and so on.[4] In order to understand the transformation of HRM systems in China, we need to highlight the differences between pre-reform and reform periods.

Pre-reform Period (1949–79)

The 'employment relations model' in China had been anchored in that of the state-owned enterprises (SOEs) that had once dominated industrial production. Their work units (*danwei*) had in turn embodied the so-called 'iron rice bowl' (*tie fan wan*) what ensured 'jobs for life' and 'cradle to grave' welfare for mostly urban industrial SOE employees (see Lu and Perry, 1997).

The development of such an employment relations system during the pre-reform period was covered under the so-called socialist superiority values in the following significant ways:

1. Employment security, seniority, social welfare, and party/management leadership (central control) were labelled the 'advantages' of the 'socialist system';
2. Trade unions mainly had a 'window-dressing' role but this was explained away as leading to 'industrial harmony';
3. Narrow wage differentials were praised as 'egalitarian';
4. Lifetime employment with a seniority-based wage system was central;
5. The traditional kinship system was also changed to a 'revolutionary' relationship, as relationships (*guanxi*) with powerful leaders now determined the path of an individual career;
6. The goals of the work-unit (*danwei*) not only required individual sacrifice for the unit but also for the nation. However, this modified employment relations system did not always necessarily benefit individual employees and work;
7. Political interests replaced economic interests as dominating influences in the employment relations system;
8. As a consequence, workers lost their motivation for production and both economic and management systems collapsed at the end of the Cultural Revolution in 1976.

The Reform Period (1979–Present)

In the reform period, the main task was reforming the pre-reform employment relations system and transforming it into a new one embodying employment relations and HRM, hence:

1. New policies were mainly centred on the reform of wages, employment, welfare and management, as we now hope to show in the discussion that follows (Zhu, 1995);
2. The reforming initiatives of the government have been broadly defined as breaking the 'three irons': 'iron rice bowl' refers to lifetime employment, 'iron wages' refer to the fixed wage system, and 'iron chair' refers to the inflexibility of changing positions of shop-floor and manager. In contrast, more flexible systems such as the labour contract system, floating wage system, and shop-floor and manager engagement systems were established (Yuan, 1990);
3. Under Deng's new ideological position, policy shifted to restore the principle of 'distribution according to work' and link individual performance, skills and position with their income in order to boost individuals' motivation for greater production (Zhu and Campbell, 1996);
4. New types of wage systems were introduced, such as the 'piece-work wage system', the 'bonus system' and later the 'structural wage system', as well as the 'floating wage system' (Li, 1992) and 'post-plus-skills wage system' (Warner, 1997). This new wage policy was designed to break one of the three irons – 'iron wages'. This step was important because the economic reform process called for greater efficiency in factor allocation, with labour flexibility a priority;
5. Allowing variations in rewards based on productivity was part and parcel of this reform. Moreover, labour was to be encouraged to move from less productive firms to more efficient ones;
6. Immobility of labour has been a feature of the old system dominated by the SOEs, where there was overmanning and zero turnover of workers. New initiative was to create labour market and encourage labour mobility.

A new Labour Law was codified in 1994 and put into effect in 1995. By virtue of the legal norms it prescribes, individual labour contracts (*geren hetong*) were introduced and they set out to undo the so-called 'iron rice bowl', were then firmly enshrined in collective contracts (*jiti hetong*), possibly reminiscent of Western-style collective bargaining arrangements, introduced with the State's blessing. As part of the reforms that have promoted the creation of a 'labour market' in China

(Ng and Warner, 1998), the system of 'lifetime employment' has in recent years been gradually phased out (Ding *et al.*, 2000; 2002).

Creating an effective labour market has been high on the reformers' agenda since then. However, improvements in labour mobility could not to take place overnight. Even by the late 1990s, the level of job mobility was relatively low in many SOEs, although rising in the non-State sector such as in joint ventures (JVs) and foreign-owned enterprises (FOEs) especially in large cities like Shanghai.

HRM Implications

With the reforms of the employment system, a new terminology of HRM came to China in the mid-1980s (see Child, 1994; Warner, 1995, 1999). Initially, HRM as an academic concept was introduced by joint teaching arrangements between Chinese and foreign universities, as well as in management practices in foreign-owned enterprises, mainly from Japan, the USA and Europe (Warner, 1995). The Chinese translation of HRM is *renli ziyuan guanli* which means 'labour force resources management'. But in fact, some people now use it misleadingly as a synonym for personnel management (PM) (*renshi guanli*) and indeed treat it as such (Warner, 1997). This form of older PM practice is still very common in SOEs and a fair degree of conservatism continues to pervade the administration of personnel in such enterprises. Certainly, it is still somewhat far from the initial concept of HRM as understood in the international business community[5] (Poole, 1997).

In parallel, attempts were made to import 'enterprise culture', code for adopting and adapting the Japanese model (Chan, 1995). This is normally found in firms entering JV arrangements with Japanese MNCs or where the Japanese have set up wholly owned firms on site. Some aspects of the Japanese management system such as the quality control circles (QCC) and total quality control (TQC) have been practised in both local and foreign companies. However, the system is closely adapted to local laws and practices.

The term HRM is in fact mostly *de rigueur* in the more prominent Sino–foreign JVs, particularly the larger ones. Even in such firms, management seems to be more inward-looking, focusing on issues like wage, welfare and promotion as found in the conventional personnel arrangements rather than strategic ones like long-term development normally associated with HRM.

Clearly, at this time, there is not a homogeneous model of HRM in Chinese enterprises. Individual enterprises are reforming their HRM systems differently on the basis of their existing conditions and the respective impact of economic reform.

CHANGING EMPLOYMENT RELATIONS AND HRM IN TAIWAN

The Taiwanese management system is also rooted in traditional Chinese culture and values, predominantly in the form of small size family businesses, coupled with strong family control and extensive subcontracting networks (Chen, 1995). However, in the first half of the twentieth century, Taiwan was colonized by Japan and Japanese influence was widespread, including its management system. Taiwan gradually developed large businesses in the capital-intensive sector owned and/or controlled by the State under the Nationalist government since the late 1940s (Hamilton, 1999; Lee, 1995).

Generally speaking, the characteristics of the Taiwanese management system can be summarized as follows: hierarchy, paternalism, strong personal loyalty and commitment, and the importance of personal connections (*guanxi*) in business and individual lives (Chen, 1995). These characteristics are rooted in Confucianism, a belief system that values harmony, and the tendency to see individuals in a family and socially dependent context.

Different stages of economic development were accompanied by differing management patterns. In Taiwan, for instance, its economic development since the 1960s can be divided into two stages: the export expansion period between 1961 and 1980 and the technology-intensive industries expansion period from 1981 to recent years (Lee, 1995; Zhu *et al.*, 2000). HRM in Taiwan also changed over the two periods.

The Export Expansion Period (1961–80)
The main characteristics of HRM during the export expansion period can be identified as follows.

Recruitment
Recruiting blue-collar workers relied heavily on informal channels, such as employee referral and company network. For the recruitment of white-collar workers, formal channels were preferred (Lee, 1995: 92). Since most middle- and high-ranking management positions were filled either by the owners' family members or by internal promotions, little outside recruiting activity took place (Lee, 1995: 92).

Training
Company-sponsored training was not popular during this period. Apprenticeships were also not common in Taiwan. However, as a rule, more skilled workers received formal on-the-job training (OJT) than did semi-skilled and unskilled workers, and foreign-owned companies offered more OJT programmes than did local companies (Lee, 1995: 93).

Compensation

Packages include basic pay and various types of bonus, such as those based on the year-end results, competition, invention, long-service and so on (Chen, 1998: 160). It was common for Taiwanese companies to adopt the Japanese seniority-based wage system for basic pay (Lee, 1995: 110). With the traditional culture of avoiding conflict between management and employees, most workers can be promoted up the scale of their job title if their annual performance is 'above-average' (Chen, 1998: 161).

Trade unions

These worker bodies were controlled by the government during this period (Zhu *et al.*, 2000). The ruling *Kuomintang* (KMT) – now known as the *Guomingdang* Party – guided most unions through local government control over the election of union officials, fostering KMT branches at workplaces and 'supervision' by larger affiliates of the sole national union peak council, the Chinese Federation of Labour (CFL) (Zhu *et al.*, 2000: 38). Thus the government was able to maintain a low minimum wage and control the adjustment of wage rates in the public sector (Lee, 1995: 98).

Expansion of Technology-Intensive Industries (1981–Present)

During this period, not only did the structure of the economy change quickly, but employment relations, human resource management practices, and the government's labour policies were similarly affected (Lee, 1995). The industrial system became more complex and formal, and government policy became more pro-labour orientated as mentioned above.

Changes in industrial structure and government policy and legislation had a profound impact on HRM and the structure of organization in Taiwan. To cope with the increase in production costs employers adopted many strategies, such as employing foreign workers at lower wages, with government permission (companies can employ foreign workers up to 30 per cent of total employees) (Zhu *et al.*, 2000), improving the efficiency of the workforce by providing more training, introducing automated machinery to substitute labour, and subcontracting their work (Lee, 1995:105). In addition, in order to obtain a further comparative advantage many companies from Taiwan relocated their operations to low-wage countries, especially to mainland China and south-east Asia (Zhu and Warner, 2001).

However, different kinds of enterprise have different approaches toward change in the labour market and to the challenges of global economic competition. Two major variables here are predominately family-based small and medium enterprises (SMEs) and predominately state-owned large enterprises (LEs).

SMEs have been seen as the most dynamic and flexible sector determining Taiwanese economic growth (see Hamilton, 1999; for China, see Garnaut *et al.*, 2001). However, since the mid-1980s, more and more SMEs have felt that the environment was becoming less favourable for their business in Taiwan: higher business costs and more regulations affected their business operations. In addition, international competition forced them to reorganize their businesses in order to survive. The major changes included internationalization of business operations, bringing in professional management and more flexible HRM and marketing strategies.

Most SMEs still maintain a centralized decision-making process. However, there is now a tendency for owners to gradually withdraw from routine management activities. Some high-ranking managers are trained and promoted within the companies and are not necessarily family members. Management professionalism becomes increasingly important as a response to criticism of managerial nepotism. During the recent financial crisis, many companies realized that more effective management skills were crucial for their business survival. Therefore, middle-level managers and skilled employees had to be recruited externally from formal employment agencies. Most SMEs now pay attention to both pre-training and continuous trainging in order to cope with market changes and link the skills of employees with the needs of production. The compensation package has not been changed and the philosophy of 'harmony' still plays an important role in wage determination. Therefore, the wage gap between top managers and the lowest employee level is about fivefold, which is much lower than that in FOEs, with sometimes over 20 times (for example, in US firms) (Zhu and Warner, 2001).

Trade unions have generally been weak in Taiwanese SMEs. Although the Trade Union Law (1975) required unions to be established in workplaces in most sectors with more than 30 employees (Lee, 1988: 188–91; cf Warner, 1995), the reality is that even now a large number of SMEs are without union organization. In addition, the major tasks of unions in these firms are rather narrowly defined, such as communicating with and assisting management, organizing annual union meetings and collective agreements with management every three years. There is a general feeling that managers in SMEs do not want union involvement in decision-making (Zhu and Warner, 2001).

On the other hand, state-owned large enterprises (LEs) in Taiwan for years enjoyed monopoly status in key sectors. They were mostly in the strategic industrial areas that had received strong support from the government. However, in recent years, privatization and marketization have dominated their economic decision-making and these enterprises are facing restructuring and reform.

Generally speaking, LEs have well-established systems of external recruitment of managers. Using examination, interview and evaluation procedures, SOEs can recruit the most capable people from outside their organizations. For a long time, people sought positions within LEs for security, better pay and welfare, good working environment, and social prestige; it made recruitment even more competitive. Therefore, so far the qualifications of managers in these enterprises remain the highest, with university graduates and post-graduates of high quality. In addition, public recruitment of employees is the main recruiting channel for LEs. However, the public sector is not allowed to employ foreign workers. In terms of training, both on-the-job training and professional training are provided by the enterprises. The compensation package has not been changed as well. In fact, among all types of enterprises, LEs seem to have the highest salary-levels. Bonuses are paid as group incentives equivalent to three or four-months' wages (Zhu and Warner, 2001).

Trade unions in the Taiwanese public sector have been subservient to the government for a long time (Frenkel et al., 1993). Even now, trade unions in these state-owned LEs are not wholly independent, although they have a strong membership base. The functions of these unions were described as 'promoting enterprise productivity as well as protecting workers' interests'; they also provide a useful bridge between employees and management in order to guarantee smooth industrial relations (Zhu et al., 2000).

As Lee (1995: 101) notes, the Taiwanese government's labour policies have also changed over the recent decades (see Ng and Warner, 1998: 152ff). The employment relations system became more complex and formal and government policy took on a more pro-labour orientation. The outcome was that the government amended several labour laws in the 1980s, including the Collective Agreement Law in 1982 (in conjunction with the Labour Union Law enacted in 1929 and last amended in 1975), the Labour Disputes Law and the Labour Insurance Act in 1988 and the Vocational Training Act in 1983 (Lee, 1995:101; Chen, 1998:155–6). It also enacted new laws such as the Labour Standards Law in 1984, last amended in 1996, the Employment Service Act in 1992, and the Equal Rights in the Workplace Act in 1993 (Lee, 1995:101; Chen, 1998:155–6). In short, Taiwan developed a less repressive labour environment, one that may be said to be more 'liberal' and more appropriate to a more externally-driven market economy and which may presage future trends on the Mainland.

DISCUSSION AND EVALUATION

Comparatively speaking, we can see that HRM policies and practices in China and Taiwan were both plainly under the influence of traditional culture (Redding, 1995) and the changing political and economic environments (Zhu *et al.*, 2000).

What were the main features of this analytical comparison? A number of characteristics that are clearly 'Chinese' come to mind here. Key characteristics such as *collectivism, hierarchy, harmony, loyalty, and strategic thinking* can, for instance, be found in both management systems. These characteristics are reflected in HRM, for example, in group-oriented production activities (teamwork), group-based performance evaluation and incentives, relatively narrow gaps in salaries between management and employees, co-operative and harmonized labour management relations, and seniority-based wage systems (in particular during the pre-reform systems). In addition, strategic thinking and management have had to deal with such changes, in particular during the period of economic transition. In recent years, both increasing global competition and the Asian financial crisis have forced enterprises to adopt more flexible policies and management systems. New political environments, reformed legal frameworks and economic pressures have also added new dimensions of HRM.

How has the comparison been affected by economic factors? Both China and Taiwan experienced rapid economic growth and industrial-ization over the post-Second World War period and particularly in recent decades, although the current international economic down-term has had a more negative effect on Taiwan than on China. In addition, Taiwan has relied on the 'market' for some time now, albeit backed by robust state support, China has only recently emerged from the strait-jacket of the 'command economy' compared with its close neighbour. As a result China has moved from the *status quo ante* in terms of its employment model, to one more like that of its neighbour and will probably do so even more in future years (see Table 1).

We can illustrate this point in terms of labour markets in the respective economies (see Tomba, 2002). Today, although the two economies respectively enjoy greater 'labour-market flexibility' in admittedly varying degrees, this may vary between the one with greater state support and the one with less. In China, the 'iron rice bowl' system is being phased out (Ding *et al.*, 2000), as it enters an era of greater openness in its product and factor markets, with WTO entry

TABLE 1
COMPARISON OF STATIST AND MARKET-DRIVEN EMPLOYMENT MODELS

Statist Model	Market-Driven Model	
	Socialist Market Economy	Capitalist Market Economy
China: pre-reform	China: post-reform	Taiwan
State ownership	Diversifying	Diverse ownership
Command economy	Market-socialism	Market economy
Personnel Management	Evolving HRM	Semi-mature HRM
'Iron rice bowl'	Nascent labour market	Mature labour market
'Jobs for life'	Individual contracts	Unregulated
Labour bureaux	Transitional system	Market choice
Egalitarian pay and perks	Hybrid reward system	Performance pay
On-site accommodation	Emergent housing market	Mature housing market
Free medical care	Hybrid mix	Market choice
One top-down union	Institutional stasis	Pluralist unions
State wage-determination	Nascent bargaining	Institutionalized bargaining

and the accompanying flood of direct foreign investment. Performance-driven rewards systems had already been adopted, in the 1980s and 1990s, by 'nominally socialist' mainland China. Social security has also been diluted – with the demise of the 'iron rice bowl' – and is now dependent on individual workers' contributions supplemented by employers. Collective contracts offer the prospect of a nascent collective bargaining system – as noted earlier (see Warner, 1995; Ng and Warner, 1998). More MNCs will establish their operations in China and 'international standardized HRM' policies and practices will be implemented in their Chinese businesses, albeit with certain modifications. On the other hand, increasing unemployment, migrant workers and regional wage disparity, as well as SARS, complicate the agenda (see Warner, 1999).

In Taiwan, although its economy has enjoyed a better outcome in terms of coping with the negative influence of the Asian crisis of 1997 and the latest global economic slow-down compared with other Asian tigers, high unemployment and low economic growth have also been common in recent years. A number of firms have relocated their major business operations to mainland China. Lack of confidence in the Taiwanese Democratic Progress Party (DPP) government did not help to improve the economic situation. Insecurity in Taiwan also puts at risk the opportunities for further SOE reform and restructuring of family-based SMEs.

Such are the main elements that have affected the respective paths of HRM development in the two economies. As China moves closer to the market, it may resemble Taiwan rather more in future years, especially as the non-state sector in the former expands (see Garnaut et al., 2001) and the SOE sector shrinks within limits.[6] In terms of Table 1, the two economies are moving in a similar direction but differences still remain between them still remain. It may be interpreted as a case of 'relative convergence' or even possibly 'cross-vergence' with 'Chinese characteristics'.

CONCLUSIONS

By comparing our findings with the initial hypotheses raised at the beginning of the paper, we can offer the following observations.

The more economic systems tend to have cultural affinities, the more likely their management systems will have 'family resemblances' in general, under the influence of globalization. However, this proposition only seems to be partially correct, given the fact that the development of management systems in China and Taiwan are moving towards closer ties across Taiwan Straits, with greater investment and trade due to their cultural affinities and economic needs, and the influence of globalization such as WTO accession. A growing number of Taiwanese companies investing in mainland China are also bringing their own management systems along with their business operations, although a number of Taiwanese companies have experienced business failure in the mainland and the difficulties of transferring Taiwanese management systems into the mainland. However, familiarity and adaptation between the two systems may increasingly be the case.

The more economic systems tend to have cultural affinities, the more their HRM systems will be likely to 'converge' in the long run, under the influence of globalization. This proposition, however, on the basis of the above analysis, seems not to be the case. Although traditional culture continues to influence HRM as we have seen, (such as group-oriented production activities, group-based performance evaluation and incentives, relatively small differences in salary between management and employees, co-operative and harmonious labour management relations, and so on), other differences remain vis-à-vis the stage of economic development and technology, market environment, as well as government policy and regulation. We must therefore remain cautious in applying the term 'cross-vergence' rather than 'convergence' to the above situation.

In conclusion, it can be argued that there will at least be a degree of 'relative convergence' (see Chan, 1995; Warner, 2000, 2002) given the evidence presented here. The trends towards globalization may in many significant respects only strengthen tendencies towards greater similarities in HRM policies and practices over the coming decades, although both societies can be expected to retain their distinct identities.

NOTES

1. In a momentous decision, China signed up to become the 143rd member of the WTO on 11 December 2001.
2. Comparisons with Taiwan on this and other points are set out in ch. 8 of Tang and Ward (2002: 207–209)
3. The term 'Confucian Capitalism' and its conceptual and empirical bases have been in a recent, highly interesting book by Yao (2002).
4. The contribution by the outgoing leader, Jiang Zemin, might be possibly added here but has not yet been regarded as a major ideological innovation. He was formally replaced by Hu Jintao in March 2003.
5. We realize that opinions may differ on this point but can state that as yet the term HRM is more often than not used rather loosely in Chinese practice, according to any precise definition of the term as used in Western literature on the subject.
6. There is little doubt that the size of the private sector in China's economy is now so large that it may have reached a critical point in defining the nature of the system. The state sector's share of industrial production had fallen to less than 25 per cent by the start of the new decade.

REFERENCES

Appelbaum, E. and Batt, R. (1994), *The New American Workplace: Transforming Work Systems in the United States*. Ithaca., NY: ILR Press.

Bamber, G. and Lansbury, R. (eds.) (1998), *International and Comparative Employment Relations*. London: Sage.

Chan, A. (1995), 'Chinese Enterprise Reforms: Convergence with the Japanese Model?', *Industrial and Corporate Change*, Vol.4, No.1, pp.449–70.

Chen, M. (1995), *Asian Management Systems: Chinese, Japanese and Korean styles of Business*. London: Routledge.

Chen, S.J. (1998), 'The Development of HRM Practices in Taiwan' in C. Rowley (ed.), *Human Resource Management in the Asia Pacific Region: Convergence Questioned*. London: Frank Cass, pp.152–69.

Child, J. (1994), *Management in China During the Era of Reform*. Cambridge: Cambridge University Press.

Chu, C.N. (1995), *The Asian Mind Game: A Westerner's Survival Manual*. Crows Nest: Stealth Productions Australia.

Delery, J. E. and Doty, D. H. (1996), 'Modes of Theorizing in Strategic HRM: Tests of Universalistic, Contingency, and Configurational Performance Predictions', *Academy of Management Journal*, No.39, pp.802–35.

Ding, D.Z ., Goodall, K. and Warner, M. (2000), 'The End of the Iron Rice Bowl: Whither Chinese HRM?', *International Journal of Human Resource Management*, Vol.11, No.2, pp.217–36.

Ding, D.Z., Goodall, K. and Warner, M. (2002), 'The Impact of Economic Reform on the Role of Trade Unions in China', *International Journal of Human Resource Management*, Vol.13, No.3, pp.431–49.

Douw, L., Huang, C. and Ip, D. (eds.) (2001), *Rethinking Chinese Transnational Enterprises: Cultural Affinity and Business Strategies*. London: Curzon/IIAS.

Fairbank, J.K. and Goldman, M. (1998), *China: A New History*. Cambridge, MA: Harvard University Press.

Frenkel, S., Hong, J.C. and Lee, B.L. (1993), 'The Resurgence and Fragility of Trade Unions in Taiwan' in S. Frenkel (ed.), *Organized Labor in the Asia-Pacific Region: a Comparative Study of Trade Unionism in Nine Countries*. Ithaca, NY: ILR Press, pp.162–86.

Garnaut, R., Li, G.S., Yang, Y. and Wang, X. (2001), *Private Enterprise in China*. Canberra: Asia Pacific Press.

Gregory, J.S. (2003), *The West and China since 1500*. London: Palgrave and New York: St Martin's Press.

Hamilton, G.G. (ed.) (1999), *Cosmopolitan Capitalists: Hong Kong and the Chinese Diaspora at the End of the 20th Century*. Seattle: University of Washington Press.

Holbig, H. and Ash, R. (eds.) (2002), *China's Accession to the World Trade Organization: National and International Perspectives*. London: RoutledgeCurzon.

Lee, J.S. (1988), 'Labor Relations and the Stages of Economic Development: The Case of the Republic of China' in *Proceedings of the Conference on Labor and Economic Development*. Taipei: Institute for Economic Research, China Productivity Center, pp.177–204.

Lee, J.S. (1995), 'Economic Development and the Evolution of Industrial Relations in Taiwan, 1950–1993' in A. Verma, T.A. Kochan and R.D. Lansbury (eds.), *Employment Relations in the Growing Asian Economies*. London: Routledge, pp.88–118.

Li, T.C. (1992), 'Zhuanhuan Qiye Jingying Jizhi De Xuanze' (The Choice for Changing Enterprise Management System) in China Enterprises Management & Training Centre (ed.), *Qiye Zhuanhuan Jingying Jizhi: Lilun Yu Shijian (Changing Enterprises Management System: Theory and Practice)*. Beijing: China People's University Press.

Lu, X. and Perry, E. J. (eds.) (1997), *Danwei: The Changing Chinese Workplace in Historical and Comparative Perspective* Armonk, NY: M.E. Sharpe.

Magarinos, C.A., Long, Y. and Sercovich, F.C. (2002), *China in the WTO: The Birth of a Catching-up Strategy*. London: Palgrave and New York: St Martin's Press.

McGreal, I. (1995), *Great Thinkers of the Eastern World: The Major Thinkers and the Philosophical and Religious Classics of China, India, Japan, Korea and the World of Islam.* New York: Harper Collins.

McKinley, W., Sanchez, L. and Schick, A.G. (1995), 'Organizational Downsizing: Constraining, Cloning, Learning', *Academy of Management Executive*, Vol.9, No.3, pp.32–44.

Ng, S.-H. and Warner, M. (1998), *China's Trade Unions and Management*. London: Macmillan and New York: St Martin's Press.

Nolan, P. (2001), *China and the Global Business Revolution*. London: Palgrave and New York: St Martin's Press.

Noronha, C. (2002), *The Theory of Culture-Specific Total Quality Management: Quality Management in Chinese Regions*. London: Palgrave and New York: St Martin's Press.

Pfeffer, J. (1994), *Competitive Advantage through People*. Boston, MA: Harvard Business School Press.

Poole, M. (1997), 'Industrial and labour relations' in M. Warner (ed.), *IEBM Concise Encyclopedia of Business and Management*. London: International Thomson Business Press, pp.264–82.

Pye, L.W. (1985), *Asian Power and Politics*. Cambridge, MA: Harvard University Press.

Redding, G. (1995), *The Spirit of Chinese Capitalism*. Berlin: De Gruyter.

Rowley, C. (1997), 'Comparisons and Perspectives on HRM in the Asia Pacific', *Asia Pacific Business Review*, Vol.3, No.4, pp.1–18.

Rowley, C. and Bae, J.S. (2002), 'Globalization and Transformation of Human Resource Management in South Korea', *International Journal of Human Resource Management*, Vol.13, No.3, pp.522–49.

Schlevogt, K.A. (2002), *The Art of Chinese Management: Theory, Evidence and Applications*. Oxford: Oxford University Press.

Tang, J. and Ward, A. (2003), *The Changing Face of Chinese Management*. London: Routledge.

Tomba, L., (2002), *Paradoxes of Labour Reform: Chinese Labour Theory and Practice from Socialism to Market*. London: RoutledgeCurzon.

Warner, M. (1995), *The Management of Human Resources in Chinese Industry*. London: Macmillan and New York: St Martin's Press.

Warner, M. (1997), 'Management-Labour Relations in the New Chinese Economy', *Human Resource Management Journal*, Vol.37, No.4, pp.30–43.

Warner, M. (ed.) (1999), *China's Managerial Revolution*. London: Frank Cass.

Warner, M. (ed.) (2000), *Changing Workplace Relations in the Chinese Economy*, London, Macmillan and New York: St Martin's Press.

Warner, M. (2002), 'Globalization, Labour Markets and Human Resources', *International*

Journal of Human Resource Management, Vol.13, No.3, pp.1–15.

Whiteley, A., Cheung, S. and Zhang, S.Q. (2000), *Human Resource Strategies in China*. Singapore: World Scientific.

Yao, S. (2002), *Confucian Capitalism: Discourse, Practice and Myth of Chinese Enterprise*. London: RoutledgeCurzon.

Yuan, L.Q. (1990), *Zhongguo Laodong Jingji Shi (The History of Chinese Labour Economy)*. Beijing: Beijing Economic Institute Press.

Zhu, Y. (1995), 'Major Changes Under Way in China's Industrial Relations', *International Labour Review*, No.124, pp.36–49.

Zhu, Y. and Campbell, I. (1996), 'Economic Reform and the Challenge of Transforming Labour Regulation in China', *Labour and Industry*, Vol.7, No.1, pp.29–49.

Zhu, Y., Chen, I. and Warner, M. (2000), 'HRM in Taiwan: An Empirical Case Study', *Human Resource Management Journal*, Vol.10, No.4, pp.32–44.

Zhu, Y. and Warner, M. (2000), 'An Emerging Model of Employment Relations in China: A Divergent Path from the Japanese', *International Business Review*, Vol.9, No.3, pp.345–61.

Zhu, Y. and Warner, M. (2001), 'Taiwanese Business Strategies vis-à-vis the Asian Financial Crisis', *Asia Pacific Business Review*, Vol.7, No.3, pp.139–56.

Zhu, Y. and Warner, M. (2003), 'HRM in East Asia' in Anne-Wil Harzing (ed.), *International Human Resource Management*, London: Sage, ch.9.

The Diffusion of Human Resource Management Practices among Chinese Firms: The Role of Western Multinational Corporations

INGMAR BJÖRKMAN

There is a long-standing debate about the impact of multinational corporations on the host country (Moran, 1993). Most of this discussion has been on the direct economic implications of multinational firms, for example on the foreign trade balance, domestic competition, long-term economic development and local employment. In spite of calls for research into the influence of the organizational patterns of multinational enterprises on host countries (Westney, 1993), there has been much less work on the impact of foreign firms' operations on non-economic aspects of local society. We know that multinational firms tend to introduce parts of the parent company's practices into their foreign subsidiaries. For instance, Western corporations bring Western managerial accounting procedures to their affiliates in China (Firth, 1996). Evidence from China also suggests that Western firms tend to implement human resource management (HRM) practices that are more similar to those of the parent company than those of local Chinese firms (Björkman and Lu, 2001). This contrasts with developed countries such as the USA, where foreign companies tend to adapt their HRM practices to a much higher degree to the host environment (Rosenzweig and Nohria, 1994). The question addressed in this paper is how Western corporations through the HRM practices that they introduce into China influence the HRM practices adopted by Chinese firms.

Already several decades ago, it was suggested that the process of industrialization and the spread of modern technologies would lead to a convergence of economic systems across countries (Kerr *et al.*, 1962). The 'convergence' hypothesis has fuelled extensive debate also in the field of HRM. Proponents of the convergence hypothesis propose that there is a tendency for countries to become more alike in terms of HRM policies and practices under the impact of globalization and the emergence of international 'best practices'. Although numerous studies have shown that considerable differences in HRM remain across countries due to cultural and institutional factors, also within Asia (Rowley and Benson, 2002), there are clear indications of some degree of convergence taking place. In this essay, it is argued that multinational corporations through their activities in Asia significantly contribute to the diffusion of Western-style HRM practices among local corporations.

So far, we do not seem to know much about the introduction of Western-style HRM in China. Although several scholars (for example, Warner, 1996); Benson and Zhu, 1999; Benson *et al.*, 2000; Ding *et al.*, 2000; Zhu and Warner, 2000) have described and analysed some of the changes taking place in Chinese HRM (or 'personnel management') during recent years, there is a paucity of research on the way in which Western corporations through their practices have induced changes in Chinese society. Notably, Western companies are likely to contribute to the diffusion of Western-style HRM practices and policies among local Chinese organizations (Benson and Zhu, 1999). In this study, I use two selected HRM practices, performance appraisal (or 'management') systems and performance-based compensation, to illustrate the effects that Western multinational corporations may have on local business practices.

The objective is to develop testable propositions that can be used as a foundation for future empirical research. In the following I shall first review research on Chinese performance appraisal and compensation systems and how these systems tend to differ from Western HRM practices. The subsequent section examines research into HRM practices in Western-owned units in China. I then argue that the institutionalization perspective provides a useful theoretical lens for understanding the diffusion of business practices, and drawing on this perspective I develop a range of propositions concerning factors influencing the spread of Western-style HRM practices among Chinese firms. In the discussion section I discuss possible avenues for research, including the potential impact of Western-style HRM practices on changes in local values.

WESTERN VERSUS CHINESE HRM PRACTICES

Any presentation of 'Western' performance appraisal and compensation systems obviously constitutes an over-simplified summary of the diverse practices that exist across (as well as within) countries. For instance, several comparative studies have established that there remain sizeable differences in HRM among countries in

Western Europe (for example, Brewster and Larsen, 1992; Gooderham *et al.*, 1999). Nonetheless, there appears to be at least some degree of homogenization taking place among Western countries with US management practices being the dominant Western model that is emulated by firms of different nationalities (Ferner and Quintarilla, 1998). The description of 'Western' performance appraisal and compensation systems below is an attempt to summarize some key features of these systems. To describe local 'Chinese' HRM practices is also riddled with problems as there may be considerable differences across ownership structure, size, industry, and geographical location (Child and Stewart, 1997). The presentation is based on a review of research on the Chinese state-owned enterprises, which until recently were the dominant actors in the Chinese economy. Our aim is to describe Chinese HRM in the mid to late 1990s, the time when the stock of foreign direct investments in China really started to increase.

Western Performance Appraisal Systems

Performance appraisal is currently used in the vast majority of large Western companies. Traditionally, appraisal schemes have concentrated on past and current performance. The main motivation for introducing an appraisal system used to be to provide a basis for wage increases or new levels of merit pay. Today, performance appraisal processes are often paired with the identification of training needs and long-term potential. Evaluation of the extent to which past goals have been achieved, analysis of factors hampering goal achievement and feedback concerning how to improve performance, and the setting of new goals are also commonly included. The most sophisticated forms of performance appraisal systems, where the personal objectives of the appraisee are agreed upon, and the outcomes of appraisal are linked to training and development (and sometimes also to financial bonuses) are called 'performance management systems' (Holdsworth, 1991).

In most Western companies, the performance of an employee is appraised by his/her immediate superior. Additionally, in a growing number of Western firms, employees – managers in particular – are also appraised by peers, subordinates and sometimes even by customers (Waldman *et al.*, 1998). New objectives are typically set as the outcome of discussions between the person and his/her superior. The process of completing appraisals can be as simple as filling out a narrative report once a year about an employee's quality and output of work, or it may involve sophisticated measurement techniques, such as rankings, ratings, behavioural checklists, critical incidents, and comparisons with objectives (Sparrow and Hiltrop, 1994). The appraisal criteria used most often by Western firms are employee behaviour, including character traits, abilities and skills; and output (Murphy and Cleveland, 1991). Over time, in parallel with the change in purpose and content of performance appraisal, the appraisal criteria have generally changed from personal character through more observable behaviour to focusing on the key task-related results (Holdsworth, 1991).

Performance Appraisal in Chinese State-owned Enterprises

Several studies have been published on HRM practices in domestic state-owned Chinese companies (for example, Child, 1994; Easterby-Smith *et al.*, 1995; Warner; 1996). Research indicates that performance appraisal 'with Chinese characteristics' has been widely practised in Chinese state-owned enterprises (Nyaw, 1995; Easterby-Smith *et al.*, 1995). According to Nyaw (1995), the unique feature of Chinese performance appraisal practices is that great emphasis is placed on the 'moral' aspect such as political attitude, team spirit, and diligent work for the motherland (see also Hempel, 2001). A comparative study of Chinese and Dutch firms also showed that clear criteria for performance appraisal were much more seldom used in Chinese companies (Verburg *et al.*, 1999). In their case analyses of large Chinese state-owned firms, Easterby-Smith *et al.* (1995) found that appraisal in Chinese state-owned enterprises was often carried out by self-evaluation and 'democratic' sounding of opinions. In practice, this meant that the appraisee wrote a self-evaluation, and these comments were reviewed by superior managers and transferred to his or her personal file. It was common to gather opinions from a wide range of employees in order to strive for a 'democratic' evaluation (Easterby-Smith *et al.*, 1995). Only relatively few firms seem to have objective setting as an integrated part of the performance appraisal system.

The differences between Chinese and Western performance appraisal practices seem to encompass sources of appraisal, evaluation criteria, appraisal methods, and objective setting. Table 1 summarizes these differences.

Western Compensation Systems

Money sends strong signals about what is valued in people's contribution to the organization, and pay systems are commonly used as strategic tools in Western companies. Compensation systems can be composed of two basic parts, basic salary and variable pay based on performance of the individual, group and/or organization. Performance-based compensation systems are widely used by Western

TABLE 1
PERFORMANCE APPRAISAL PRACTICES
IN CHINESE AND WESTERN COMPANIES

	Chinese	Western
Sources of Appraisal	Self-evaluation and democratic sounding of opinions by peers and subordinates in addition to superior	Usually immediate manager
Evaluation criteria	Broad, rather unspecified evaluation criteria related to task but also to 'moral' and ideological behaviour as well as personal characteristics	Performance criteria related to specific task objectives
Appraisal discussion	No appraisal discussion, limited inter-personal feedback	Appraisal discussion common, direct feedback on performance
Objective setting	Top-down (if included)	Based on superior-subordinate interaction

Source: Adapted from Easterby-Smith *et al.*, 1995; Lindholm *et al.*, 1999)

companies, and the component contingent on performance tends to be significant. For example, according to a survey conducted in the United States in 1997, executives received 38.7 per cent bonus payment. Performance-based pay has been predominately linked to individual employee performance, and both quantitative measures and subjective superior judgement have been used to determine the variable pay received by the employee. Variable pay systems transfer some of the business risk from the owner to the employees.

The salary differences across employees tend to be very significant. In the United States, the average CEO in a large firm made 326 times more money than the average worker in 1997 (Tang et al., 1998). Although the salary differences tend to be smaller in other Western countries, the disparities increased considerably in the 1990s also outside the United States.

Compensation in Chinese State-owned Enterprises

Until the mid-1980s, government bodies determined the wages in Chinese state-owned enterprises. After the Communist takeover in 1949, there was strong ideological opposition to individual material incentives and the emphasis was on collective welfare benefits and non-material incentives (Chow, 1992). In the 1980s, wage reforms were carried out in China, with job characteristics playing an increasingly important role in determining employee salaries. Whereas in 1985 age was by far the most important predictor of an employee's earnings in state-owned enterprises, by 1990 job level in the company had replaced age as the most significant predictor, and more advanced education and training had begun to make a difference to people's pay levels (Child, 1995). Income differences were still relatively small (Child, 1995), although apparently the internal differences increased in the early 1990s (Easterby-Smith et al., 1995).

Performance-based pay was introduced as a part of the wage reforms in the 1980s. By the mid to late 1990s, state-owned enterprises had increasingly introduced performance-based systems (Goodall and Warner, 1999b; Verburg et al., 1999). However, in reality 'many enterprises have begun to pay equal (or almost equal) bonuses to all employees' (Warner 1995, 244), and 'although there is evidence of individualized payment being discussed in China there is still much resistance to its implementation – and the preference remains for group incentive schemes' (Easterby-Smith et al., 1995, 49). In other words, although the state-owned companies had been allowed and even encouraged to introduce performance-based pay systems, by the mid to late 1990s there had been only relatively limited changes in the entrenched compensation practices. Table 2 summarizes differences commonly found been Western and Chinese compensation systems.

TABLE 2
COMPENSATION SYSTEMS COMMONLY FOUND
IN CHINESE AND WESTERN COMPANIES

	Chinese	Western
Salary differences	Small	Large
Use of performance-based compensation	Fairly common	Common
Individual performance component (if existing)	Uncommon and/or insignificant	Common and significant with incentives as a function of the performance of the individual

THE DIFFUSION OF WESTERN-STYLE HRM IN CHINA

HRM in Western Firms in China

Research on the first Western-owned units established in China in the early 1980s indicated that there was a relatively high degree of local adaptation of HRM practices (Child, 1991). This pattern has clearly changed over the past 20 years (Björkman and Lu, 2001). Lu and Björkman (1997) conducted an interview-based survey of 72 foreign investment enterprises in 1996–97. Data were collected both with the help of a standardized questionnaire and open-ended questions. Their results indicated that Western companies had introduced performance management practices that were much more similar to their home country operations than to those of local Chinese firms. There was also a significant difference concerning compensation systems, although the difference between the degree of global standardization versus local adaptation of the practices of the foreign-owned companies was somewhat smaller. Hence, their conclusion was clear, Western firms tend to a high degree to introduce their own performance appraisal and compensation systems in their Chinese units. Other recent studies have obtained similar results. For instance, surveys conducted by the consultancy firm Hewitt Associates have shown that a growing number of foreign firms uses performance-based pay in China. Whereas in 1998 50 per cent of the surveyed companies reported variable pay plans, in 1999 70 per cent reported some form of variable compensation (Fiedler, 1999).

The potential impact of Western HRM practices on local practice is arguably greater the less Western corporations locally adapt their practices; conversely, the more foreign practices are introduced, the greater the potential influence on local practices and values. In view of the available evidence on MNC operations in China, a relevant research question is to what extent Western multinational firms through their HRM practices have influenced Chinese society. The most direct influence would be on how human resources are managed in local Chinese firms.

Changes in HRM in Chinese Firms

The overall conclusion in recent work on HRM in Chinese state-owned firms appears to be that gradual changes have been taking place in the 1990s (Ding et al., 2000). For instance, in their case studies of three Chinese companies (one state-owned enterprise, two joint stock companies), Benson et al. (2000) reported that all companies had some element of individual performance built into the wage system, but that income differences still remained relatively small and that '[M]anagers still seem to win the co-operation of workers by uniformly increasing wages and benefits' (Benson et al., 2000, 189).

While it seems to be relatively clear that changes in HRM are taking place, little rigorous work has been conducted to shed more light on how to explain the direction of these changes. The Japanese personnel management and industrial relations system has had a significant impact on Chinese personnel practices since the beginning of the twentieth century, but the changes taking place in the 1990s indicate a clear departure from the Japanese influence (Zhu and Warner, 2000). The spread of HRM through foreign-owned enterprises in China appears to have been significant in the 1990s (Benson and Zhu, 1999; Ding *et al.*, 2000). However, there is a dearth of scholarly work on the degree of Western-style HRM in Chinese organizations and no efforts have been made to explain differences across Chinese organizations in their propensity to adopt Western-style HRM practices.

The Institutionalization Perspective

In this study it is argued that the institutionalization perspective is conducive for examining why Chinese firms differ in their propensity to adopt Western-style HRM practices. The institutionalization perspective of organizational analysis is far from homogeneous (Scott, 1987). However, a common point of departure for most scholars is that organizations are under pressure to adapt and be consistent with their institutional environment. They are assumed to search for legitimacy and recognition, which they do by adopting structures and practices defined as, or rather, taken for granted as appropriate in their environment. Thus, it is not (only) technical rationality that determines organizational action and structure, but rather the organization is under pressure to become isomorphic with its environment. In other words, organizations are expected gradually to resemble other (successful) organizations in the environment in which they are embedded.

DiMaggio and Powell (1983) suggest that there are three major ways in which isomorphism is produced, coercive isomorphism, where a powerful constituency (for example, the government) imposes certain patterns on the organization; mimetic isomorphism, where organizations in situations of uncertainty adopt the pattern exhibited by organizations in their environment that are viewed as successful; and normative isomorphism, where professional organizations act as the disseminators of appropriate organizational patterns which are then adopted by organizations which are under the influence of the professional organizations. In the context of China, Western multinational corporations are likely to serve as a source of mimetic isomorphism and may also contribute to a professionalization of the HR profession. It should be noted that a convergence of HRM practices between local Chinese and Western multinational corporations may occur at different levels, ranging from guiding principles and basic assumptions of HRM to actual HRM practices, including tools and procedures (Becker and Gerhart, 1996; Bae and Rowley, 2001). The different levels are not necessarily aligned, in particular when local firms are adopting new HRM systems. Hence, Chinese firms may copy Western-style HRM practices, including particular HRM tools, without necessarily sharing basic assumptions and guiding principles with the Western corporations. The institution-alization perspective is particularly suited to examining the diffusion of structural organizational properties (Meyer and Rowan, 1977), of which HRM tools and procedures are examples.

So far, scholars studying Chinese management have mostly focused on coercive isomorphism as an outcome of state-legislated reforms. After 1949, Chinese state-owned enterprises were under considerable coercive pressure. However, the so-called 'three systems reforms' in 1992 involved the introduction of labour contracts, the endorsement of financial rewards, and contributory social insurance (Ng and Warner, 1998). In combination with the 1994 Labour Law, these changes contributed to the creation of an institutional framework within which changes in HRM practices could take place. By the end of the twentieth century, it was mainly large state-owned firms that were to some extent restricted in terms of their HRM practices by the Chinese authorities (Benson and Zhu, 1999).

The reforms in the 1990s did not point directly to any specific kind of HRM practices to be adopted by Chinese firms. Rather, the changes in the political–legal context created a situation where there was no strongly institutionalized model of HRM (Goodall and Warner, 1999a). Following Ding *et al.* (2000), I argue that Western multinational corporations have brought into China HRM systems and practices that may influence the kind of practices that Chinese firms adopt. The Chinese state-owned companies are today facing competitive pressures, and in a situation where they face uncertainty and lack a local model of how to manage human resources successfully, managers may view foreign corporations as successful role models whose practices they should mimic (DiMaggio and Powell, 1983; Westney, 1993). In situations of uncertainty, stakeholders may also begin to exert pressure on managers to implement new management practices (Abrahamson, 1996). In the situation facing Chinese managers responsible for deciding on how to manage people in their organizations, in particular mimetic isomorphic mechanisms but also normative processes may be at play.

Factors Influencing the Adoption of Western-Style HRM

This section will outline some factors that are hypothesized to influence the adoption of Western-style HRM practices by Chinese firms. 'Western-style HRM practices' should here be perceived as a continuum from high to low, and companies are likely to differ in the extent to which they adopt a certain practice. The most direct influence of Western multinational enterprises and their HRM is likely to be as role models who trigger mimetic behaviour on the part of Chinese firms with which they have direct relationships. The impact of various kinds of partnerships between Chinese and Western firms is therefore discussed first, followed by propositions concerning the impact of other mimetic and normative factors.

Partnerships

Chinese companies that enter into partnerships with Western companies are those that are most directly exposed to Western management practices. In one of the very few empirical studies carried out on the adoption of Western-style management practices in China, Firth (1996) found that Chinese state-owned enterprises that had joint ventures with Western partners appeared to incorporate the management accounting practices seen in capitalist nations to a much greater extent than did state-owned firms without joint venture operations. The direct exposure to Western management within the context of a joint venture may serve as a visible model of 'appropriate' practices. Additionally, the costs and efficiency of introducing Western-style practices are likely to be lower for companies that at least to some extent are familiar with these practices in their own partly-owned operations; in other words, the direct experience is likely to enhance the absorptive capacity (Cohen and Levinthal, 1990) of the focal Chinese organization. In fact, to learn Western management techniques may even have been one of the motives for establishing the joint venture. There is also some evidence from case study research (Benson and Zhu, 1999) that Chinese firms with foreign joint venture partners have been more likely to adopt HRM practices from their joint ventures. Therefore,

> Proposition 1: Chinese firms with joint ventures with Western partners more likely will adopt Western-like HRM practices.

Joint ventures differ in the extent to which they use Western HRM practices (Goodall and Warner, 1999a; Björkman and Lu, 2001). Some joint venture may use more Western-like practices, which then provide the basis for imitation by the Chinese partner. In other words, the more Western-like the HRM practices of the jointly-owned operation, the more Western-like the practices implemented in the Chinese organization are likely to be. Hence,

> Proposition 2: The more Western-like HRM practices in the

joint venture(s) with Western partner(s), the more likely the Chinese firm will adopt Western-like HRM practices.

The physical closeness of a joint venture to that of the parent is also likely to expose the Chinese partner more to the practices of the joint venture. Extensive research has shown that social networks are important in determining the organizations as well as the action or structure that are imitated by others (for example, Galaskiewcz and Wassserman, 1989; Haunschild, 1993). When units are geographically close, managers in the local organization are particularly likely to receive information through interpersonal networks and through direct involvement in the joint venture's operations. Therefore,

> Proposition 3: The closer the Chinese firm is to its joint venture(s) with Western partner(s), the more likely the Chinese firm will adopt Western-like HRM practices.

Although joint ventures with Western companies may be viewed as the highest degree of formal integration, Chinese firms may be exposed to Western-like management practices also through other kinds of collaboration. For instance, most Chinese–Western joint ventures and wholly-owned Western subsidiaries use local Chinese suppliers. The former often work closely with their suppliers to improve their operations. Some Western firms even organize management training programmes for their customers and business partners. For instance, several Western multinational corporations in the telecommunications equipment sector arrange programmes where Western management practices, including HRM, are extensively discussed. Similar to the case when Chinese firms have joint ventures with Western firms, non-equity business relationships between local and Western firms may trigger diffusion of practices through imitation. I therefore put forward the following propositions,

> Proposition 4: The more a Chinese firm's business operations are integrated with those of Western-owned units in China, the more likely the Chinese firm will adopt Western-like HRM practices.

Other sources of mimetic behaviour

However, ideas about new practices are not only diffused through direct partnerships. Scholars working within the institutionalization literature argue that the appropriate level of analysis is the organizational field, that is, organizations where the participants are mutually aware of each other, share a similar set of activities and recognize each other as referents (DiMaggio and Powell, 1983). How to define an organizational field is ultimately an empirical question, but it has been applied to regional economies and to broad groups of organizations such as the Fortune 200 (Mezias, 1990) and Fortune 500 (Fligstein, 1985) in the USA. Within one organizational field, new management practices spread more quickly than across fields (O'Neill, Pounder and Buchholtz, 1998). It has been shown that when there is a high degree of institutionalization, that is, when a large number of organizations share a certain salient practice or policy that is seen as *the* way to handle a certain issue, there is a higher probability that additional organizations will copy them (Tolbert and Zucker, 1983). Late adopters jump on the bandwagon as the increasing number of users leads to stronger isomorphic pressures. Research on corporate acquisitions has also found that companies tend to imitate the actions of visible companies within the same industry (Baum, Li and Usher, 2000). In a similar vein, when there is a large number of 'model' organizations with similar practices and/or policies, there is arguably a higher probability that new firms will embrace the practices. Building on this body of work, I put forward the following propositions:

Proposition 5: The higher the number of Western-owned units in the geographical region, the more likely the Chinese firm will adopt Western-like HRM practices.

Proposition 6: The higher the proportion of Western-owned competitors the Chinese firm is facing in China, the more likely the Chinese firm will adopt Western-like HRM practices

Normative factors

As pointed out by DiMaggio and Powell, one form of isomorphism is normative and stems primarily from a process of professionalization. DiMaggio and Powell (1983) suggest that two aspects of professionalization are important sources of isomorphism,

> One is the resting of formal education and of legitimization in a cognitive base produced by university specialists; the second is the growth and elaboration of professional networks that span organizations and across which new models diffuse rapidly. Universities and professional training institutions are important centers for the development of organizational norms among professional managers and their staff. Professional and trade associations are another vehicle for the definition and promulgation of normative rules about organizational and professional behavior. Such mechanisms create a pool of almost interchangeable

individuals who occupy similar positions across a range of organizations (DiMaggio and Powell, 1983, 152).

The emergence of an HR profession in China may serve as a conduit of new ideas about HRM. Hence, I expect that there is a positive relationship between the professionalization of the HR function and the introduction of new HRM practices. If a professionalization of the HR function takes place in China, empirically it would seem likely that the model for HRM would be obtained from societies in which the function is already institutionalized. One of the ways in which the professionalization process may take place is through the activities of semi-formal networks. In several locations in China, such as Tianjin, Beijing, and Guangzhou, there are networks consisting of HR professionals from foreign-owned firms. Some of these networks are closed to outsiders (a new member must be recommended by an existing member), but others are open to all foreign investment enterprises. HR professionals admit that the interaction in such networks has influenced their own firm's HR management policies and practices, as the networking provides good opportunities for benchmarking with other organizations (Björkman and Lu, 1999). The degree of professionalization is likely to differ in different parts of China, among others as an effect of the number of firms with Western-style HRM practices in the region in question. The following proposition is offered:

> Proposition 7: The higher the degree to which the HR function is professionalized in the geographical region, the more likely the Chinese firm will adopt Western-like HRM practices.

CONCLUSIONS

We currently have some knowledge about the use of Western-like HRM practices in the foreign subsidiaries of multinational corporations. While there is a growing body of research on the international convergence and divergence of HRM, there is a paucity of empirical research on factors explaining the adoption of Western-style HRM practices in Asia. This essay takes steps towards rectifying this situation by developing a range of propositions concerning how HRM practices in the units owned by Western corporations impact on organizational practices in Chinese firms. While the paper has focused on the influence of multinational corporations on the adoption of Western-style HRM in Chinese organizations, the propositions developed here can and should also be empirically tested in other contexts. Of interest would for instance be to conduct a comparative study of multiple countries in Asia.

Although we have asserted here that the HRM practices employed by Western firms influence HRM in local Chinese companies, one-to-one copying of Western HRM systems is implausible. To duplicate other companies' practices is difficult even in domestic contexts. Institutional, cultural and language factors are likely to play important roles as the HRM practices are modified as they are implemented in Chinese firms (Zhu and Warner, 2000). Therefore, large-scale surveys of the degree to which Chinese firms have adopted Western-style HRM need to be supplemented with detailed analyses of the process of 'translation' and process of modification of the HRM practices in local Chinese organizations. Research should also be conducted on the convergence between Western and Chinese firms of HRM systems at different levels, ranging from specific HRM practices to the guiding principles and basic assumptions underlying the practices (Becker and Gerhart, 1996; Bae and Rowley, 2001). The influence of other sources of 'appropriate' HRM than Western multinational firms – such as business school academics, consulting firms and successful local firms – should also be investigated by scholars aiming at augmenting our understanding of the emerging HRM practices in China.

Western-style performance appraisal and performance-based pay systems discussed here are at least partly at odds with behavioural norms and traditional Chinese values. The Chinese culture is built on a long Confucian tradition of familism and authoritarianism, creating norms of dependence and acceptance of hierarchy (Redding, 1990). These societal values are at odds with the development of individual responsibility and initiative (Child, 1991), which are central ingredients of Western performance appraisal practices, and may also restrict the possibilities to introduce pay based on performance at the expense of hierarchical position. The role of 'face' and harmony are also significant aspects of social life in China. The manager who criticizes a subordinate, whether in private or in the presence of others can cause that subordinate to 'lose face'. The issue of face might complicate direct performance feedback between managers and subordinates. It is also conceivable that individuals lose face and that group harmony is upset if they receive lower salaries than their peers. Finally, there is some indication that the Chinese tend to exhibit a high level of uncertainty avoidance (Worm, 1997). This may be of relevance when performance-based compensation systems are introduced since these systems increase the financial risk of the employee. International HRM scholars have advised multinational corporations not to apply HRM practices that fit poorly with the local culture as such practices may not have the intended effects on employee and organizational performance (Milliman *et al.*, 1998). For instance, cultural factors have been shown to influence significantly appraisals of performance (Farh, Dobbins, and Cheng, 1991). To date, little rigorous empirical work has been carried out on the performance effects of Western-style HRM practices in China and research on this topic should have high priority.

However, my point is not only that the Chinese cultural features discussed above may undermine the introduction of Western-style practices in China. Rather, I would like to suggest that to the extent that 'foreign' practices are implemented they require behavioural changes on the part of the local employees. Hence, I propose that the introduction of Western style may have an indirect impact on the values held by Chinese people as the HRM practices may be at odds with and thus 'challenge' existing values. This proposition is made based on the assumption that as people are induced to behave in ways that are at odds with existing societal values and behaviour norms, they will at least to some extent adapt their values accordingly. Therefore, one might for example hypothesize that the longer tenure individuals have in organizations with Western-style performance appraisal and performance-based compensation practices,

1. The less hierarchical values will they have,
2. The less importance they will attach to 'face',
3. The less they will attach to maintaining harmonious personal relationships, and
4. The lower degree of uncertainty avoidance they will exhibit.

In conclusion, researchers are encouraged to study not only factors explaining the adoption of Western-style HRM practices by local firms but also the effects that these practices may have on values held by people who are exposed to them both in the present and future years.

REFERENCES

Abrahamson, E. (1996), 'Management Fashion', *Academy of Management Review*, Vol.21, pp.254–85.
Bae, J. and Rowley, C. (2001), 'The Impact of Globalization on HRM, the Case of South Korea', *Journal of World Business*, Vol.36, pp.402–28.
Baum, J.A., Li, S.X. and Usher, J.M. (2000), 'Making the Next Move, how Experimental and Vicarious Learning Shape the Location of Chains' Acquisitions', *Administrative Science Quarterly*, Vol.45, pp.766–801.
Becker, B. and Gerhart, B. (1996), 'The Impact of Human Resource Management on Organizational Performance, Progress and Prospects', *Academy of Management Journal*, Vol.39, pp.779–801.
Benson, J., Debroux, P., Yuasa, M. and Zhu, Y. (2000), 'Flexibility and Labour Management,

Chinese Manufacturing Enterprises in the 1990s', *International Journal of Human Resource Management*, Vol.11, pp.183–96.

Benson, J. and Zhu, Y. (1999), 'Markets, Firms and Workers in Chinese State-owned Enterprises', *Human Resource Management Journal*, Vol.9, No.4, pp.58–74.

Björkman, I. and Lu, Y. (1999), 'A Corporate Perspective on the Management of Human Resources in China', *Journal of World Business*, Vol.34, No.1, pp.16–25.

Björkman, I. and Lu, Y. (2001), 'Institutionalization and Bargaining Power Explanations of Human Resource Management Practices in Chinese–Western Joint Ventures', *Organization Studies*, Vol.22, pp.491–512.

Brewster, C. and Larsen, H.H. (1992), 'Human Resource Management in Europe, Evidence from Ten Countries', *International Journal of Human Resource Management*, Vol.3, pp.409–33.

Child, J. (1991), 'A Foreign Perspective on the Management of People in China', *International Journal of Human Resource Management*, Vol.2, pp.93–107.

Child, J. (1994), *Management in China During the Age of Reform*. Cambridge: Cambridge University Press.

Child, J. (1995), 'Changes in the Structure and Prediction of Earnings in Chinese State Enterprises during the Economic Reform', *International Journal of Human Resource Management*, Vol.6, pp.1–30.

Child, J. and Stewart, S. (1997), 'Regional Differences in China and their Implications for Sino–foreign Joint Ventures', *Journal of General Management*, Vol.23, No.2, pp.65–86.

Chow, I.H. (1992), 'Chinese Workers' Attitude towards Compensation Practices in the People's Republic of China', *Employee Relations*, Vol.14, No.3, pp.41–55.

Cohen, W. and Leventhal, D.A. (1990), 'Absorptive Capacity: A New Perspective on Learning and Innovation', *Administrative Science Quarterly*, Vol.35, pp.128–52.

DiMaggio, P. and Powell, W. (1983), 'The Iron Cage Revisited, Institutional Isomorphism and Collective Rationality in Organizational Fields.' *American Sociological Review'*, Vol.48, pp.147–60.

Ding, D.Z., Goodall, K. and Warner, M. (2000), 'The End of the 'Iron Rice Bowl', Whither Chinese Human Resource Management?' *International Journal of Human Resource Management*, Vol.11, pp.217–36.

Easterby-Smith, M., Malina, M.D. and Lu, Y. (1995), 'How Culture Sensitive is HRM? A Comparative Analysis of Practice in Chinese and UK Companies', *The International Journal of Human Resources Management*, Vol.6, pp.31–59.

Farh, J.-L., Dobbins, G.H. and Cheng, B.-S. (1991), 'Cultural Relativity in Action, A Comparison of Self-Ratings Made by Chinese and U.S. workers', *Personnel Psychology*, Vol.44, pp.129–47.

Ferner, A. and Quantanilla, J. (1998), 'Multinationals, National Business Systems and HRM, the Enduring Influence of National Identity or a Process of "Anglo-Saxonization"'. *International Journal of Human Resource Management*, Vol.9, pp.710–31.

Fiedler, E. (1999), 'Manage for Success by Paying for Performance', *China Staff*, Dec. 1999–Jan. 2000, pp.13–18.

Firth, M. (1996), 'The Diffusion of Managerial Accounting Procedures in the People's Republic of China and the Influence of Foreign Partnered Joint Ventures', *Accounting, Organizations and Society*, Vol.21, pp.629–54.

Fligstein, N. (1985), 'The Spread of the Multidivisional Form among Large Firms, 1919–79', *American Sociological Review*, Vol.50, pp.377–91.

Gabreneya, W.K. Jr. and Hwang, K.-K. (1996), 'Chinese Social Interaction, Harmony and Hierarchy on the Good Earth' in Bond, M. (ed.), *The Handbook of Chinese Psychology*. Hong Kong: Oxford University Press.

Galaskiewicz, J. and Wasserman, S. (1989), 'Mimetic Processes within an Interorganizational Field, an Empirical Test', *Administrative Science Quarterly*, Vol.34, pp.454–79.

Gomez-Meija, L. and Welbourne, T. (1991), Compensation Strategies in a Global Context. *Human Resource Planning*, Vol.14, No.1, 29–42.

Goodall, K. and Warner, M. (1999a), 'HRM Dilemmas in China, The Case of Foreign-invested Enterprises in Shanghai', *Asia Pacific Business Review*, Vol.4, No.4, pp.1–21.

Goodall, K and Warner, M. (1999b), 'Enterprise Reform, Labor–Management Relations, and

Human Resource Management in a Multinational Context', *International Studies of Management & Organization*, Vol.29, No.3, pp.21–36.

Gooderham, P.N., Nordhaug, O. and Ringdal, K. (1999), 'Institutional and Rational Determinants of Organizational Practices, Human Resource Management in European Firms, *Administrative Science Quarterly*, Vol.44, pp.507–31.

Haunschild, P. (1993), 'Inteorganizational Imitation: The Impact of Interlocks on Corporate Acquisition Activity', *Administrative Science Quarterly*, Vol.38, pp.564–92.

Hempel, P.S. (2001), 'Differences between Chinese and Western Managerial Views of Performance', *Personnel Review*, Vol.30, pp.203–26.

Holdsworth, R. (1991), 'Appraisal' in Neale, F. (ed.), *The Handbook of Performance Management*. Exeter: Short Run Press Ltd.

Kerr, C., Dunlup, J., Harbison, E.H. and Myers, C. (1962), *Industrialism and Industrial Man*. London: Heineman.

Lindholm, N. (2000), *Globally Standardized Performance Management Policies in Multinational Companies' Subsidiaries in China*. Helsinki: Swedish School of Economics and Business Administration, doctoral thesis.

Lindholm, N., Tahvanainen, M. and Björkman, I. (1999), 'Performance Appraisal of Host Country Employees, Western MNCs in China' in C. Brewster and H. Harris (eds.), *International HRM, Contemporary Issues in Europe*. London: Routledge.

Locke E.A. and Latham G.P. (1984), *Goal Setting, A Motivational Technique that Works!* Englewood Cliffs, NJ: Prentice-Hall, Inc.

Lu, Y. and Björkman, I. (1997), 'MNC Standardisation Versus Localisation, MNC Practices in China–Western Joint Ventures', *International Journal of Human Resource Management*, Vol.8, pp.614–28.

Luo, Y. (2000), *Multinational Corporations in China*. Copenhagen: Copenhagen Business School Press.

Mezias, S.J. (1990), 'An Institutional Model of Organizational Practice, Financial Reporting at the Fortune 200', *Administrative Science Quarterly*, Vol.35, pp.431–57.

Meyer, J. and Rowan, B. (1977), 'Institutionalized Organizations, Formal Structure as Myth and Ceremony', *American Journal of Sociology*, Vol.83, pp.340–60.

Milliman, J., Nason, S., Gallagher, E., Huo, P., Von Glinow, M.A. and Lowe, K.B. (1998), 'The Impact of National Culture on Human Resource Management Practices, the Case of Performance Appraisal', *Advances in International Comparative Management*, Vol.12, pp.157–83.

Moran, T.H. (1993), 'Introduction, Governments and Transnational Corporations' in T.H. Moran (ed.), *Governments and Transnational Corporations*. London: Routledge.

Murphy, K.R. and Cleveland J.N. (1991), *Performance Appraisal, an Organizational Perspective*. Needham Heights, MA: Allyn and Bacon.

Ng S.-H.and Warner, M. (1998), *China's Trade Unions and Management*. London, Macmillan.

Nyaw, M.-K. (1995), 'Human Resource Management in the People's Republic of China' in Moore L.F. and Jennings P.D. (eds.), *Human Resource Management on the Pacific Rim*. Berlin: Walter de Gruyter.

O'Neill, H.M., Pouder, R.W. and Buchholtz, A.K. (1998), 'Patterns in the Diffusion of Strategies across Organizations, Insights from the Innovation Diffusion Literature', *Academy of Management Review*, Vol.23, pp.98–114.

Redding, S.G. (1990), *The Spirit of Chinese Capitalism*. Berlin: de Greyter.

Rosenzweig, P.M. and Noria, N. (1994), 'Influences on Human Resource Management Practices in Multinational Corporations', *Journal of International Business Studies*, Vol.25, pp.229–51.

Rowley, C. and Benson, J. (2002), 'Convergence and Divergence in Asian Human Resource Management.' *California Management Review*, Vol.44, No.2, 90–109.

Scott, Richard (1987), 'The Adolescence of Institutional Theory', *Administrative Science Quarterly*, Vol.32, pp.493–511.

Sparrow, P. and Hiltrop, J.-M. (1994), *European Human Resource Management in Transition*. New York: Prentice Hall.

Stinchcombe, A. (1965), 'Social Structure and Organizations' in J.G. March (ed.), *Handbook of Organizations.* Chicago: Rand McNally.

Tang, T.L.P., Tang, D.S.H., Tang, C.S.Y. and Dozier, T.S. (1998), 'CEO Pay, Pay Differentials and Pay–Performance Linkages', *Journal of Compensation and Benefits*, Vol.14, No.3, 41–6.

Tolbert, P.S. and Zucker, L.G. (1983), Institutionalized Sources of Change in the Formal Structure of Organizations, the Diffusion of Civil Service Reforms, 1880–1935', *Administrative Science Quarterly*, Vol.23, pp.22–39.

Verburg, R.M., Drenth, P.J.D., Koopman, P.L., van Muijen, J.J. and Wang, Z.-M. (1999), 'Managing Human Resources Across Cultures, a Comparative Analysises of Practices in Industrial Enterprises in China and The Netherlands', *International Journal of Human Resource Management*, Vol.10, pp.391–410.

Waldman, D., Atwater, L.E. and Antonioni, D. (1998), 'Has 360 Degree Feedback Gone Amok?' *Academy of Management Executive*, Vol.12, pp.86–94.

Warner, M. (1995), 'Managing China's Human Resources', *Human Systems Management*, Vol.14, pp.239–48.

Warner, M. (1996), 'Human Resources in the People's Republic of China, the "Three Systems" Reforms', *Human Resource Management Journal*, Vol.6, No.2, pp.32–43.

Westney, E. (1993), 'Institutionalization Theory and the Multinational Corporation' in S. Ghoshal and D.E. Westney (eds.), *Organization Theory and the Multinational Corporation*. New York: St Martin's Press.

Worm, V. (1997), *Vikings and Mandarins, Sino–Scandinavian Business Cooperation in Cross-Cultural Settings*. Copenhagen: Copenhagen Business School Press.

Zhu, Y. and Warner, M. (2000), 'An Emerging Model of Employment Relations in China, a Divergent Path from the Japanese?', *International Business Review*, Vol.9, pp.345–61.

The Significance of
Tripartite Consultation in China

SIMON CLARKE and CHANG-HEE LEE

Progressively deepening economic reform in the People's Republic of China since the mid-1980s has led to radical changes in labour relations.[1] The traditional guarantees of employment, wages and welfare have been eroded as state-owned enterprises (SOEs) have been progressively freed from state control and subjected to increasingly competitive market pressures and as economic growth has seen the rapid expansion of new forms of non-state enterprise in which none of the traditional guarantees exist. The subordination of enterprises to the constraints of the market was tempered through the 1980s and 1990s by a degree of state intervention, particularly but not exclusively in SOEs, to preserve the 'socialist' character of the 'socialist market economy'. However, the institutional framework and the financial resources required to maintain such intervention have been progressively eroded as responsibility for economic management and financial solvency has been passed to the enterprises. The withdrawal of support for the once privileged SOE employees has provoked a rapid increase in spontaneous industrial conflict and social protest right now and in the near future (Blecher, 2002; Cai, 2002).

The dismantling of the detailed management of labour relations by the Party-state has been accompanied by the gradual development of a new institutional framework for the regulation of industrial relations, often drawing on the example of developed market economies, in a bid to preserve social peace. This new framework has centred on the legal and contractual regulation of labour relations, a system for the tripartite resolution of labour disputes and, since the mid-1990s, the development of workplace 'collective consultation' between trade unions and employers (Warner and Ng, 1999). The most recent such development has been the establishment of a system of 'tripartite consultation' between representatives of government, employers and employees at national, provincial and municipal levels.

TRIPARTITE SOCIAL DIALOGUE

Social dialogue has long been sponsored by the International Labour Organization (ILO) as the most effective means of 'forging democratic, economically productive societies that incorporate social justice' (Treblicock *et al.*1994: 3). Tripartism is a form of 'corporatist' regulation, because it implies the institutional representation of corporate interests, but it also implies that the representatives of the three parties are independent of one another, and so presupposes an element of 'pluralism' in the political system (Treblicock, 1994: 7).

According to the ILO, the enabling conditions for social dialogue are 'strong, independent workers' and employers' organizations with the technical capacity and access to the relevant information to participate in social dialogue'; 'political will and commitment to engage in social dialogue on the part of all the parties'; 'respect for the fundamental rights of freedom of association and collective bargaining'; and 'appropriate institutional support' (ILO, 2002; cf. Treblicock, 1994: 7–8).

China ratified the ILO Tripartite Consultation Convention 144 in November 1990, but doubts about the commitment of the Chinese government to tripartism have centred on its unwillingness to grant the trade unions and employers' organizations the independence that underpins their ability to represent their constituencies and so that is regarded by the ILO as the key presupposition of real social dialogue. Comparative studies suggest that 'the domination of one or both of the social parties by the ruling political party may lead to a so-called tripartite accord, but not to true social dialogue' (Treblicock, 1994: 8). The ILO considers that 'social dialogue differs greatly from country to country, though the overriding principles of freedom of association and the right to collective bargaining remain the same' (ILO, 2002). It is these rights that the Chinese government has systematically denied to Chinese workers, China having been subject to five complaints to the Committee on Freedom of Association of the ILO Governing Body since 1989 (China Labour Bulletin, 2001), the most recent being a complaint lodged by the International Confederation of Free Trade Unions (ICFTU) in March 2002. Nevertheless, the Chinese government has recently made its effort to develop the institutions of tripartite social dialogue at various levels. The primary aim of this essay is to assess how far China has progressed in developing 'true social dialogue'.

HYPOTHESES

The 'pluralist' dimension, that is a precondition of 'true social dialogue', has been conspicuously absent from the Chinese political system, in which power at all levels has been concentrated in the hands of the Party-state and the function of the All-China Federation of Trade Unions (ACFTU) has been to serve as the 'transmission belt between the Communist Party and the masses'. Nevertheless, the dismantling of many of the mechanisms of top-down state administrative control of the economy has led some commentators to speculate about the possible emergence of the bottom-up representation of economic interests (Chan, 1993; Unger and Chan, 1995; Ogden, 2000), in which the trade unions could become the independent representatives of the employees in the workplace. China's critics, most notably the ICFTU, have insisted that the continued repression of independent labour organizations is evidence that there has been no advance towards freedom of association, and that the new institutions only represent an adaptation of the former intensive state regulation of labour relations to new economic conditions, with the Party exercising its control indirectly, through the ACFTU, so that 'the autonomy which the ACFTU has been talking about in the past decade can be compared to that of a civil service reform' (Leung, 2002: 2). Other commentators have not ruled out the possibility of the development of a voluntaristic system of regulation of industrial relations, whether on a 'Western' or an 'Asian' model, but have doubted that this would be possible while the trade union and employers' organizations remain firmly under the control of the Party-state (Warner, 1995: 44; Ng and Warner, 1998: 165).

There is little doubt that Chinese workers do not enjoy the right of freedom of association and, without that right and the right to strike, it is doubtful that they could be said to enjoy the right to collective bargaining. However, it might be that to disqualify the new system of tripartite consultation from serious consideration on those grounds is to adopt an excessively purist definition of 'true social dialogue'. Indeed, the central hypothesis of this essay is that it may turn out to be precisely the requirements of 'true social dialogue' that provide the lever that will induce the Chinese government to concede greater freedom of representation to employees.

The pace of change of labour and employment relations in China has accelerated since the middle of the 1990s as the Chinese government has accepted and even embraced the closer integration of China into the global capitalist economy. The consequent intensification of the subordination of labour to capital has implied an increase in the potential for conflict between employers and employees, the threat of which attests to the need to develop appropriate institutions to regulate such conflict. While the Party-state has continued to use the ACFTU as an instrument for the mobilization and control of the urban population, it has become increasingly aware that, if the ACFTU is to be effective as such an instrument, it has to articulate the aspirations and grievances of its members. This is by no means to argue that the development of a pluralistic system of industrial relations is a necessary consequence of the development of an advanced industrial society (Kerr *et al.*, 1962), but implies only that it would be politically very difficult for the Chinese Communist Party to respond to widespread labour conflict with purely authoritarian methods (and even less likely that it would respond by declaring the dictatorship of the proletariat). Pluralism, which can be seen as an institutionalization of Jiang Zemin's theory of the 'three represents', provides a specific means by which the Chinese Communist Party can seek to resolve the dilemma with which it has confronted itself of fostering the most rapid possible development of capitalism while still claiming to represent the interests of the working class.

The hypothesis that we want to explore in this paper is that the introduction of the new tripartite system marks the recognition of the need to develop the effective representation of the interests of employers and employees and so contains the potential for a transition in the direction of a pluralistic form of corporatist regulation, in which the trade union and employers' organizations are able effectively to represent their constituencies in negotiation with each other and with the government. If this is the case, international support for the development of tripartite social dialogue in China should be encouraged as a means of fostering the recognition of the fundamental human rights of labour by the Chinese government.

METHODOLOGY

This contribution is based on the observations of a field visit to China in May–June 2002 with a view to assessing the development of tripartite social dialogue institutions in China. In the course of the mission we met specialists from ACFTU, the Ministry of Labour and Social Security (MOLSS) and the China Enterprise Confederation (CEC) and representatives of the three parties involved in the National Tripartite Consultative Committee (NTCC) and the Beijing, Dalian and Chengdu Municipal Tripartite Consultative Committees (TCC), as well as with the employer representative on the Sichuan provincial TCC. All information reported here derives from these interviews and related documentary materials, unless otherwise stated. In each case, we met separately trade union, employer and government representatives. We did not have a prepared agenda for these meetings, but covered more or less the same ground in each one and sought, where appropriate, to verify information provided by one party against that provided by the others. In addition to meetings with the TCC representatives, we visited four enterprises in each city, where we again had separate meetings with management and trade union representatives. These meetings covered, amongst other things, their relations with higher representative bodies and their participation in tripartite structures of dispute handling and consultation. Our respondents were well-informed and, in general, forthcoming. We also had the opportunity to discuss our observations with our colleagues on the field trip and our preliminary findings with leading officials of ACFTU, MOLSS and CEC in Beijing at the end of the trip.

THE TRIPARTITE CONSULTATION SYSTEM

The National Tripartite Consultative Committee (NTCC) was established in August 2001 and instructions were sent to all provincial governments to establish their own TCCs by the end of 2002. The second meeting of the NTCC in February 2002 decided to extend tripartism to municipalities and townships across the country. By the end of 2001 there were already 15 provincial TCCs and by June 2002 their coverage extended to 20 out of 31 regions.

The project has four dimensions. First, to establish a consistent and appropriate legal and regulatory framework for the conduct of industrial relations in the enterprise. Second, to sponsor the extension of the principles of 'democratic management' and 'collective consultation' to all enterprises of all property forms. Third, to establish a framework for the consideration of the government's substantive social, labour and welfare policies. Fourth, to intervene directly to forestall or resolve conflicts which escape the bounds of the established framework of conflict resolution. All three parties see tripartism primarily as a means of maintaining social peace by ensuring 'harmonious labour relations' in the enterprise.

Terms of Reference

Article 34 of the 2001 Trade Union Law provides that 'Administrative departments for labour under the people's governments at various levels shall, together with the trade unions at the corresponding levels and the representatives of enterprises, establish trilateral consultation mechanisms on labour relations and jointly analyse and settle major issues regarding labour relations.' Beyond this, there is not yet any legislative basis for the functioning of the TCCs, which determine their own procedures within the framework of broad guidelines laid down by the NTCC, transmitted through MOLSS to its provincial

Departments and municipal Bureaux. Nevertheless, Article 34 already indicates two of the weaknesses of the system of tripartite consultation, which we will discuss in more detail later. First, it confines tripartite consultation to issues pertaining to labour relations and, correspondingly, identifies MOLSS and its branches as the representative of the government, whereas many of the most pressing issues extend far beyond the sphere of labour relations and are primarily the responsibility of other government departments. Second, it refers to the representatives of enterprises, rather than of employers, which raises the question of the very basis of tripartism, since tripartism usually presupposes the independent representation of government, employers and employees, while the reference to 'enterprises' signifies the traditional concept of the unity of interests of employer and employee.

Our impression was that the Labour Ministry and its representatives at all levels regard the TCC as a channel through which it can consult the social partners, rather than a decision-making body in its own right, and the employers play little active role, but ACFTU clearly has higher hopes for the new forum.

The ACFTU has been the driving force behind the application of tripartism, which it sees at national and provincial level as a means of influencing legislation and government policy. ACFTU campaigned very actively, and successfully, over the 1994 Labour Law (Ogden, 2000: 283–4) and, most recently, the 2001 revision of the Trade Union Law and there is a whole series of important new laws in the pipeline: on labour contracts, on collective agreements, on the settlement of labour disputes, possibly a law on wages. ACFTU is also very concerned about such issues as the compensation for laid-off workers and the funding of active labour market policies. Tripartite consultation provides a means by which ACFTU can institutionalize and consolidate its influence on legislation and policy formation, which has hitherto rested heavily on the position of its President, Wei Jianxing, as a senior member of the Politburo, which he left in November 2002.

ACFTU sees tripartism at the local level as a way of using the lever of tripartite agreements, and in particular using the power of the labour administration at the corresponding level, to pressure recalcitrant employers and extend the signing of collective contracts (and trade union organization) in enterprises where the ACFTU organization is weak. Anita Chan has suggested that 'the nascent tripartite structure is weighted against the union federation' because 'at the apex it is under the "leadership" of the CCP, and at the local levels it is under the thumb of local governments' (Chan, 2000: 50).

However, so long as ACFTU can call on the backing of the Party, the tripartite structures can give it the leverage to overcome its weakness at the local and enterprise levels.

The National Tripartite Consultative Committee

The National Tripartite Consultative Committee is chaired by a Deputy Minister of Labour, with vice-chairs from the other two parties. The quarterly meetings are held alternately in the offices of the three parties. The most contentious issue in the preparatory discussions concerned the composition of the committee, with ACFTU insisting strongly that the number of representatives should represent the importance of each party, with ACFTU having the largest delegation. After tough bargaining the parties finally agreed that, in addition to the chair and vice-chairs, ACFTU is represented by five department heads, MOLSS has four representatives – all directors-general of departments, and the employers' representative, the China Enterprise Confederation (CEC), is represented by three senior officials. The CEC could console itself with the fact that the body is purely consultative and all decisions are taken by consensus, so that the size of the delegations has a purely symbolic significance, but such symbolism is by no means unimportant and the employers have continued to press the issue of their representation.

The agendas of the first two meetings of the NTCC were dominated by issues which most concerned ACFTU. The only issue which actively engaged the employers was that of their representation on the Committee.

The first meeting of the NTCC in November 2001 defined the functions of the committee, decided to extend tripartite consultation to all provinces, and approved three documents: one, to promote further the collective contract system; the second, to strengthen the labour disputes settlement procedure; and the third, on the co-ordination of labour inspection with the trade unions. ACFTU viewed the outcome of the meeting very positively, in having provided for the first time a framework for the tripartite discussion at the national level of issues surrounding labour relations in the enterprise.

The second meeting in February 2002 reviewed the progress of tripartism, reconsidered the composition of the Committee and resolved to extend tripartism across the country at the municipal level. ACFTU attaches great importance to this because conditions differ so much from one locality to another that little can be achieved substantively at the national or even the provincial level. At national and provincial levels, the agenda of the TCC is dominated by the consideration of policy statements and proposed laws and regulations, while substantive issues are more likely to be addressed at municipal level and it is primarily at municipal level that the TCC can put pressure on particular enterprises. The second meeting also decided on a tripartite system of labour inspection and to survey industrial relations at enterprise, municipality and provincial levels to give guidance for the promotion of labour contracts and collective agreements.

Tripartite Consultation at Municipal Level

While the national and provincial TCCs focus on broad policy and regulatory issues, and on issuing instructions to the lower levels, the municipal TCCs are at the sharp end of the tripartite system because they deal directly with the enterprises in which the conflicts arise that tripartism is supposed to avert. In this section we will discuss the progress made in tripartite consultation at the municipal level on the basis of our interviews in Beijing, Dalian and Chengdu. The Beijing TCC was established in 2001 and that in Chengdu in March 2002. The Dalian TCC has a longer history, having been set up in 1999 as a development of the tripartite labour arbitration system that had been established in Dalian in 1987.

The municipal Tripartite Consultative Committees that we studied had a similar organizational structure. The TCCs were smaller than the NTCC and had equal representation, with three representatives from each party, and the chair rotated, rather than being held by the MOLSS representative. It is indicative of the status of the TCC that the top officials do not participate in it, the representatives being at vice-chairman and head of department level. The TCC is supported by a secretariat, provided by each of the three parties in turn, which draws up the agenda, prepares the meetings, provides the premises (and finance) and writes the minutes, in consultation with the other parties. Any disagreements that may arise are not ironed out by the secretariat before the meetings, as is the case with the NTCC, but are argued out in meetings of the committee. The Beijing TCC meets quarterly, while the Dalian and Chengdu TCCs only meet twice a year, although any of the three parties can call a special meeting if necessary. The Dalian TCC has established three sub-committees to handle its core work.

In each city, the Labour Bureau is attempting to establish tripartite committees at county and district level, but this has proved very difficult because the authorized employers' representative, CEC, does not have many branches at that level. This difficulty has been partially overcome by drafting in some of the major local employers to represent the employers' association where CEC is absent. On this basis Beijing had established TCCs in five districts by May 2002 and

Dalian had established tripartite structures in all 13 of its subordinate administrative units. Chengdu had not yet developed any such structures but it was under strong pressure from the provincial government and Party organization to do so. By this time, TCCs had already been set up in all cities and counties under the jurisdiction of Jiangsu and Henan provinces (*ACFTU Bulletin*, 5, 2002).

All three parties see the priority task of tripartite consultation as forestalling or resolving industrial conflict and social protest. The principal means of doing this are by encouraging the extension of collective bargaining and wage consultation in enterprises; monitoring the observance of labour legislation; reviewing the social and labour policies of the city administration; considering specific social and labour problems as they arise; and intervening to resolve serious labour disputes. As at the national level, ACFTU has been the driving force in defining the agenda of the municipal TCCs, while the employers have played an almost entirely passive role. The leader of the employers' delegation on the Dalian TCC could not remember a single example of an issue that they had raised through the tripartite system. Even in relation to wage guidelines, Dalian Employers' Confederation is happy to leave this in the expert hands of the Labour Bureau. Tripartite consultation provides a channel through which enterprises can petition the city government rather than a means for their participation as employers in the consideration of labour issues.

THE LIMITS OF TRIPARTISM IN CHINA

Although tripartite consultation is still in its infancy in China, it is already possible to identify a number of problems that might lead us to doubt that it will fully meet the expectations of its proponents. The main problems that we have identified are

1. The limited terms of reference of tripartite consultation,
2. The potential duplication of the established methods of dispute resolution, and
3. The limited representative base of the three parties.

Terms of Reference

The terms of reference of tripartite consultation confine it to labour relations issues and this is reinforced by the fact that the government side is represented by MOLSS, which effectively limits its terms of reference to issues which fall within the competence of MOLSS. In particular, tripartite consultation cannot deal with any issues which require the government to make expenditure commitments, since

MOLSS does not have the authority to make such commitments. This limitation is partially overcome in Dalian by inviting representatives of other departments to TCC meetings when that is appropriate, but it appears that such participation is only to provide relevant information, not in a decision-making role. The central issue facing the Chengdu TCC was the move of a big downtown industrial zone to the suburbs to make way for commercial and housing development in the city centre. This will affect the jobs of 100,000 workers and there is anxiety that many of them may lose their jobs in the move. The relocation programme is a programme of the city government, so it is not clear what, if anything, the TCC can do about it. The employers see their role as being to encourage enterprises to maintain employment through economic expansion and the role of the trade unions as being to explain to the workers the need for the move.

The issue of wages – normally central to tripartite consultation – does not fall within the remit of any of the TCCs that we studied. The minimum wage is set locally by the Labour Bureau, on the basis of procedures laid down by Beijing, without any substantive consultation with either employers or the trade unions. Similarly, the Labour Bureau issues annual wage guidelines, which indicate the range within which wage increases should fall, but these guidelines again are not subject to tripartite consultation, though the opinions of ACFTU may be consulted in a rather perfunctory manner.

Consultation over other issues takes place through traditional channels of bipartite consultation of ACFTU and CEC with, for example, the Director General of the State Council and the Ministry of Finance. A bipartite 'Labour/Government Consultation System', covering such issues as employment promotion, social security and job creation had been set up in 13 cities and provinces by March 2002, and efforts to extend the system to county level were under way (*ACFTU Bulletin*, 7, 2002). This means that the most important issues that affect the lives of workers fall outside the framework of tripartite consultation.

Dispute Resolution

The limited terms of reference of the TCCs is particularly relevant to their proclaimed role of dispute resolution. Most social protests have centred on issues such as allegations of management corruption, the non-payment of wages and social benefits, inadequate compensation for laid-off workers, or the abandonment of laid-off workers when their compensation runs out at the end of three years. Such means of forestalling conflict as the prosecution of corrupt managers, the provision of more favourable compensation or the creation of more jobs for laid-off workers lie beyond the terms of reference of the TCC and the competence and authority of MOLSS. This considerably restricts the ability of the TCC to intervene effectively to resolve disputes.

The only example of the successful resolution of a labour dispute through the intervention of a TCC reported to us occurred in Dalian. This was the case of a three-day spontaneous strike of 2,100 workers in a Singapore-funded enterprise in 2001 over illegal lay-offs and the failure to pay wages and social insurance payments. The Dalian Labour Bureau immediately set up a working group of the TCC, headed by the Director of the Labour Bureau, which visited the enterprise and persuaded the workers to return to work pending negotiations. The Labour Bureau drew the employers' attention to the relevant laws and regulations and persuaded them to meet their legal obligations.

A comparable case in Sichuan did not involve any tripartite intervention. Over 1,000 workers struck at the Guangyuan Textile Factory in March 2002 when the management, already in arrears in their payments to the pension fund and suspected of having bankrupted the company by stripping its assets, announced the sale of the factory, threatening the livelihoods of the employees. The workers took to the streets, where they were met with force and some of their leaders were detained (*China Labour Bulletin*, 19 March 2002). In this case, the dispute was not referred to tripartite intervention and the provincial government intervened directly.

The contrast between these two cases illustrates the limitation of the current system of tripartite social dialogue as a means of resolving serious labour disputes. The Dalian strike could be resolved by the Labour Bureau reminding the employers of their obligations under labour legislation, but the Sichuan strike involved much wider issues which the Department of Labour could not address but required the intervention of the provincial government.

Representatives of the social partners argued for the involvement of the TCC in dispute resolution on the grounds that the existing dispute resolution procedures are cumbersome and there is still a shortage of qualified arbitrators, so it can take a year or more for a case to be resolved. However, while direct intervention can accelerate the hearing of a case, it threatens to undermine the existing dispute resolution procedure by giving complainants an incentive to engage in direct action to secure the accelerated consideration of their cases. Moreover, social unrest has not been provoked by cumbersome arbitration procedures, because the majority of serious disputes never even enter the formal dispute resolution procedure,[2] partly for the same reason that the TCC is not competent to resolve them, that they involve issues that directly involve the government and so cannot be resolved within a purely industrial relations framework.

Social unrest has not been provoked by cumbersome procedures as much as by the failure of the trade unions to take up their members' grievances at an early stage. Like the vast majority of strikes and social protests, those in Dalian and Guangyuan had not involved the trade union and many of the workers' complaints had been directed against their trade union. This draws our attention to the second major weakness of the system of tripartism in China, the fact that the participants do not act as the independent representatives of the three parties, which is the precondition for any system of tripartite consultation. We have already noted that MOLSS does not have the authority to represent the government as a whole, but CEC does not effectively represent the interests of employers, nor does ACFTU effectively represent the interests of employees. On the one hand, the base of both organizations is in the SOEs and they have little penetration of the private or foreign-invested sectors. On the other hand, both organizations are more strongly influenced by the Party and the government than they are by their own membership.

Status of the Parties

According to almost all the officials we interviewed, there have been no significant disagreements, conflicts or disputes among the three parties at TCC at any level and consensus was achieved on all issues. This is a very strange situation, since the system of tripartite social dialogue exists, and was established in China, precisely to resolve conflicts and disputes, which are an inherent feature of labour–management relations in a market economy and which the Chinese government fears could be a serious destabilizing force. The main reason for this consensus is the fact that, while the transition towards a market economy has created conflicts of interests between employers and workers, the workers' and employers' organizations at higher level are not structured in such a way as to represent views and interests of their grassroots level. While both CEC and ACFTU are at best just beginning to disentangle themselves from their subordination to the Party-state, they still lack the political orientation and organizational capacity to represent their members at the grassroots level and therefore tend to emphasize the common interest of employers and employees in the development of the enterprise.

China Enterprise Confederation

The China Enterprise Management Association (CEMA) was established in 1979. In 1988 it merged with the Chinese Enterprise Directors' Association (CEDA), which had been established in 1983. The two organizations retain their separate names and have different membership, but the same staff services both organizations. In April 1999 CEMA was renamed the China Enterprise Confederation (CEC). CEMA was established by the State Trade and Economic Commission (STEC) as China began to experiment with the decentralisation of the management of SOEs at the beginning of the 1980s. Its purpose was to maintain links between STEC and the SOEs that had formerly been under the direction of the State Planning Commission, circulating information, providing training and holding conferences. It was originally funded and supervised by STEC and largely staffed by retired state officials. CEMA was recognised as the official Chinese employers' association when China re-entered the ILO in 1983, but did nothing to develop its capacity as an employers' association within China until the late 1990s. Following the first tripartite experiments, in 1998 the STEC authorised CEC to act as the representative of all enterprises in industrial relations matters and in 1999 issued instructions to all provincial governments requiring them to delegate this authority to CEC. Nevertheless, CEC is still primarily an enterprise association, rather than an employers' organization.

CEC no longer receives state funding, and is officially registered as a social organization, but it still has a close relationship with TEC. In Dalian, TEC participates in the TCC on the employers' side as a legacy from the days when it served as the representative of the employers on the Labour Arbitration Committee set up in 1987. TEC is still the supervising authority of the Dalian Enterprise Confederation, and the President of DEC is the Deputy Director of TEC. The Chengdu Enterprise Confederation has made even less progress in moving beyond its role as a bureaucratic quasi-state organization. It is still supervised by TEC, which appoints its General Secretary and his Deputy. Its five district organizations are managed by TEC and most are still affiliated to TEC, although there are plans to secure their independence.

In accordance with its new-found role as representative of employers, CEC has begun to develop its representative capacity, establishing new functional departments and seeking to employ labour relations specialists. However, it is hampered in these developments by four factors.

1. CEC has very limited funds. Although originally sponsored by the government, CEC now has to live on its affiliation fees and revenues from the services it provides. As a social organization, it is only permitted to charge a maximum affiliation fee of 2–3,000 yuan per year, regardless of the size of the affiliating enterprise.
2. CEC membership is still dominated by large SOEs. It has been

seeking to recruit non-state enterprises into membership but they have their own enterprise associations which have been set up under other government departments to serve their specific needs (Ogden, 2000). As an interim measure, CEC has appointed the presidents of some of these associations to vice-presidential positions in CEC at both national and local levels.

3. Most of the employers we spoke to still see CEC not as representative of employers in industrial relations, but as a channel for interaction with and access to government officials. This perception is reinforced by the fact that no CEC official we interviewed at any level could recall ever having had any serious disagreement over any issue with ACFTU! A CEC national officer commented, 'we are a socialist state, so to protect workers' rights is necessary. As a socialist state it has to take into consideration the interests of all parties. My opinion is only my own. Our government has a deeper and broader understanding.'

4. CEC does not have an effective representative structure through which employers can make their views known to the leadership and the leadership can be accountable to the members. The policies and activities of CEC are still decided primarily by its leadership and the leaders consult members and government officials at their discretion. One enterprise director, a satisfied member of CEC, regarded it as an organization 'run by the government and staffed by laid-off government bureaucrats'.

All our interviews with CEC officers, and the comments of ACFTU and MOLSS officials, reinforced our impression that CEC's priorities in tripartism continue to reflect their subordination to TEC, as the transmission belt from the government to the enterprise, rather than their role as representative of employers. They see their role not as being to represent the employers in the face of the demands of the trade unions so much as to represent the responsibilities of enterprises to contribute to social stability by providing jobs. The CEC's contribution is its role in trade and investment promotion, persuading enterprises to create more job opportunities, training employers to abide by the law and supporting the government's policy of encouraging the expansion of collective bargaining and democratic management.

ACFTU regards the weakness of CEC as a major obstacle to the development of tripartism, but this is rather a complacent view since, to a considerable extent, the weakness of CEC is only the mirror image of the weakness of ACFTU. It is only when trade unions present a serious challenge to employers that employers respond by joining employers' organizations which can defend and represent employers' interests vis-à-vis labour's offensive. The fact that CEC has no disagreements with ACFTU is not so much a sign of its failure to represent the interests of employers as of the failure of ACFTU effectively to represent the interests of employees.

ACFTU

There is no doubt among international observers about the ACFTU's subordination to the Party-state. According to ACFTU's Constitution, the trade unions 'are a bridge and a bond linking the Party and the masses of the workers and staff members, an important social pillar of the state power of the country'. However, with the disengagement of the state from economic management, this has ceased to be the serious barrier it once was to ACFTU's ability to fulfil its trade union functions. The Communist Party and the Chinese state have recognized that, in new economic conditions, social stability depends on the trade unions more effectively defending and representing the rights and interests of their members through the negotiation of collective agreements, which will respond to the particular conditions in each enterprise. For ACFTU, tripartite consultation is both the pinnacle of the system of collective consultation based in the enterprise and the means of extending that system to all enterprises, of all property forms. The effective implementation of the system of tripartite consultation consequently depends on the effective implementation of the system of collective consultation, a term preferred to the more adversarial 'collective bargaining' (Warner and Ng, 1999: 303–4), and the ability of ACFTU to represent its members' interests in the enterprise.

ACFTU has an ambiguous role to play in the reform process. On the one hand, as a trade union, its role is to defend the rights and interests of employees, which increasingly come into conflict with the interests of employers as the latter place profitability over the jobs, wages and welfare of their employees. On the other hand, the ACFTU has a responsibility, imposed on it by the Party, to maintain social stability. The more progressive elements in ACFTU do not see a contradiction between these two roles, since they believe that social stability can best be maintained if the trade unions can effectively defend the rights of their members. This may not demand militant action, but it does depend on the trade union in the enterprise acting as the effective representative of the employees, rather than fulfilling its traditional role as a branch of enterprise management. In practice, the leaders of enterprise trade union organizations continue to identify with management and give priority to the development, and now the profitability, of the enterprise over the defence of the immediate rights and interests of their members (Cooke 2002: 21; Ding, Goodall and Warner, 2002: 444; Chan 1998; Ding, Lan and Warner 2001).

Like CEC, ACFTU's organization is predominantly in SOEs, where it generally has near 100% membership. ACFTU is attempting to expand its membership in the private sector, partly for its own institutional reasons, but also, with the encouragement of the Party, as a means of establishing some form of social control in non-state enterprises and of forestalling the formation of free trade unions. The ACFTU organizing strategy for the private sector is to establish local federations of SME trade unions and then to launch a recruiting campaign. There is no evidence that much effort is put into such recruiting or that these initiatives have been very effective (Fu, Taylor and Li, 2001).

The character of enterprise trade unionism in China, with its base in SOEs and its identification with management, means that ACFTU generally shares the commitment of the government and employers to economic development and the continued deepening of reform as the means of creating jobs and improving the living standards of its members, to be achieved by the goodwill of employers with the encouragement of government, rather than through the collective organization of employees.

DISCUSSION

Tripartite consultative bodies are rapidly being established throughout China in the hope that tripartite consultation can forestall or resolve the growing number of labour disputes that are not resolved through the formal disputes procedures. On the basis of a study of the new tripartite institutions at national level and in three cities, we have to conclude that the tripartite system as presently constituted is unlikely to live up to the hopes placed in it both now and in the future. This is for two principal reasons. On the one hand, the terms of reference of the tripartite bodies are too narrow, in confining them to the consideration of narrowly defined 'labour relations' issues and in confining government participation to officials of MOLSS. On the other hand, the presupposition of tripartite consultation, the independent representation of the interests of the three parties, is absent. ACFTU and CEC membership is largely confined to SOEs, neither organization has internal structures through which employer and employee interests are articulated and both are strongly subject to guidance by the Party-state, retaining their traditional functions as 'transmission belts' respectively from the Party to the working class and from the government to the enterprise.

The subordination of trade unions and employers' organizations to the Party-state is clearly in gross violation of what the ILO regards as the most fundamental precondition for real social dialogue. However, in all our interviews with trade union and employer representatives at municipal and national levels we found a clear commitment to developing the capacity of their respective organizations as independent representatives, able to articulate the interests, aspirations and grievances of their members within the system of social dialogue. In the first instance, at least, the principal barrier to such an independent articulation of the interests of employers and employees is not the subordination of ACFTU and CEC to the Party-state, so much as the subordination of trade union primary organizations to enterprise management, which means that ACFTU primary organizations continue to put the interests of 'the enterprise' (and consequently of its management) above those of its employees.

ACFTU has been the most active proponent of tripartite consultation as a means of protecting its members and maintaining social peace. For ACFTU, TCC provides an institutional lever by which ACFTU can push its agenda of protecting its members through better law enforcement and promoting collective consultation at the enterprise. On the one hand, the more progressive ACFTU officers are well aware of the need to activate their members and their primary organizations if tripartite consultation is to prove more effective. From this point of view, tripartite consultation, while providing additional leverage for ACFTU to influence government decisions and to facilitate the institutionalization of collective consultation, cannot be a substitute for effective collective bargaining at the enterprise level. On the other hand, the mainstream of ACFTU seems to take a more traditional view, that tripartite consultation is an extension of administrative and political instruments through which they can compensate their organizational weakness at the workplace by tripartite enforcement of laws and regulations. There is no doubt that elements in the Party, and particularly in government, would respond negatively to a growing display of independence by the trade unions, but such conservative elements will not necessarily prevail over those who understand that such independence is a necessary condition for the effective and peaceful regulation of industrial conflict.

CONCLUSION

China is going through a period of rapid economic and social change and the likelihood is that tripartite structures will evolve in a positive direction. On the one hand, both ACFTU and CEC are conscious of their limitations as representative bodies and both are seeking to extend their membership beyond the state sector. The more progressive elements in ACFTU are aware of the need to break the dependence of enterprise trade unions on management, and CEC is developing its capacity to represent employers. On the other hand, bipartite and tripartite consultation is developing in other areas, alongside the formal tripartite structures, and it is likely that the scope of tripartism will continue to expand, whether by expanding the terms of reference of the Tripartite Consultative Committees or by developing parallel bipartite and tripartite bodies.

In this regard, recent industrial relations developments in Vietnam, where the first attempt towards tripartite social dialogue is being made, are noteworthy. In spite of the similarity with China in terms of the overall political structure, and particularly the Party–union relations, Vietnam has shown a flexible approach to industrial relations issues. For example, the official employers' organization in Vietnam, the Vietnam Chamber of Commerce and Industry (VCCI), has a strong private sector membership base, which allows them better to represent all types of employers' voice than their counterpart in China. Moreover, there are other competing employers' associations in some provinces, which are invited to participate in the tripartite structures. In turn, the strong and flexible representation of employers tends to put pressure on the Vietnam General Confederation of Labour (VGCL) better to represent their members at both enterprise and provincial level. Also, according to the draft regulation on tripartite consultation, it is foreseen that the tripartite consultative committee will have an annual meeting with the Prime Minister to discuss a broad range of social and economic policy issues. The stronger membership basis of VCCI in the non-state sector, flexibility on employers' representation in tripartite consultation, and the broader agenda and participation of the government in tripartite consultation are encouraging factors, which can possibly lead to a different path of industrial relations development in Vietnam from the current Chinese approach, in spite of the political structure and ideology they share.

China is by no means alone among the post-socialist countries in seeking to develop tripartite consultation and social dialogue as a means of maintaining social peace in a period of dramatic and fundamental economic and social change. The ACFTU is also by no means alone in facing the dilemma of wanting to encourage its primary organizations to become more active, while seeking to preserve social peace to justify its existence in the eyes of the state. The leaders of the Federation of Independent Trade Unions of Russia (FNPR) are well aware of the fact that to break their dependence on the state they have to build a base in the enterprise, but they rarely support employees in open conflict with their employers for fear of retaliation from the state (Ashwin and Clarke, 2002). It is by no means only under those regimes in which the government is under the control of a single party that the state tries to limit the ability of the trade unions to represent their members. This is why China has so much to gain from the international experience of the ILO and the ACFTU from international trade union co-operation both now and in the future.

ACKNOWLEDGMENTS

We are very grateful to the other members of the mission, Anita Chan of the Australian National University, Hao Jian and Chen Qiaoling of the ILO Beijing office and particularly to Shi Meixia of the Institute of Labour Studies under the Ministry of Labour and Social Security, Beijing, and to the Labour Bureaux representatives in Beijing, Dalian and Chengdu who organized our programme.

We are also grateful to Bill Taylor, Li Qi and Malcolm Warner for helpful comments on a previous draft of the paper.

The views expressed in this paper are those of the authors and are not in any way endorsed by the ILO or any other body. A longer version of this paper and related materials is available at www.warwick.ac.uk/~syrbe/china.

NOTES

1. There is a large literature on labour relations in contemporary China. For an overview see Warner, 1995; Ng and Warner, 1998; O'Leary, 1998; Warner, 2000; Zhu and Warner, 2000; Chiu and Frenkel, 2000; Chan, 2001.
2. Not one of 34 'labour chaos' events reported by Jiang (2000) had involved a prior reference to arbitration. We are grateful to Li Qi for this reference.

REFERENCES

Ashwin, S. and Clarke, S. (2002), *Russian Trade Unions and Industrial Relations in Transition*. Basingstoke and New York: Palgrave.

Blecher, Marc C. (2002), 'Hegemony and Workers' Politics in China', *China Quarterly*, Vol.170, June, pp.283–303.

Cai, Yongshun (2002), 'The Resistance of Chinese Laid-off Workers in the Reform Period', *China Quarterly*, No.170, June, pp.327–44.

Chan, A. (1993), 'Revolution or Corporatism? Workers and Trade Unions in Post-Mao China', *Australian Journal of Chinese Affairs*, Vol.29, pp.31–61.

Chan, A. (1998), 'Labour Relations in Foreign-Funded Ventures, Chinese Trade Unions, and the Prospects for Collective Bargaining' in G. O'Leary (ed.), *Adjusting to Capitalism: Chinese Workers and the State*. Armonk, NY: M.E. Sharpe.

Chan, A. (2000), 'Chinese Trade Unions and Workplace Relations in State-owned and Joint-venture Enterprises' in M. Warner (ed.), *Changing Workplace Relations in the Chinese Economy*. Basingstoke: Macmillan, pp.34–56.

Chan, A. (2001), *China's Workers Under Assault*. Armonk, NY: M.E. Sharpe.

China Labour Bulletin (2001), 'China and the ILO', *China Labour Bulletin*, 58, Jan.–Feb.

Chiu, S.W.K. and Frenkel, S.J. (2000), *Globalization and Industrial Relations and Human Resources Change in China*. Bangkok: ILO Regional Office for Asia and the Pacific.

Cooke, F.L. (2002), 'Ownership Change and Reshaping of Employment Relations in China: A Study of Two Manufacturing Companies', *Journal of Industrial Relations*, Vol.44, No.1, pp.19–39.

Ding, D.Z., Goodall, K. and Warner, M. (2002), 'The Impact of Economic Reform on the Role of Trade Unions in Chinese Enterprises', *International Journal of Human Resource Management*, Vol.13, No.3, pp.431–49.

Ding, D.Z., Lan, G. and Warner, M. (2001), 'A New Form of Chinese Human Resource Management? Personnel and Labour–Management Relations in Chinese Township and Village Enterprises: a Case-Study Approach', *Industrial Relations Journal*, Vol.32, No.4, pp.328–43.

Fu, L., Taylor, B. and Li, Q. (2001), 'City Trade Unions and the Regulation of Industrial Relations in FIEs in China: a Last Chance for the ACFTU to be Relevant?', *Labour in a Globalising World: The Challenge for Asia*, Hong Kong: City University of Hong Kong, January.

ILO (2002), 'Social Dialogue'. Infocus Programme on Social Dialogue, Labour Law and Labour Administration, www.ilo.org/public/english/dialogue/ifpdial/index.htm

Jiang, Zhenchang (2000), 'Qianxin yu jinqi dalu gongchao: jiti xingdong duandian' (Wage Arrears and Labour Chaos in Mainland China: Opinions of Collective Action). *Zhongguo dalu yanjiu (Mainland China Studies)*. Vol.43, No.9, pp.81–101.

Kerr, C., Dunlop, J. T., Harbison, F. and Myers, C.A. (1962), *Industrialism and Industrial Man*, London: Heinemann.

Leung, T. (2002), 'ACFTU and Union Organizing', *China Labour Bulletin*, 26 April 2002 (www.china-labour.org.hk/iso).

Li, Q. (2000), 'A Study of Labour Relations in State-owned Enterprises in China: the Continued Dominance of the State and the Failure of the Collective Contract System.' PhD Thesis. Hong Kong: City University of Hong Kong.

Ng, S.H. and Warner, M. (1998), *China's Trade Union and Management*. Basingstoke: Macmillan.

Ogden, S. (2000), 'China's Developing Civil Society: Interest Groups, Trade Unions and Associational Pluralism' in M. Warner (ed.), *Changing Workplace Relations in the Chinese Economy*. Basingstoke: Macmillan, pp.263–97.

O'Leary, G. (ed.) (1998), *Adjusting to Capitalism: Chinese Workers and the State*. Armonk: M.E. Sharpe.

Treblicock, A. *et al.* (1994), *Towards Social Dialogue: Tripartite Cooperation in National Economic and Social Policy-Making*. Geneva: ILO.

Unger, J. and Chan, A. (1995), 'China, Corporatism and the East Asia Model', *Australian Journal of Chinese Affairs*, Vol.33, Jan., pp.25–33.

Warner, M. (1995), *The Management of Human Resources in Chinese Industry*. Basingstoke: Macmillan.

Warner, M. (2000), *Changing Workplace Relations in the Chinese Economy*. Basingstoke: Macmillan.

Warner, M. and Ng, S.H. (1999), 'Collective Contracts in Chinese Enterprises: A New Brand of Collective Bargaining under Market Socialism', *British Journal of Industrial Relations*, Vol.32, pp.295–314.

Warner, M. and Zhu, Y. (2000), 'The Origins of Chinese "Industrial Relations"' in M. Warner (ed.), *Changing Workplace Relations in the Chinese Economy*. Basingstoke: Macmillan, pp.15–33.

Zhu, Y. and Warner, M. (2000), 'An Emerging Model of Employment Relations in China: a Divergent Path from the Japanese?', *International Business Review*, Vol.9, pp.345–61.

Sharing Knowledge and Decision Power in Sino-Foreign Joint Ventures

DOMINIQUE JOLLY

Because of the growing openness of the Chinese economy, an increasing number of foreign companies is operating in mainland China. The country has become the largest recipient for Foreign Direct Investment (FDI) amongst the emerging countries. The size and the dynamic of the Chinese market are so impressive that foreign companies are convinced that they cannot afford to be absent. The entry of the People's Republic of China (PRC) into the World Trade Organization (WTO) in 2001 will probably act as a new stimulus to this trend. Sino–foreign joint ventures are still the dominant pattern for entry into the market – even if, according to Vanhonacker (1997), an increasing number of foreign companies operate as Wholly Foreign Owned Enterprises (WFOE).

The management of Sino–foreign joint ventures raises many practical problems. Such joint ventures were even discredited by some writers such as Deng (2001) for the management challenges they pose. The literature has dealt with issues such as role of government (Osland and Cavusgil, 1996; De Bruijn and Jia, 1997), trust, control and governance (Yan and Gray, 1994; Child, 1998; Goodall and Warner, 2002), partner selection (Luo, 1998), knowledge transfer (Zhao *et al.*, 1997; Si and Bruton, 1999; Bruun and Bennett, 2002), *guanxi* (Ambler, 1995; Farh *et al.*, 1998), human resource management (Tsang, 1994; Ding *et al.*, 2000), etc. This study focuses on two main issues at the core of the management of these joint ventures:

1. *Sharing decision-making power*
   By definition, whether they are Chinese or not, equity joint ventures call for a sharing of control and decision-making power because they result from the pooling of resources from at least two distinct partners. How is this done in Sino–foreign joint ventures? What is the role of each partner? What are the

decision-mechanisms used in these joint ventures? What are the rules and procedures? Is there a relationship between ownership structure and the distribution of decision-making power?

2. *Sharing knowledge*

   For over 20 years, the PRC government has required the formation of joint ventures as a way of transferring technologies and management skills to China from the West. Technological transfers were viewed as compensation for gaining access to Chinese markets. Is this solely a one-way transfer, that is, are there any learning opportunities for the foreigner? What is the dynamic of knowledge transfers between partners? What are the barriers to knowledge sharing? What, on the contrary, are the incentives to knowledge sharing?

This study is divided into four parts. Section one offers an overview of what has been said in the literature regarding these two issues – about inter-firm alliances as well as more specifically on Sino–foreign joint ventures. Section two presents the methodology developed for this research. Sections three and four report on the research results and discuss its implications.

THEORETICAL BACKGROUND AND HYPOTHESIS

This first section uses the conceptualization and the empirical results produced by previous research to generate two hypotheses:

1. The higher the decision-making in the hierarchy, the more the decision-making power is shared by the partners;
2. Knowledge transfers are hampered by exogamic barriers but stimulated by business incentives.

Literature examined encompasses inter-firm alliance theories, resource-based literature, as well as more specifically empirical works conducted in Sino–foreign joint ventures.

The first hypothesis relates to the sharing of decision-making power that comes from the pursuit of a joint goal in a specified area by at least two partners. My research draws upon previous research done on the governance of equity joint ventures which refers to management control and the sharing of decision-making power. Research has shown that governance faces issues such as partners' opportunistic behaviour, asymmetrical interests and even conflicting objectives between partners. My study differs from previous studies in that it distinguishes between strategic, functional and operational decisions.

The second hypothesis builds on one of the key idiosyncratic feature of inter-firm alliances, that is the sharing of resources in the co-operation by at least two distinct partners. Knowledge is one very specific type of resource. Research on the knowledge transfer dynamic in inter-firm alliances has shown that, contrary to tangible assets which cannot be recreated without money, one given partner can use the co-operation for observing, understanding and learning the knowledge of its counterpart – he/she can even transfer this knowledge to his/her own organization and reproduce it at limited cost. Thus, understanding the barriers and incentives to knowledge transfer is a very important matter. I will now introduce the conceptual and empirical arguments underlying the formulation of these two research hypotheses.

Decision-making Mechanisms Inside the Joint Venture

Because they want to ensure the most effective use of the resources they pool into the joint venture, each partner wants to exert control on the joint venture's destiny (Killing, 1982). Joint ownership and joint management are not easy tasks. Joint ventures pose the problem of opportunistic behaviour (Hill, 1990; Gugler, 1991; Gulati *et al.*, 1994). Asymmetrical interests are also a source of conflict in the joint venture. Companies share the same bed, but they have different dreams! (Si and Bruton, 1999). Conflicting objectives may hamper the decision-making process.

Hennart (1988) distinguishes between equity and non-equity joint ventures. In equity joint ventures, the distribution of equity is a function of the resources brought into the joint venture by each partner. Holding a share of the equity opens the door to control.

Control has been defined by Geringer and Hébert (1989) as: 'the process by which one entity influences, to varying degrees, the behaviour and output of another entity through the use of power, authority and a wide range of bureaucratic, cultural and informal mechanisms' (pp.236–7) so as to lead to the attainment of its objectives. Control refers to the ability to influence strategic decision. It is a mechanism through which parent firms implement their strategies and protect their interests. This can be done through, for example, the appointment of members to the board of directors (they approve the venture's business plan, profit distribution, major investments and other important financial decisions) or the nomination of key personnel such as top executives.

A case study of four Sino–American joint ventures conducted by Yan and Gray (1994), with both US and Chinese partners, shows that the relative bargaining power of each partner shapes the pattern of management control; bargaining power is defined as the resources under the control of the partner and the number of alternatives available (for example, the number of possible partners). Foreign companies wanting to increase their control should bring key resources into the joint venture. Research conducted by Child and Yan (1999) in 67 manufacturing Sino–foreign joint ventures shows that the equity share has a direct effect on board representation and also on strategic control – whilst non-equity contributions have an impact on operational control. The analysis of the composition and function of the board of directors in Sino–foreign joint ventures conducted by Goodall and Warner (2002) shows that drawing up the joint venture's strategic plans, approving budgets and short-term plans, as well as setting dividends, are perceived (by Chinese as well as by expatriates) as the most important roles.

However, research on the relationship between joint venture control and performance yields mixed results. Dominant control by the foreign partner has shown an increase in performance (Killing, 1982). Nevertheless, some research has also shown the opposite. Research conducted by Calantone and Zhao (2001) on a sample of 312 Sino–foreign joint ventures tends to show that control should be a function of the familiarity of the foreign partner with the local culture and market. If the foreign firm emphasizes gaining access to local knowledge through the Chinese partner, then it should reduce its control. On the other hand, if the foreign company is familiar with local settings and if it wants to increase market power, then it should increase its control. In summary, the literature has shown: a positive relationship between resources pooled in the joint venture, bargaining power and the equity share; a positive relationship between the equity share and management control; but, a mixed result regarding the link between control and performance.

This review of the literature reveals that only a few studies in the Chinese context paid attention to the type of decision made within the joint venture. The present research has been carried out with a distinction between three types of decision: strategic, functional and operational. Strategic decisions deal with the company's long-term orientations. This concerns decisions about positioning vis-à-vis competitors, the development of competitive advantage, and the expansion of activities through diversification and vertical integration. Strategic decisions are usually considered to have a greater impact on a company's future than functional decisions such as finance, marketing, human resource management, etc. Because equity is, by definition, shared in an equity joint venture, it has been hypothesized that decisions regarding the future of the joint venture will be taken jointly by the Chinese and the foreign partner. Operational decisions such as scheduling, production control, financial reporting, merchandising and programming are usually considered as having only a short-term impact on company development. Functional decisions are generally positioned as a kind of mid-way between strategic and operational decisions. Because operational decisions need to be localised and because the cost of taking these numerous decisions jointly would be too high, it is assumed that the partners of a joint venture will decide to entrust the responsibility of operational decisions to the local partner. The following hypothesis is proposed:

1. The higher the decision in the hierarchy of decision types (strategic, functional, operational), the more the decision-making power is shared by the two partners. In other words, strategic decisions involve both partners while operational decisions are most often delegated to the local partner – functional decisions being half-way between these two extremes.

Barriers and Incentives to Knowledge Exchanges

Doz *et al.* (1989), Hamel (1991) as well as Richter and Vettel (1995) showed that inter-firm alliances could be a channel for transfers between partners. This point is particularly interesting when these transfers relate to intangible assets such as the knowledge carried by individuals: intimate knowledge of a market or a country, expertise in a management method embodied in an organization, use of a complex technology, etc. Contrary to tangible assets, such knowledge can be duplicated at low cost. In this context, alliances have more appeal than licences or commercial transactions (Kogut, 1988).

If adequate mechanisms exist, a partner can appropriate one of these intangible assets through co-operation with its ally. Basically, the transfer occurs through the in and out moves of personnel between the joint venture and the parent companies. Inkpen (1996) identified four organizational mechanisms. These are: regular meetings between the joint venture and parent-company staffs, study visits of parent-company members to the joint venture in operation, frequent rotations of personnel between joint venture and parent company, and participation of the joint venture managers in parent-company strategy meetings. Mowery *et al.* (1996) have shown that the formation of equity joint ventures is likely to promote the transfer of technological competences – while the formation of non-equity joint ventures is weaker in this respect.

The argument suggested here is that knowledge appropriation differs significantly depending on the distance between allies' profiles – and, as a consequence on the relatedness between the resources brought by the partners. Jolly (2002) suggested distinguishing between two types: so-called *endogamic* alliances (between associates that are close) and the *exogamic* alliances where the two parties are quite different from each other. In the case of endogamies, the differences between parent companies are not strong enough for significant lessons to be drawn from the observation of the ally's practices. Because allies' profiles converge, the resources brought into the alliance are weakly differentiated. As a consequence, transfers are limited. When two allies have close technology portfolios, comparable organizational know-how and managerial competencies, they have limited chances to learn from one another. Nevertheless they can learn together, that is create new knowledge collectively. In summary, the absence of significant differences in endogamies considerably limits transfer between allies. In the case of exogamy, the situation is exactly the opposite. Co-operation is established between parents presenting contrasting profiles. The coexistence of differentiated profiles within the same alliance fosters the interbreeding of resources. Each ally has the opportunity to learn new competences which are only revealed by observation of the other party.

Sino–foreign joint ventures are precisely one case of exogamic partnerships. Because they combine resources of different kinds, partners gain advantages which they could not obtain individually. The foreign partner generally seeks to benefit from the *guanxi* of his Chinese partner, to acquire the intelligence of the local milieu as well as access to distribution networks, raw materials suppliers, utilities and the labour market. On the other hand, the Chinese company aims at capturing the industrial know-how and (product and process) technologies of its ally, and more generally speaking its managerial skills (Beamish, 1993; Yan and Gray, 1994; Luo, 1998; Si and Bruton, 1999; Liu and Pak, 1999).

The resource-based literature (Wernerfelt, 1984; Hamel and Prahalad, 1990; Barney, 1991; Grant, 1991) puts a strong emphasis on competitive edge and the contribution of knowledge to the formation of competitive advantages (Whitehill, 1997; Teece, 2000; McEvily and Chakravarthy, 2002). As a consequence, a very basic hypothesis derived from the competitive value of knowledge is that companies try to erect barriers to the imitation of their specific knowledge.

As stressed by Bruun and Bennett (2002), this is the case in China for joint ventures as well as for WFOE. A survey conducted with 200 British companies by Zhao *et al.* (1997) identifies several obstacles to transferring technologies: excessive bureaucracy in Chinese enterprises as well as in government ministries and agencies, time-consuming negotiations and unsatisfactory protection of transferred technology.

Nair and Stafford (1998) conducted in-depth interviews with Western executives (experienced in Sino–Western alliances); they identified complexity, cultural differences, language barriers and bureaucracy as being challenges for strategic decisions. Cultural differences were also identified as an obstacle to knowledge transfers by Liu and Vince (1999). Protecting intellectual property was identified as a barrier to technology transfers by Weldon and Vanhonacker (1999). The following hypothesis can therefore be formulated:

2. Knowledge transfers between Chinese and foreign partners are hampered by exogamic barriers – such as cultural differences or language barriers – but stimulated by business perspectives.

Research Model

Figure 1 offers an articulated summary of the two parallel research tracks explored in this essay.

FIGURE 1
RESEARCH MODEL

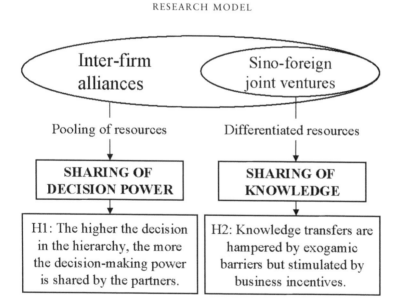

METHODOLOGY

Data Sources and Treatment

Data collection was based on face-to-face interviews conducted during autumn 2001 with general managers in Sino–foreign joint ventures employing a minimum of 100 employees. A semi-structured questionnaire was designed mixing closed and open questions relating to the management of the joint venture. Experts on Chinese business were asked to review the questionnaire. An English and a Chinese version of the questionnaire was used.

Only part of the data collected with this questionnaire was used for the present analysis. The issues raised here were treated exclusively with open questions. This approach is well adapted to the issues raised in this study for the following reasons: open questions do not impose any constraints, do not create any bias, give maximum of freedom to the respondent, let him answer spontaneously, open new dimensions and finally allow the researcher to draw on a wide range of answers. On the other hand, some respondents might find the lack of directiveness difficult to deal with. Furthermore, data generated by open questions require specific treatment in order to uncover any crude statistics. The data was processed in three steps:

1. An examination of questionnaires so to extract all the possible answers and draw a list of all items generated by all the respondents for each question;
2. Codification of each questionnaire on the basis of the scale previously developed;
3. Capture of the codified answers so to establish a data counting.

Sample and Respondents

A total of 67 questionnaires was collected. The major characteristics of the firms in the sample are shown in Tables 1 and 2. Absolute and relative frequencies are given.

A large majority (86 per cent) of the Chinese partners of the joint ventures in this sample are based in the Shanghai area: 51 in Shanghai and 7 in adjacent provinces; this allows checking for regional differences. Foreign partners come mostly from North America and Europe, particularly France and Germany. Only one foreign partner is from Singapore; none are from Taiwan or Hong Kong. This means that this sample is practically unbiased by overseas Chinese companies.

Equity distribution is presented here using Killing's (1982) classification: shared management, dominant partner, independent. In only 12 cases in the sample is ownership strictly balanced (50/50). Most of the time, the foreign partner is the dominant one (23 + 16 > 5 + 6). On average, the foreign partner holds 57 per cent of the share (with 43 per cent for the Chinese partner). Nevertheless, more than one third of the joint ventures (5 + 16) exhibit a significantly unbalanced ownership distribution, that is where one of the two partners owns more than 60 per cent of the shares.

Regarding size – as has already been mentioned, there is no joint

TABLE 1
SAMPLE PROFILE: ORIGIN OF PARTNERS AND SHAREHOLDING

Categories	No.	%
Origins of Chinese partners (n=67)		
Shanghai	51	0.76
Adjacent Provinces: Jiangsu, Anhui	7	0.10
Beijing	7	0.10
Other Provinces: Hubei, Yunnan	2	0.03
Origins of foreign partners (n=67)		
North America: USA, Canada	19	0.28
Western Europe: France	19	0.28
Germany	10	0.15
UK	4	0.06
Others	9	0.13
Asia: Japan, Australia, Singapore	6	0.09
Equity distribution of joint ventures (n=62)		
Chinese partners over 60%	5	0.08
Chinese partners 51–60%	6	0.10
Balanced ownership (50/50)	12	0.19
Foreign partners 51–60%	23	0.37
Foreign partners over 60%	16	0.26

venture in this sample with fewer than 100 employees. Most of the companies included are small (100–500) or medium-sized companies (500–2000). The average staff is 907 employees – of whom 875 are Chinese and 33 expatriates, that is only 3.8 per cent of the staff comes from abroad. Similar results are shown in data on turnover (Pearson correlation = 0.643**). The sample includes joint ventures from the very beginning of the 'Open Door Policy' (1983–1990) as well as early followers (1991–1995). Some other companies were created even more recently. The average duration of operation is seven years. Not surprisingly, age is correlated with staff (Pearson correlation = 0.453**). In summary, most of the companies in the sample have significant experience of doing business with a partner.

It is worth noting that this data collection relies mainly on the perceptions of Chinese managers (56/67) whereas most of the research done in the past has relied on the perceptions of foreign managers.

DECISION MECHANISMS INSIDE THE JOINT VENTURE

Decision-making mechanisms in the joint venture were analysed at three levels: strategic decisions, functional decisions (finance, marketing, human resource management, etc.), and operational decisions (scheduling, production control, financial reporting,

TABLE 2
SAMPLE PROFILE: SIZE AND AGE OF JOINT VENTURES

Joint venture	Category		No.	%
Size (n=66)	Small	100–500	39	0.59
	Medium	500–2000	18	0.27
	Large	Over 2000	9	0.14
Annual turnover (n=58)	Small	< 10 million	12	0.21
	Med.–small	10–100 million	28	0.48
	Med.–large	100–1000 million	13	0.22
	Large	> 1000 million	5	0.09
Date of set-up (n=65)	1983–90		7	0.11
	1991–95		31	0.48
	1996–2001		27	0.41

merchandising, etc). The aim was to understand the rules and procedures adopted by the joint venture partners for implementing their joint decision-making power.

Analysis of the data collected reveals two distinct patterns of answers. This point enabled us to cast light on the decision mechanism issue from two distinct angles: some respondents (23) took a hierarchical perspective whilst others (19) looked at the distribution of roles between the Chinese and foreign partners. Unfortunately, a significant part of the questionnaires (25) were not exploitable, because of incomplete answers. This might show the sensitivity of respondents regarding the issue of decision mechanisms.

The Hierarchical Perspective

Table 3 exhibits the distribution of the sub-sample of 23 respondents who took the hierarchical perspective. Absolute and relative frequencies are given. Three types of decision-makers were inferred from the analysis of the answers to the questionnaire: board of directors, company general managers and department heads. These three categories clearly demonstrate a hierarchy: department heads report to company general managers who in turn are accountable to the board of directors. The board, meeting usually once or twice a year, is the main link between the joint venture and its parent companies.

These data – even if they are based on a limited sample – are in line with the usual idea that strategic decisions are generally decided by the board of directors, while functional decisions are most of the time taken by general managers, and finally, operational decisions are under the responsibility of department heads. There is nothing new in this very traditional hierarchy. These data only show that distribution of

TABLE 3
TYPES OF DECISION IN RELATION TO HEIRARCHY

	Strategic		Functional		Operational	
	No.	%	No.	%	No.	%
Board of directors	20	0.87	1	0.04	0	0.00
Company general manager	3	0.13	20	0.87	6	0.27
Department head	0	0.00	2	0.09	16	0.73

power according to the type of decisions in Sino–foreign joint ventures is no different from the usual pattern observable in the West.

If strategic decisions are usually taken by the board of directors, we should keep in mind that in Sino–foreign joint ventures, the board of directors is composed both of Chinese and foreign partners. Here is one piece of evidence that partially sustains the hypothesis presented above.

The Chinese/Foreign Perspective

Table 4 exhibits the distribution of the sub-sample of 19 respondents who took the Chinese/foreign perspective. Three types of decision-making power distribution were identified from the analysis of the answers to the questionnaire.

These data show that the foreign partner tends to exert an

TABLE 4
CHINESE/FOREIGN DECISION POWER

	Strategic		Functional		Operational	
	No.	%	No.	%	No.	%
Foreign partner decides alone	15	0.79	11	0.61	6	0.33
Chinese partner decides alone	0	0.00	2	0.11	5	0.28
Both partners decide	4	0.21	5	0.28	7	0.39

overwhelming position for two out of the three types of decision considered. This is especially true for strategic decisions – where there is not a single case where the Chinese partner decides alone. This also holds true for functional decisions: the Chinese partner is involved in only seven cases while the foreign partner is involved in 16 cases. Nevertheless, the situation for operational decisions seems to be much more balanced (13 foreign versus 12 Chinese).

These results can be explained if we bear in mind the fact that in the sample of this study, the foreign partner has, on average, a larger share in the equity distribution of the joint venture (57 per cent versus

43 per cent for the Chinese partner). The foreign partner has a dominant equity position in 63 per cent of the cases analysed. Another explanation is that the Chinese have limited experience of operating on boards of directors.

Thus we can conclude that our hypothesis is not verified. Furthermore, data tend to show exactly the inverse pattern. The more important the decision for the future of the company, the less the decision-making power is shared: strategic decisions are concentrated in the hands of the foreign partner, while the Chinese have the power to decide (either alone or jointly with the foreigner) only in the case of operational decisions.

BARRIERS AND INCENTIVES TO KNOWLEDGE EXCHANGES

The underlying factors of the dynamic of knowledge exchanges between partners of Sino–foreign joint ventures were analysed according to opposing dimensions. The research first investigated the barriers to knowledge exchanges. However, adopting a more heterodox approach, the research also tried to identify the incentives that might stimulate knowledge exchanges. It was hypothesized that knowledge transfers between Chinese and foreign partners are hampered by exogamic barriers but stimulated by business perspectives.

Barriers to Knowledge Transfers between Partners

Table 5 presents the barriers identified in this research. Nine different types of barrier were found. Absolute and relative frequencies of quotation are given in the two last columns. Whilst the first four items of the list were frequently cited, the five at the bottom of the list received limited attention. The first two items 'cultural differences' and 'language differences' cover no less than 50 per cent of the total answers. This shows how important communication is in the management of these joint ventures. These frequently cited barriers give strong credence to the research hypothesis, as they all stem from exogamic differences between partners.

Not surprisingly, 'cultural differences' come at the top of the list. This is in line with Chen and Boggs (1998) who showed that perceptions of co-operation are more favourable when joint venture partners' firms are from culturally similar countries. As a matter of fact, differences between Confucian and Western values find themselves face-to-face in Sino–foreign joint ventures. Here is a fundamental barrier to knowledge transfers between allies. When cultural frameworks differ, the same fact or the same event might not mean the same thing for the two parties. Similarly, a given piece of

TABLE 5
BARRIERS TO KNOWLEDGE TRANSFER

	Type of barrier	No.	%
1	Cultural differences	46	0.277
2	Language differences	37	0.223
3	Differentiated approaches to management	21	0.127
4	Unwillingness to share technology	18	0.108
5	Antagonistic intentions	13	0.078
6	Inappropriate human resources	9	0.054
7	Political regulations	8	0.048
8	Market differences	7	0.042
9	Technical differences	7	0.042
Total		166	1.000

knowledge may be interpreted differently by two persons of different cultural backgrounds. Even more complex, certain behaviour may not be interpreted or valued the same way. Such differences create tremendous tensions in knowledge transfers between allies. First, partners have to identify these cultural differences and attempt to understand them. Secondly, they need to be willing to accept them. And finally, they need to find ways to adapt to each other, to reconcile their differences – otherwise they won't be able to collaborate.

'Language differences' are also an obvious barrier to knowledge transfers and they also came top of the list. Chinese has its own writing system unknown by most foreigners. Chinese is a tonal language with subtle variations which are very difficult to reproduce for many foreigners. Moreover, pronunciation of the same written character varies dramatically from one place to another. All these significant differences represent a major barrier to communication (incomparable to learning French or Spanish for an English-speaking person). As a consequence, most foreign managers face the handicap of not being able to communicate properly in Chinese. In such circumstances, managing and motivating the Chinese work force seems an impossible task. Nevertheless, Chinese managers are less handicapped than their foreign colleagues. This is because an increasing number of people in China (especially in the younger generation) are trained in foreign languages from childhood.

These first two barriers exist in the joint venture but they also represent a prominent obstacle for foreign managers wanting to learn about the Chinese business environment in which they operate. Given their objectives – to gain access to distribution networks, figure out the mentality of Chinese customers, set up contracts with utilities and other suppliers, etc. – having a limited understanding of the local culture will constitute a severe handicap.

'Differentiated approaches to management' came third in the list of barriers to knowledge transfers. It must be kept in mind that the Deng Xiao Ping 'Open Door' and 'Four Modernisations' policies started only after 1978 (after the turmoil of the cultural revolution). This means that most of the Chinese managers who now work in Sino–foreign joint ventures were trained during the era of communism (the Mao heritage is still with us!) and most of their work experience has been in state-owned companies. Their approach to management is that of a planned economy. Such a background does not help to deal with management methods, techniques and styles imported to the joint ventures by their Western counterparts. Hierarchy, objectives, accountability, quality, work ethic, group work, empowerment (to quote only a few) probably do not have the same meaning for a Chinese as for a foreign manager. For example, Chinese managers are known to emphasise respect for age, hierarchy and face-saving. They are also more group oriented. Such differences create differential learning capabilities among partners and, as a consequence, different learning rhythms (Kumar and Nti, 1998). Such differences also do not facilitate mutual understanding with Western counterparts and call for efforts on both sides if such barriers are to be overcome. Once again, the situation is tremendously different for young managers who are now coming onto the job market. They have a stronger awareness of Western management models – as they grew up in sharply different conditions from the older generation and might even have been trained abroad.

The fourth barrier on the list is the 'unwillingness to share technology'. Technology is almost always an asset pooled in the joint venture by the foreign partner. If transferred technologies are sources of competing advantage for the partner holding them, it can easily be understood that the foreigner will try to slow down the learning process of the Chinese partner. The foreign partner is simply afraid to create a new competitor because of technology spill-over. The issue is even more complex when the technological competitive advantage is based on tacit knowledge. This inarticulate knowledge is difficult to explain in explicit and formalized language. It is by definition not codified or codifiable. Inter-firm alliances are known to be a channel for the transfer of such types of knowledge. The problem is that tacit knowledge is difficult to protect because it can easily flow from one partner to another through day-to-day and shoulder-to-shoulder contacts between personnel working inside the joint venture itself.

Finally, the five remaining criteria in Table 5 receive limited attention. They can be considered as exogamic barriers easier to overcome than the previous ones. 'Antagonist intentions' express the fact that Chinese and foreign partners do not have the same learning objectives when entering a joint venture. Interestingly, it seems that the challenge of 'inappropriate human resources' or 'political regulations' do not significantly impede knowledge transfer. The low ratings for 'market differences' and 'technical differences' seem to imply that managers appear to know how to deal with these differences.

Incentives to Facilitate Technological Transfers

Table 6 gives results regarding incentives to facilitate knowledge transfers. The first two items overwhelm the rest of the list. In comparison, the five remaining items received far less interest. They express business perspectives. This result is in line with hypothesis 2.

TABLE 6
INCENTIVES FOR KNOWLEDGE TRANSFER

	Type of incentive	No.	%
1	Increase profits	48	0.308
2	Expand market share and brands	42	0.269
3	Develop technological edge in China	19	0.122
4	Learn local policy	15	0.096
5	Increase business scale and scope	15	0.096
6	Optimize the relationship of two partners	10	0.064
7	Staff training	7	0.045
Total		156	1.000

As already mentioned above, most of the respondents are Chinese (56/67). They naturally perceive knowledge transfers positively. They assume that, so long as these transfers allow to 'increase profits' as well as to 'expand market share and brands', partners have incentives for transfers. Thus the Chinese respondents give a strong competitive value to imported intangible assets (new technologies, industrial know-how but also brands and managerial abilities). Such an argument makes sense for the joint venture itself and also for the foreign partner as one of the shareholders in the joint venture.

The third criterion in the list, 'develop technological edge in China', also makes sense. According to De Meyer (2001), there is even an increasing expectation and demand emanating from Chinese authorities concerning technological transfers for transferring the latest, the state-of-the-art (rather than established) technologies. The focus on innovative technology is important in businesses such as, telecommunications, computers, pharmaceutical products, automotive, etc. where consumers are very sensitive to technical issues. Most of the writings stress that Chinese products are outmoded and produced in facilities where technology and manufacturing equipment are obsolete (see, for example, Zhang and Goffin, 1999). The importation of new technologies can obviously help to create positive differences when compared to competitors. This argument prevails for the Chinese partner as well as for the foreign one. Other items on the list cover several different issues but are less significant than those cited above.

CONCLUSION

Synthesis

This research has shown two points. First, the study has enriched the perspective of previous ones on decision-making in Sino–foreign joint ventures by distinguishing three types of decision-making. Analysis on the way decisions are taken has shown that distribution of decision-making power is no different from the usual pattern observable in the West: strategic decisions are taken by the board of directors, functional decisions by company general managers and operational decisions by department heads. However, contrary to what was hypothesized, foreign partners tend to exert an overwhelming impact on strategic and functional decisions.

Second, several factors interplay in the dynamic of knowledge exchange between Chinese and foreign partners inside the joint venture itself. Amongst the most significant barriers are 'cultural differences' inducing different perceptions of the same fact, event or even behaviour, 'language differences' raising strong obstacles to interpersonal communications, 'differentiated approaches to management' as well as 'unwillingness to share technology' pooled in the joint venture by the foreign partner for fear of creating new competitors. On the other hand, the perspective of increasing profits, expanding market share and brands act as strong incentives for knowledge transfers.

Effects of the WTO

In the future, the WTO will probably tend to fluidify knowledge transfers in Sino–foreign joint ventures. Three arguments can be put forwards. First, as the WTO represents a commitment to improved intellectual property rights, it will reduce patent infringement and counterfeiting. In industries such as pharmaceuticals, this will secure relationships and increase the level of confidence. As such this should act as a facilitator for technology transfers. Second, China is now boosting its legal modernization process to produce a more sophisticated and transparent legal system. The alignment of China's market system regulations to WTO rules aims at conforming to internationally recognized laws and standards for trade. This alignment will reduce differences between China and other countries (at least at the legal and the regulatory levels). This reduction of differences is conducive to a reduction of exogamic barriers, which means that, once again, the WTO will act as facilitator of expertise and capabilities transfer. Finally, facilitation principles creating greater freedom will induce more rapid growth. Therefore, the reinforcement of business perspectives will also act as a stimulus for knowledge transfers.

However, the effect of WTO on the sharing of decision-making power in joint ventures is unclear. On the one hand, it can be argued that increasing predictability will induce foreign companies to give a more equitable share of decision-making power to their Chinese partners. On the other hand, as different sectors (including finance, insurance, telecommunications) will gradually be opened to overseas investors and because the WTO will reduce barriers to foreign companies – reduce and finally eliminate quotas and/or tariff rates, in such as the automotive industry or for agricultural imports – foreign direct investment will be encouraged. As a consequence, foreign companies might be more and more tempted to operate alone and give up their involvement in joint ventures.

Practical Implications

Managers should pay serious attention to knowledge transfers that occur between the joint venture and each of the partners' organizations. Foreign managers need to consider the way they share decision-making power with their Chinese partner. It is quite understandable that foreign companies want to keep control of the destiny of their joint ventures as shown by this research. However, the prominent foreign position demonstrated by this research is questionable. It is reasonable to suggest that the Chinese partner will ask for more control. If these expectations are not met, Chinese partner co-operation might fade in the future. Foreign partners might lose the support of their counterpart and the benefits of operating in co-operation.

Traditionally, foreign companies have been reluctant to transfer state of the art knowledge to China – whether this be technological or managerial. In the past, foreign companies used to emphasize strategies for protecting transferred assets and slowing down the learning pace of the Chinese partner. However times have changed; secured political reforms, reduced market uncertainties, better informed consumers, improved local suppliers, improving technological capabilities and infrastructures as well as increasing competition (from foreign and local firms) should urge foreign companies to facilitate transfers so as to benefit from a low cost and increasingly experienced technical and managerial work force.

Further Research

One challenging research issue for the future is related to the impact of the current learning process. Sino–foreign joint ventures that have been set up over the past 20 years gave the opportunity to each partner to learn from its counterpart. Is it possible to suggest that the learning process has now been completed? Or, do foreign and Chinese companies still have things to learn from each other? Or, has one partner been more successful than its counterpart in achieving its learning goals? If knowledge has been successfully transferred, then partners have lost one good reason to collaborate; so there only remains benefits such as scale effects (reaching a critical mass or the optimal scale, gaining scope economies, spreading risks, etc.). If one partner has been able to absorb knowledge more easily than the other, then this will modify their respective bargaining power.

ACKNOWLEDGMENTS

I gratefully acknowledge my colleagues at Shanghai University, Professor Yu Ying Chuan and Professor Dong Qin, for supporting the implementation of this research. I would like also to express my appreciation of the work done by my Executive MBA students at Shanghai University in conducting the interviews. I finally thank my research assistants at Ceram Sophia Antipolis, Yuan Guang Liang and Tao Rong Rong, for their help in data analysis.

NOTE

1. A copy of the questionnaire is available from the author on request.

REFERENCES

Ambler, T. (1995), 'Reflections in China: Re-orienting Images of Marketing', *Marketing Management*, Summer, Vol.4, No1, pp.22–31.

Barney, J.B. (1991), 'Firm resources and sustained competitive advantage', *Journal of Management*, Vol.17, pp.99–120.

Beamish, P. (1993), 'The characteristics of joint ventures in the People's Republic of China', *Journal of International Marketing*, Vol.1, pp.27–48.

Bruun, P. and Bennett, D.J. (2002), 'Transfer of Technology to China: A Scandinavian and European Perspective', *European Management Journal*, Vol.20, No1, pp.98–106.

Calantone, R.J. and Zhao, Y.S. (2001), 'Joint Ventures in China: A Comparative Study of Japanese, Korean, and US Partners', *Journal of International Marketing*, Vol.9, No1, pp.1–23.

Chen, R. and Boggs, D. (1998), 'Long term co-operation prospects in international joint ventures: perspectives of Chinese firms', *Journal of Applied Management Studies*, Vol.7, No.1, pp.111–127.

Child, J. (1998), 'Trust and International Strategic Alliances: The Case of Sino–foreign Joint Ventures', in Lane and Bachmann (eds), *Trust within and between organizations*. Oxford: University Press, pp.241–272.

Child, J. and Yan, Y. (1999), 'Investment and Control in International Joint Ventures: The Case of China', *Journal of World Business*, Vol.34, No1, pp.3–15.

Deng, P. (2001), 'WFOEs: The most popular entry mode into China', *Business Horizons*, Vol.44, No4, pp.63–73.

De Bruijn, E.J. and Jia, X. (1997), 'Joint ventures in China face new rules of the game', *Research Technology Management*, Vol.40, No2, pp.48–55.

De Meyer, A. (2001), 'Technology Transfer Into China: Preparing for a New Era', *European Management Journal*, Vol.19, N°2, pp.140–144.

Ding, D.Z., Goodall, K. and Warner, M. (2000), 'The end of the 'iron rice-bowl': whither Chinese human resource management?', *International Journal of Human Resource Management*, Vol.11, No2, pp.217–236.

Doz, Y.L., Hamel, G. and Prahalad, C.K. (1989), 'Collaborate with your competitors and win', *Harvard Business Review*, Vol.67, No1, pp.133–139.

Farh, J.-L., Tsui, A.S., Xin, K. and Cheng, B.-S. (1998), 'The Influence of Relational Demography and *Guanxi*: The Chinese Case', *Organization Science*, Vol.9, No4, pp.471–488.

Geringer, J.M. and Hébert, L. (1989), 'Control and Performance of International Joint Ventures', *Journal of International Business Studies*, Vol.20, No2, pp.235–254.

Goodall, K. and Warner, M. (2002), 'Corporate Governance in Sino–foreign Joint Ventures in the PRC: The View of Chinese Directors', *Journal of General Management*, Vol.27, No3, pp.77–92.

Grant, R.M. (1991), 'The Resource-Based Theory of Competitive Advantage: Implications for Strategy Formulation', *California Management Review*, Spring, pp.114–135.

Gugler, P. (1991), *Les alliances stratégiques transnationales*, Éditions Universitaires Fribourg (Suisse).

Gulati, R., Khanna, T. and Nohria, N. (1994), 'Unilateral Commitments and the Importance of Process in Alliances', *Sloan Management Review*, Vol.35, No3, pp.61–70.

Hamel, G. (1991), 'Competition for competence and inter-partner learning within international strategic alliances', *Strategic Management Journal*, Vol.12, pp.83–103.

Hamel, G. and Prahalad, C.K. (1990), 'The Core Competence of the Corporation', *Harvard Business Review*, May-June, pp.79–91.

Hennart, J.-F. (1988), 'A transaction Costs Theory of Equity Joint Ventures', *Strategic Management Journal*, Vol.9, pp.361–374.

Hill, C.W.L. (1990), 'Co-operation, Opportunism, and the Invisible Hand: Implications for Transaction Cost Theory', *Academy of Management Review*, Vol.15, No3, pp.500–513.

Inkpen, A.C. (1996), 'Creating Knowledge through Collaboration', *California Management Review*, Vol.39, No1, pp.123–140.

Jolly, D. (2002), 'Alliance strategy: linking motives with benefits', *European Business Forum*, Issue 9, pp.47–50.

Killing, J.P. (1982), 'How to make a global joint venture work', *Harvard Business Review*, Vol.60, No3, pp.120–127.

Kogut, B. (1988), 'Joint ventures: Theoretical and Empirical Perspectives', *Strategic Management Journal*, Vol.9, pp.319–332.

Kumar, R. and Nti, K.O. (1998), 'Differential Learning and Interaction in Alliance Dynamics: A Process and Outcome Discrepancy Model', *Organization Science*, Vol.9, No.3, pp.356–367.

Liu, H. and Pak, K. (1999), 'How Important is Marketing in China Today to Sino–foreign Joint Ventures', *European Management Journal*, Vol.17, No5, pp.546–554.

Liu, S. and Vince, R. (1999), 'The cultural context of learning in international joint ventures', *Journal of Management Development*, Vol.18, No8, pp.666–675.

Luo, Y. (1998), 'Joint ventures success in China: How should we select a good partner?', *Journal of World Business*, Vol.33, No2, pp.145–167.

McEvily, S.K. and Chakravarthy, B. (2002), 'The Persistence of Knowledge-Based advantage: An Empirical Test for Product Performance and Technological Knowledge', *Strategic Management Journal*, Vol. 23, No4, pp.285–306.

Mowery, D.C., Oxley, J.E. and Silverman, B.S. (1996), 'Strategic Alliances and Interfirm Knowledge Transfer', *Strategic Management Journal*, Vol.17, No10, pp.77–91.

Nair, A.S. and Stafford, E.R. (1998), 'Strategic Alliances in China: Negotiating the Barriers', *Long Range Planning*, Vol.31, No.1, pp.139–146.

Osland, G.E. and Cavusgil, S.T. (1996), 'Performance Issues in U.S.-China Joint Ventures', *California Management Review*, Vol.38, No2, pp.106–130.

Richter, F.-J. and Vettel, K. (1995), 'Successful Joint Ventures in Japan: Transferring Knowledge Through Organizational Learning', *Long Range Planning*, Vol.28, No3, pp.37–45.

Si, S.X. and Bruton, G.D. (1999), 'Knowledge transfer in international joint ventures in transitional economies: The China experience', *Academy of Management Executive*, Vol.13, No1, pp.83–90.

Teece, D.J. (2000), 'Strategies for Managing Knowledge Assets: The Role of Firm Structure and Industrial Context', *Long Range Planning*, Vol.33, No1, pp.35–55.

Tsang, E.W.K. (1994), 'Human Resource Management Problems in Sino–foreign Joint Ventures', *International Journal of Manpower*, Vol.15, No9/10, pp.4–21.

Vanhonacker, W.R. (1997), 'Entering China: An unconventional approach', *Harvard Business Review*, Vol.75, No2, pp.130–137.

Weldon, E. and Vanhonacker, W. (1999), 'Operating a Foreign-Invested Enterprise in China: Challenges for Managers and Management Researchers', *Journal of World Business*, Vol.34, No1, pp.94.-107.

Wernerfelt, B. (1984), 'A Resource-based View of the Firm', *Strategic Management Journal*, Vol.5, N°2, pp.171–180.

Whitehill, M. (1997), 'Knowledge-based strategy to deliver sustained competitive advantage', *Long Range Planning*, Vol.30, No4, pp.621–628.

Yan, A. and Gray, B. (1994), 'Bargaining power, management control, and performance in United States-China joint ventures: A comparative case study', *Academy of Management Journal*, Vol.37, No6, pp.1478–1517.

Zhang, L. and Gaffin, K. (1999), 'Joint Venture Manufacturing in China: An Explanatory Investigation', *International Journal of Operations and Production Management*, Vol.19, No.5/6, pp.474–90.

Zhao, H., Bennett, D., Vaidya, K. and Wang, X.M. (1997), 'Perceptions on the Transfer of Technology to China: A Survey of British Companies', *Technology Management: Strategies and Applications*, Vol.3, pp.241–259.

Adjustment of Third-Country National Expatriates in China

JAN SELMER

International staffing issues have become more pressing in this era of globalization. Although many companies prefer to select parent country nationals (PCNs) to manage their overseas operations (Harvey, 1995), firms typically face a shortage of such employees with the required international skills and knowledge for international operations (see Caligiuri and Cascio, 1998; Ettorre, 1993). Therefore, it is surprising that the literature on third country nationals (TCNs) mostly have focused on issues of compensation and benefits (see Hait, 1992; Heitzman, 1990: Parker, 2001) of such employees while other aspects have been largely neglected. A few notable published exceptions to this general trend deal with TCNs as expatriates (Zeira, 1975), TCN policies (Chadwick, 1995), and the strategic employment of TCNs (Reynolds, 1997). Surprisingly, since one reason for making use of TCNs is their supposed superior cross-cultural effectiveness (Reynolds, 1997), no study is known to have compared how TCNs and PCNs adjust to a foreign cultural context.

Therefore, the purpose of this study is to compare the degree of adjustment of TCNs and PCNs in the same host location, China. Since TCNs are often regionalists, that is, thought of as being the most suitable candidates to fill higher positions in countries in the same region (Reynolds, 1997), the study makes a distinction between Asian TCNs and Western TCNs. Hence, three expatriate groups in China are compared: Asian TCNs, Western TCNs, and PCNs, the last category being all Western. This is an important study for several reasons. Firstly, a crucial assumption in using TCNs is examined by this investigation. Do they really have superior cross-cultural skills compared with PCNs? Secondly, the reason for the regional character of TCN assignments is examined. Are regional TCNs better adjusted than non-regional TCNs? This comparative investigation is undertaken for the very first time and the results could inform practitioners as well as academics about the soundness of current assumptions and future expatriate assignment practices.

China, as the place of investigation, is an important current and potential market for Western and other international business firms, further accentuated by China's entry into the World Trade Organisation. China has a huge need for foreign investment. The Chinese government has estimated that China in the next few years until 2004 will need more than $70 billion investments (Wang and Ralston, 2000). However, establishing operations in China may constitute more than a financial challenge to foreign firms. China is distinctly different from most other countries. From a Western perspective, China is frequently regarded as the most foreign of all foreign places. Chinese culture, institutions, and people may appear completely baffling (Chen, 2001). This makes China a challenging destination for Western business expatriates and their need for effective cross-cultural skills appears to be substantial. Hence, China seems a very suitable host location for comparing the extent of adjustment among different groups of business expatriates.

After a review of the sparse literature on TCNs, the concept of expatriate adjustment and its components are introduced. Hypotheses are developed and methodological issues are clarified. Following the results of the analysis, the findings are discussed and conclusions are drawn.

THIRD-COUNTRY NATIONALS

A TCN, as the term is used here, is an employee working temporarily in a host country who is neither a national of that host country nor of the country in which the corporate headquarters is located (Reynolds, 1997). This definition excludes a subsidiary's local hiring of a national from a third country living permanently in the host country. It also excludes foreign nationals assigned to headquarters. Such employees have been labelled inpatriates (Harvey and Buckley, 1997). The distinction here is that the employer is participating in the management of TCNs outside their home and headquarters countries (Reynolds, 1997). A characteristic of TCNs is that they may have lower salary and benefit requirements than PCNs (Chadwick, 1995; Dowling, Welch and Schuler, 1999; Reynolds, 1997).

While PCNs are frequently assigned abroad to protect a firm's interests and to transfer corporate know-how and practices (see Torbiörn, 1982), a national of another country may not be expected to understand or transmit corporate standards and culture as easily. Therefore, the first TCNs are typically assigned when a company already has a few foreign operations and decides to establish yet another. In such a situation, an expatriate candidate from an existing overseas operation may be regarded as superior to a comparatively more expensive PCN (Dowling, Welch and Schuler, 1999). On the other hand, it has also been argued that TCNs may have a deep understanding of corporate policies from the perspective of a foreigner and may be able to communicate such policies to others and implement them abroad in a more effective way than PCNs (Reynolds, 1997).

Senior level TCNs are particularly common in developing countries since firms have found that TCNs are more flexible and more willing to work under such conditions than PCNs. TCNs are much more common in North American firms than elsewhere, although German, Dutch and Swiss companies tend to use more TCNs than other continental European multinationals. Although the use of expatriates in Japanese companies seems to be high, the overwhelming majority of them are PCNs (Peterson, Napier and Shim, 1996; Reynolds, 1997).

To the extent that TCNs are used instead of PCNs, it is essential not to go too far since corporations may lose the strategic control over their global operations by replacing too many of their PCNs with non-parent nationals. This may weaken their corporate culture abroad contributing to a state of anarchy (Kobrin, 1988).

Nevertheless, outstanding talent can be found anywhere in the world. Effective global corporations seek out international expertise whatever its origin and build that competence into the corporate knowledge base. During periods of rapid expansion, TCNs can not only substitute for PCNs in new and growing operations, they may also offer different perspectives, complementing and expanding the sometimes narrowly focused views of both local nationals and PCNs originating from the headquarters. In short, TCNs may constitute an effective talent pool for international corporations playing an important role in the firm's globalization efforts (Reynolds, 1997).

EXPATRIATE ADJUSTMENT

Sociocultural versus Psychological Adjustment

A distinction has been proposed between sociocultural and psychological adjustment in the literature on expatriate adjustment (see Searle and Ward, 1990; Ward and Kennedy, 1992; Ward and Searle, 1991). Although conceptually interrelated, the latter deals with subjective well-being or mood states (e.g. depression, anxiety, tension, and fatigue). The former relates to the ability to 'fit in' or to negotiate interactive aspects of the host culture as measured by the amount of difficulty experienced in the management of everyday situations in the host culture (Ward and Kennedy, 1996).

The concept of psychological adjustment is based on a problem-oriented view, focusing on attitudinal factors of the adjustment process (see Grove and Torbiörn, 1985; Juffer, 1986; Oberg, 1960). The sociocultural notion of adjustment is based on cultural learning theory and highlights social behaviour and practical social skills underlying attitudinal factors (see Black and Mendenhall, 1991; Furnham, 1993; Klineberg, 1982). This distinction is consistent with the separation of behavioural from attitudinal acculturation as discussed by Jun, Lee and Gentry (1997).

The theoretical framework of Black, Mendenhall and Oddou (1991) covers sociocultural aspects of expatriate adjustment. They argued that the degree of cross-cultural adjustment should be treated as a multidimensional concept, rather than a unitary phenomenon as was the previous dominating view (see Gullahorn and Gullahorn, 1962; Oberg, 1960). In their proposed model for expatriate adjustment, Black, Mendenhall and Oddou (1991) made a distinction between three dimensions of in-country adjustment:

1. Adjustment to work;
2. Adjustment to interacting with host nationals, and
3. Adjustment to the general non-work environment.

The three dimensions of expatriate adjustment have found support in several empirical studies of US expatriates and their spouses (Black and Gregersen, 1990, 1991a, 1991b; Black and Stephens, 1989; McEvoy and Parker, 1995).

The theoretical concept of subjective well-being, corresponding to the psychological aspects of expatriate adjustment, has been well developed, especially in relation to work and work environment characteristics (see Caplan et al., 1975; Karasek, 1979; Kornhauser, 1965). In connection with the adjustment of expatriate business managers, the concept of subjective well-being has been applied in several instances (see Anderzen and Arnetz, 1997, 1999; Arnetz and Anderzen, 1992; Aryee and Stone, 1996; Nicholson and Imaizumi, 1993).

HYPOTHESES

Multinationals may assume that TCNs are not only low-cost substitutes for PCNs, but may also be the most suitable candidates to fill higher level positions in countries within the same region. Regional candidates are frequently preferred because they are presumed to have better language and cross-cultural skills. Besides being qualified, they may speak the local language and could be culturally attuned to another country in the same region (Reynolds, 1997). TCNs are frequently multilingual which may allow them to work in more than one language. TCNs could have greater cultural sensitivity, making them more interpersonally effective in another regional host country than PCNs. While PCNs may be assigned to a foreign location to gain international experience as part of a long-term management development plan (Edström and Galbraith, 1977), TCNs are frequently assigned to contribute productively to a local operation. As an assurance to get the job done, TCNs are often assigned to a host location based on earlier demonstrated skills and performance (Chadwick, 1995; Reynolds, 1997).

Another reason for inter-regional transfers of TCNs is that the globalizing corporation may have begun to identify regional talent pools to strengthen regional organizations and to make the regions more self-sufficient. Hence, the regional manager is a special type of TCN regionalist. In the cause of developing from an emerging multinational to a global corporation, many firms establish regional organizational structures to co-ordinate subsidiary activities within specific geographical boundaries (Reynolds, 1997). The greatest numbers of TCNs can be found within such regional organizational structures (Dowling, Welch and Schuler, 1999).

Given the substantial differences between China and most Western countries, providing a challenging destination for Western business expatriates, it is likely that Asian TCNs are more socioculturally effective in China than both Western TCNs and PCNs. This presumption is explored in Hypotheses 1 to 3.

Hypothesis 1
Asian TCNs will have better general adjustment to China than Western TCNs and PCNs.

Hypothesis 2
Asian TCNs will have better interaction adjustment to China than Western TCNs and PCNs.

Hypothesis 3
Asian TCNs will have better work adjustment to China than Western TCNs and PCNs.

Sociocultural adjustment, emphasizing social behaviour and practical social skills, may be encouraged by contextual circumstances, such as social pressure, to a larger extent than psychological adjustment involving less easily detectable mental predispositions. Hence, adjustment of deep-seated attitudinal factors may be more voluntary than sociocultural behavioural adjustment (Jun, Lee and Gentry, 1997). Furthermore, research generally agrees that most of an individual's values are entrenched by the end of adolescence at one's late teens (Thompson and Thompson, 1990). If expatriates do not feel obliged to adjust psychologically, the chance is that their original core value system will be kept intact. Furthermore, a typical expatriate assignment only lasts from three to five years (see Selmer, 1992; Selmer and Lee, 1994; Tung, 1988). Although exposed to a radically different value system, a relatively short stay in China is not likely to result in much change in an individual's cultural norms and attitudes. This proposition is explored in Hypothesis 4.

Hypothesis 4
There will be no difference between the three expatriate categories in terms of psychological adjustment to China.

METHOD

Sample
The specific data for this study originate with two sources. One of them was a mail questionnaire targeted at business expatriates assigned by Western firms to China. Eventually, 154 usable of 790 mailed questionnaires were returned. Subtracting 36 non-target returned questionnaires from the mailed ones, a response rate of 20.4% was attained. This is not high, but it is equivalent or higher than other international mail surveys (see Harzing, 1997; Naumann, 1993). However, the effective response rate may be higher. Available directories and listings of expatriate managers in the China are, at best, updated annually. Many of the questionnaires must have been addressed to expatriates no longer in China because of the limited average duration of expatriate assignments, but only a small number of undeliverable mailings were returned (see Black, 1990). The second data source for this investigation was a questionnaire directed at overseas Chinese business expatriates assigned to China by Western corporations. As there are no specific sources identifying this target group, the same business directories that were used to identify the expatriates working for Western companies were used and all listed executives with Chinese names were selected. Screening questions

were used to determine whether the respondents belonged to our target group and should complete the questionnaire. Since Chinese ethnicity is defined patrilineally (see Wee, 1988; Wu and Wu, 1980), only respondents who answered 'yes' to the question 'Is your father Chinese?' were retained. Furthermore, all respondents born in the PRC, and/or current PRC citizens, and/or those who had been living in the PRC for ten years or more were screened out. Of a total of 1,205 mailed questionnaires, 59 usable returns indicated that the respondent indeed belonged to the target group. Although 285 returns showed that the respondent was not an expatriate manager, the technique used here does not allow us to calculate a response rate.

The two data sets were combined and the three subgroups Western PCNs (n=103), Asian TCNs (n=47), and Western TCNs (n=46) (see Table 1) were extracted in the following way. Respondents with the same nationality at birth as the nationality of their parent organization were classified as Western PCNs, or otherwise as TCNs. Of the last group, those expatriates with a nationality at birth of an Asian country were categorized as Asian TCNs. Similarly, respondents with a nationality at birth of a Western country were labelled Western TCNs.

TABLE 1
BACKGROUND OF THE SUBSAMPLES

Background Variables	Asian TCNs (n=47)		Western TCNs (n=46)		Western PCNs (n=103)	
	Frequency	%	Frequency	%	Frequency	%
Gender:						
Male	40	85	36	78	92	89
Female	7	15	10	22	11	11
Married	39	83	31	67	83	81
Position:						
CEO	27	58	27	59	61	59
Manager	19	40	14	30	38	37
Non- managerial	1	2	5	11	4	4

The average age of the Asian TCNs was 40.35 years (SD=6.53) and on average, they had spent 3.57 years in China (SD=2.60) and had lived abroad for 8.05 years (SD=5.28), including China. The Western TCNs had a similar mean age (41.33 years; SD=8.74) and had also spent a similar average time in China (4.15 years; SD=3.95) and had, on the average, lived abroad for a similar time as the Asian TCNs (10.27 years; SD=6.52). The group of Western PCNs had similar background characteristics as the other two expatriate groups. They had an average age of 43.57 years (SD=10.13), they had lived in

China, on the average, for 4.02 years (SD=3.61) and had lived an average of 9.80 years abroad (SD=10.65).

The overwhelming majority of the Asian TCNs were born in Hong Kong (66.0%), but birth nationalities such as Taiwan, Singapore, Vietnam, Cambodia, India, Korea, and Malaysia are also represented. Exactly half of the Western TCNs were either of British (28.3%) or US (21.7%) nationality at birth. French, Australian, German, Canadian, Austrian, and Belgian birth nationalities can also be found in this sample. The sample of Western PCNs is dominated by expatriates with a US nationality at birth (42.7%). Other birth nationalities represented here are French, German, Australian, British, Danish, and Swedish. As displayed in Table 1, all three sub-samples had a similar gender distribution and marriage frequency. Consistent with other recent studies of business expatriates (see Caligiuri, 2000; Selmer, 2001; Shaffer, Harrison, and Gilley, 1999), most of the respondents were male and married. The distribution of organizational positions was similar for all three expatriate groups. Almost all the respondents were managers and most of the respondents were CEOs. Analyses of Variance (ANOVAs) confirmed that there were no significant differences between the three groups of expatriates on any of the background variables age, gender, marriage frequency, organizational position, time abroad, and time in China.

Instrument

The instrument used two separate scales for sociocultural and psychological adjustment. Expatriates completed Black and Stephens (1989) 14-item scale to assess sociocultural adjustment. This scale is designed to measure three dimensions: Work Adjustment (sample item: 'Supervisory responsibilities'), General Adjustment (sample item: 'Food'), and Interaction Adjustment (sample item: 'Speaking with host nationals'). The respondents indicated how well adjusted they were to China on a scale ranging from 1 = *very unadjusted* to 7 = *completely adjusted*. Principle component factor analysis with varimax rotation produced the three previously identified dimensions of expatriate adjustment: Three items on Work Adjustment (*alpha*=0.83), seven items on General Adjustment (*alpha*=0.89), and four items on Interaction Adjustment (*alpha*=0.87).

Expatriate psychological adjustment was measured using the General Health Questionnaire (GHQ-12) developed by Goldberg (1972). This scale is commonly applied to assess minor psychiatric symptoms, but it has also been extensively used to monitor levels of well-being in community and organizational samples (Forster, 2000), as well as to measure expatriates' subjective well-being (see Anderzen and Arnetz, 1997, 1999; Arnetz and Anderzen, 1992). Containing a number of questions concerning how people have been feeling recently, it includes sleeping difficulties, feelings of unhappiness, and respondents' ability to enjoy everyday experiences. Respondents were asked to think about how they have been feeling over the past few weeks (sample item: 'Have you recently felt that you are playing a useful part in things?'). Responses ranged from (1) 'not at all' to (4) 'much more than usual'. Reliability was acceptable ($alpha$=0.83).

RESULTS

The overall sample means, standard deviations and zero-order correlations are provided in Table 2. A review of that table reveals that the mean scores for the three adjustment variables are all close to or above the mid-level point depicted as 'somewhat adjusted', indicating a certain degree of comfortableness with the Chinese context after having spent an average of three to four years there. Also the mean score of the subjective well-being variable is above the mid-level point. All variables are significantly inter-correlated.

TABLE 2
MEANS[1], STANDARD DEVIATIONS, AND CORRELATIONS AMONG
THE VARIABLES (N=194)

Variables	Mean	SD	1	2	3	4
1. General Adjustment	4.94	1.19	1.00			
2. Interaction Adjustment	5.14	1.28	0.59**	1.00		
3. Work Adjustment	5.41	1.14	0.63**	0.63**	1.00	
4. Psychological Adjustment	2.83	0.44	0.21**	0.27**	0.35**	1.00

** $p<0.01$ (2-tailed)
[1] The higher the score, the higher the degree of adjustment.

To test the hypotheses, between-group differences were examined through 4 x 3 Multivariate Analysis of Variance (MANOVA). Table 3 displays a significant overall effect detected for the three groups of business expatriates (F=2.92; $p<0.05$) and univariate F-tests indicated significant between-group differences for work adjustment (F=4.64; $p<0.05$). Multiple range tests indicated that in terms of work adjustment, the mean score for the Asian TCNs were significantly lower than for both the Western TCNs and PCNs. These findings indicate that H3 should be rejected. Since there were no other significant differences between the Asian and Western expatriate groups on the other sociocultural adjustment variables, H1 and H2

TABLE 3
MANOVA AND *ANOVA* FOR ADJUSTMENT[1] BY EXPATRIATE GROUP[2]

Variables	Asian TCNs n = 47 Mean (SD)	Western TCNs n = 46 Mean (SD)	PCNs n = 103 Mean (SD)	Multivariate Effect	Univariate F-ratios
				2.92*	
General Adjustment	4.66 (1.15)	5.10 (1.47)	5.06 (1.03)		2.20
Interaction Adjustment	5.00 (1.26)	5.28 (1.46)	5.16 (1.21)		0.54
Work Adjustment	4.96 (1.43)ᵃ	5.57 (1.19)ᵇ	5.53 (0.94)ᵇ		4.64*
Psychological Adjustment	2.81 (0.46)	2.88 (0.41)	2.81 (0.43)		0.47

[1] The higher the score, the higher the degree of adjustment.
[2] Means with different superscripts differ significantly at $p<0.05$ (Multiple Range Tests: Scheffé)
* $p <0.05$

were not supported. However, the absence of any significant inter-group difference in terms of psychological adjustment indicates that H4 was supported.

DISCUSSION

The main result is that Asian TCNs are less well adjusted to work in China than both Western TCNs and PCNs. This is both a fundamental and surprising finding. It is fundamental, because expatriates are sent on foreign assignments, first and foremost, to perform a work task, so adjusting to the foreign work context may be crucial. The positive association between expatriate adjustment and work performance has been supported by anecdotal evidence (see Aycan and Kanungo, 1997; Ones and Viswesvaran, 1997; Tung, 1981). Emerging rigorous empirical research on this issue seems to affirm a positive relationship between the two concepts (see Caligiuri, 1997; Kraimer, Wayne and Jaworski, 2001; Parker and McEvoy, 1993). Therefore, being less well adjusted to work may have negative consequences for an expatriate's performance and could also be detrimental to the functioning of the foreign operation at large, especially if the expatriate is in a top managerial position.

The finding that both Western TCNs and PCNs are better adjusted to work in China than the Asian TCNs is surprising since the latter group of expatriates would be expected to be more culturally attuned to another Asian country (Reynolds, 1997). The majority of the Asian TCNs was born in Hong Kong which may have provided them not only with a thorough understanding of Chinese culture, but also some appropriate linguistic skills. So why are they relatively less adjusted to work in China? The answer may have something to do with how they are treated by the host country nationals at the workplace. It has been suggested that while lower and middle level TCNs could enjoy a favourable general attitude from their local colleagues at the foreign subsidiary, senior level TCNs may not be welcome by local staff. The assignment of lower-level TCNs may be perceived as highly temporary and therefore not blocking the promotion prospects of local nationals. Such TCNs may be very eager to be positively assessed by their host-country superiors. Accordingly, they could look for assistance, guidance and information from their peers and subordinates. And, they may make a special effort to adapt their behaviour to the local context to obtain this co-operation. On the other hand, the transfer of senior-level TCNs may be perceived as less temporary than in the case of lower-level TCNs, threatening to block local promotions. Besides, senior-level TCNs may not feel any pressure to adjust their managerial behaviour to the local environment. TCNs sensing an aversion from local nationals, may feel a need to demonstrate their managerial superiority in their new positions. As a result, this behaviour could increase the resentment of the host nationals, further decreasing their willingness to help their new superiors to act more effectively (Zeira, 1975).

In this case, a clear majority of the Asian TCNs was senior-level expatriates. But that was also the case for both the Western TCNs and PCNs, who were found to have a higher work adjustment than the Asian TCNs. It may be speculated that another factor may also have been involved here. It has been found that Hong Kong Chinese expatriates could encounter extraordinary adjustment problems in mainland China. This is especially the case beyond the neighbouring Guangdong Province, sharing cultural traits and the local dialect with Hong Kong (Selmer and Shui, 1999)

Limitations

As usual, this investigation has some limitations to be considered in evaluating its findings. Data on the extent of adjustment were only collected through a self-report questionnaire. Although the general condemnations of self-report methods have been found exaggerated (Crampton and Wagner, 1994), to lessen any potential problem of method bias, all items within the two categories of variables; sociocultural and psychological adjustment; were assigned to the instrument in random order. Furthermore, half of the items measuring subjective well-being had reverse-polarity, as in the original scale, to make it less easy for the respondents to give uniform answers. These precautions may generate more reliable responses as it avoids the problem of respondents depending on a cognitive set of rules in evaluating items intended to measure constructs that are supposed to be conceptually different (Lord and Maher, 1991).

Expatriate adjustment is considered to be a process over time (see Black and Mendenhall, 1991; Janssens, 1995; Ward *et.al.*, 1998). However, the method employed here only used measures of the average level of adjustment for the investigated groups of business expatriates at a certain point in time. A longitudinal approach may have produced a more rich data source where adjustment patterns over time could have been identified and compared. On the other hand, longitudinal studies pose other serious methodological challenges (see Menard, 1991).

Last, but not least, it cannot be excluded that the generality of our findings is limited due to the composition of our sample of Asian TCNs or the specific circumstances in China.

IMPLICATIONS

There are several implications for globalizing firms – their future behaviour as well as future research. The findings may have implications for both the selection, training and support of TCNs. Avoiding the conventional wisdom regarding the superior cross-cultural effectiveness of regional TCNs, firms assigning employees to other countries may prefer to select all business expatriates in the same way. A rigorous selection procedure could proceed the choice of PCNs and TCNs alike, ensuring that the best candidate available is sent to do the job. Because of the equal footing of all categories of business expatriates, companies may also want to subject all expatriates to cross-cultural training, whether they are PCNs, non-regional or regional TCNs. Also, since previous research has suggested that it may be as difficult to adjust to a similar as a dissimilar host culture (Selmer, 2002; Selmer and Shui, 1999), to impose cultural preparation for all expatriate candidates may be justified. This kind of training could be useful not only when assigning expatriate managers to very different cultures, but also for regional assignments to similar cultures, as in the case of Asian TCNs assigned to China. However, it is also likely that the training should be different for expatriates assigned to similar as opposed to dissimilar cultural contexts. Preparing expatriates for a very different cultural environment, preparations often include substantial elements of cognitive training, emphasizing factual information about the distant host country (Gudykunst, Guzley and Hammer; 1996). Training for dealing with a similar culture should probably rather focus on creating motivation for the expatriates to identify the few crucial cultural differences that exist in the close host culture.

Suggested by the results of our investigation, training activities may place specific emphasis on adjustment to work. Cross-cultural training aimed at facilitating work adjustment is not very commonly provided to business expatriates (see Brewster and Pickard, 1994; Early, 1987; Tung, 1982). This is unfortunate since efficient job interaction skills are essential for maintaining and developing the competitive strength of international firms (*see* Bartlett and Goshal, 1989; de Cieri and Dowling, 1995).

Last, but not least, the findings may justify the same magnitude of support from headquarters for TCNs as for other categories of business expatriates. Avoiding the assumption that, at least, regional TCNs do not need much help, specific types of support activities could be extended to these expatriates. For example, TCNs formerly assigned to the same foreign location can act as mentors or discussion partners (Feldman and Bolino, 1999) in identifying and analyzing work-related problems that the incumbent TCN cannot handle or even identify as associated with subtle cross-cultural differences.

Future research may preferably replicate this pioneering effort to examine the comparative cross-cultural effectiveness of TCNs. Replications involving the same and other host locations would be useful to exclude the possibility that our TCN sample or host location peculiarities introduced bias to the findings. Other potential shortcomings could be eliminated by avoiding self-reported data and using a longitudinal approach.

CONCLUSIONS

Answering the two initial questions, it seems that TCNs do not necessarily have superior cross-cultural skills compared with PCNs. Actually, the reverse may be true for regional TCNs in terms of work adjustment. Secondly, regional TCNs may not be better adjusted than non-regional TCNs, or even PCNs. In fact, regional TCNs may be even less well adjusted to their work than both non-regional TCNs and PCNs. Although primarily concerning foreign companies in China, these insights may also comprise a powerful message to globalizing firms in general not to take anything for granted when composing their international workforce both now and in future years.

ACKNOWLEDGEMENT

This study was supported by a Faculty Research Grant from the Hong Kong Baptist University, Hong Kong.

REFERENCES

Anderzen, I. and Arnetz, B.B. (1997), 'Psychophysiological Reactions During the First Year of Foreign Assignment: Results from a Controlled Longitudinal Study', *Work and Stress*, Vol.11, No.4, pp.304–18.

Anderzen, I. and Arnetz, B.B. (1999), 'Psychophysiological Reactions to International Adjustment: Results from a Controlled, Longitudinal Study', *Psychotherapy and Psychosomatics*, Vol.68, pp.67–75.

Arnetz, B.B. and Anderzen, I. (1992), 'The Internationalization of Work. Optimizing Adaptation of Employees to a Global Economy. A Multidisciplinary Study of the Expatriation and Repatriation Process' in J. Selmer (ed.), *Proceedings of the First International Conference on Expatriate Management*, Hong Kong: Hong Kong Baptist College, pp.9–10.

Aryee, S. and Stone, R.J. (1996), 'Work Experiences, Work Adjustment and Psychological Well-Being of Expatriate Employees in Hong Kong', *The International Journal of Human Resource Management*, Vol.7, No.1, pp.150–64.

Aycan, Z. and Kanungo, R.N. (1997), 'Current Issues and Future Challenges in Expatriate Management' in D.M. Sunders and Z. Aycan (eds.), *New Approaches to Employee Management, Greenwich,* CT: JAI Press.

Bartlett, C. and Goshal, S. (1989), *Managing Across National Borders: The Transnational Solution*, Boston: Harvard University Press.

Black, J.S. (1990), 'Locus of Control, Social Support, Stress, and Adjustment in International Transfers', *Asia Pacific Journal of Management*, Vol.7, No.1, pp.1–29.

Black, J.S. and Gregersen, H.B. (1990), 'Expectations, Satisfaction and Intentions to Leave of American Managers in Japan', *International Journal of Intercultural Relations*, Vol.14, pp.485–506.

Black, J.S. and Gregersen, H.B. (1991a), 'Antecedents to Cross-Cultural Adjustment for Expatriates in Pacific Rim Assignments', *Human Relations*, Vol.44, No.5, pp.497–515.

Black, J.S. and Gregersen, H.B. (1991b), 'The Other Half of the Picture: Antecedents of Spouse Cultural Adjustment', *Journal of International Business Studies*, Vol.22, No.3, pp.461–477.

Black, J.S., and Mendenhall, M. (1991), 'The U-Curve Adjustment Hypothesis Revisited: A Review and Theoretical Framework', *Journal of International Business Studies*, Vol.22, No.2, pp.225–47.

Black, J.S., Mendenhall, M. and Oddou, G. (1991), 'Toward a Comprehensive Model of International Adjustment: An Integration of Multiple Theoretical Perspectives', *Academy of Management Review*, Vol.16, No.2, pp.291–317.

Black, J.S. and Stephens, G.K. (1989), 'The Influence of the Spouse on American Expatriate Adjustment in Overseas Assignments', *Journal of Management*, Vol.15, pp.529–44.

Brewster, C. and Pickard, J. (1994), 'Evaluating Expatriate Training', *International Studies of Management and Organization*, Vol.24, No.3: pp.18–35.

Caligiuri, P.M. (1997), 'Assessing Expatriate Success: Beyond Just "Being There"' in D.M. Sunders and Z. Aycan (eds.), *New Approaches to Employee Management*, Greenwich, CT: JAI Press.

Caligiuri, P.M. (2000), 'Selecting Expatriates for Personality Characteristics: A Moderating Effect of Personality on the Relationship Between Host National Contact and Cross-Cultural Adjustment', *Management International Review*, Vol.40, No.1, pp.61–80.

Caligiuri, P.M. and Cascio, W. (1998), 'Can We Send Her There? Maximizing the Success of Western Women on Global Assignments', *Journal of World Business*, Vol.33, No.4, pp.394–416.

Caplan, R.D., Cobb, S., French, J.R.P., Van Herrison, R. and Pinneau, S.R. (1975), *Job Demands and Worker Health*, Washington, DC: National Institute for Occupational Safety and Health.

Chadwick, W.F. (1995), 'TCN Expatriate Manager Policies' in J. Selmer (ed.), *Expatriate Management: New Ideas for International Business*, Westport, CT: Quorum Books.

Chen, M.-J. (2001), *Inside Chinese Business: A Guide for Managers Worldwide*, Boston, MA: Harvard Business School Press.

Crampton, S.M. and Wagner III, J.A. (1994), 'Percept-Percept Inflation in Microorganizational Research: An Investigation of Prevalence and Effect', *Journal of Applied Psychology*, Vol.79, No.1, pp.67–76.

de Cieri, H. and Dowling, P. (1995), 'Cross-Cultural Issues in organizational Behaviour', *Trends in Organizational Behaviour*, Vol.2, pp.127–145.

Dowling, P.J., Welch, D.E. and Schuler, R.S. (1999), *International Human Resource Management: Managing People in a Multinational Context*, Cincinnati: South-Western College Publishing.

Early, P.C. (1987), 'Intercultural Training for Managers: A Comparison of Documentary and Interpersonal Methods', *Academy of Management Journal*, Vol.30, No.4, pp.685–98.

Edström, A. and Galbraith, J.R. (1977), 'Transfers of Managers as a Coordination and Control Strategy in Multinational Organizations', *Administrative Science Quarterly*, Vol.22, pp.248–63.

Ettorre, B. (1993), 'A Brave New World: Managing International Careers', *Management Review*, April, pp.10–15.

Feldman, D.C. and Bolino, M.C. (1999), 'The Impact of On-site Mentoring on Expatriate Socialization: A Structural Equation Modelling Approach', *International Journal of Human Resource Management*, Vol.10, No.1, pp.54–71.

Forster, N. (2000), 'The Myth of the 'International Manager'', *International Journal of Human Resource Management*, Vol.11, No.1, pp.126–42.

Furnham, A. (1993), 'Communicating in Foreign Lands: The Cause, Consequences and Cures of Culture Shock', *Language, Culture and Curriculum*, Vol.6, No.1, pp.91–109.

Goldberg, D. (1972), *The Detection of Psychiatric Illness by Questionnaire*, London: Oxford University Press.

Grove, C.L. and Torbiörn, I. (1985), 'A New Conceptualization of Intercultural Adjustment and the Goals of Training', *International Journal of Intercultural Relations*, Vol.9, pp.205–33.

Gudykunst, W.B., Guzley, R.M. and Hammer, M.R. (1996), 'Designing Intercultural Training' in D. Landis and Bhagat, R.S. (eds.), *Handbook of Intercultural Training*, (2nd edn), Thousand Oaks: Sage Publications.

Gullahorn, J.E. and Gullahorn, J.R. (1962), 'An Extension of The U-Curve Hypothesis', *Journal of Social Issues*, Vol.3, pp.33–47.

Hait, A.G. (1992), 'Employee Benefits in the Global Economy: What US Benefit Professionals Should Know about Internationally Mobile Employees', *Benefits Quarterly*, Vol.8, No.4, pp.21–7.

Harvey, M.G. (1995), 'The Impact of the Dual-Career Expatriate on International Human Resource Management', *Human Resource Management Review*, Vol.5, No.3, pp.223–44.

Harvey, M.G. and Buckley, M.R. (1997), 'Managing Inpatriates: Building a Global Core Competency', *Journal of World Business*, Vol.32, pp.35–52.

Harzing, A.W.K. (1997), 'Response Rates in International Mail Surveys: Results of a 22-Country Study', *International Business Review*, Vol.6, No.6, pp.641–65.

Heitzman Jr, R.E. (1990), 'International Employees: Are They Losing Out on Retirement?', *Financial Executive*, Vol.6, No.5, pp.44–50.

Janssens, M. (1995), 'Intercultural Interaction: A Burden on International Managers', *Journal of Organizational Behaviour*, Vol.16, pp.155–67.

Juffer, K.A. (1986), 'The First Step in Cross-Cultural Orientation: Defining the Problem' in R.M. Paige (ed.), *Cross-Cultural Orientation: New Conceptualizations and Applications*, Lanham, MD: University Press of America.

Jun, S., Lee, S. and Gentry, J.W. (1997), 'The Effects of Acculturation on Commitment to the Parent Company and the Foreign Operation', *International Business Review*, Vol.6, No.5, pp.519–35.

Karasek, R.A. (1979), 'Job Demands, Job Decision Latitude and Mental Strain: Implications for Job Redesign', *Administrative Science Quarterly*, Vol.24, pp.285–308.

Klineberg, O. (1982), 'Contact Between Ethnic Groups: A Historical Perspective of Some Aspects of Theory and Research' in S. Bochner (ed.), *Cultures in Contact: Studies in Cross-Cultural Interaction*, Oxford: Pergamon.

Kobrin, S.J. (1988), 'Expatriate Reduction and Strategic Control in American Multinational Corporations', *Human Resource Management*, Vol.27, No.1, pp.63–75.

Kornhauser, A. (1965), *Mental Health of the Industrial Worker: A Detroit Study*, New York: Wiley.

Kraimer, M.L., Wayne, S.J. and Jaworski, R.A. (2001), 'Sources of Support and Expatriate Performance: The Mediating Role of Expatriate Adjustment', *Personnel Psychology*, Vol.54, pp.71–99.

Lord, R. and Maher, K. (1991), *Leadership and Information Processing: Linking Perceptions and Processes*, Boston: Unwin and Hyman.

McEvoy, G.M. and Parker, B. (1995), 'Expatriate Adjustment: Causes and Consequences' in J. Selmer (ed.) *Expatriate Management: New Ideas for International Business*, Westport, CT: Quorum Books.

Menard, S. (1991), *Longitudinal Research*, Newbury Park: Sage Publications.

Naumann, E. (1993), 'Antecedents and Consequences of Satisfaction and Commitment Among Expatriate Managers', *Group and Organization Management*, Vol.18, pp.153–87.

Nicholson, N. and Imaizumi, A. (1993), 'The Adjustment of Japanese Expatriates to Living and Working in Britain', *British Journal of Management*, Vol.4, pp.119–34.

Oberg, K. (1960), 'Culture Shock: Adjustment to New Cultural Environments', *Practical Anthropologist*, Vol.7, pp.177–82.

Ones, D.S. and Viswesvaran, C. (1997), 'Personality Determinants in the Prediction of Aspects of Expatriate Job Success' in Z. Aycan (ed.), *Expatriate Management: Theory and Research*, CT: JAI Press.

Parker, G. (2001), 'Establishing Remuneration Practices across Culturally Diverse Environments', *Compensation and Benefits Management*, Vol.17, No.2, pp.23–7.

Parker, B. and McEvoy, G.M. (1993), 'Initial Examination of a Model of Intercultural Adjustment', *International Journal of Intercultural Relations*, Vol.17, pp.355–79.

Peterson, R.B., Napier, N. and Shim, W.S. (1996), 'Expatriate Management – The Differential Role of National Multinational Corporation Ownership', *Management International Review*, Vol.38, No.4, pp.543–62.

Reynolds, C. (1997), 'Strategic Employment of Third Country Nationals', *Human Resource Planning*, Vol.20, No.1, pp.33–9.

Searle, W. and Ward, C. (1990), 'The Prediction of Psychological and Socio-Cultural Adjustment During Cross-Cultural Transitions', *International Journal of Intercultural Relations*, Vol.14, pp.449–64.

Selmer, J. (1992), 'Succession of Expatriate Top Managers in Foreign Subsidiaries: A Study of Swedish CEOs in Southeast Asia', Working Paper Series No. MS 91073, Business Research Centre, School of Business, Hong Kong Baptist College, Hong Kong.

Selmer, J. (2001), 'Psychological Barriers to Adjustment and How They Affect Coping Strategies: Western Business Expatriates in China', *International Journal of Human Resource Management*, Vol.12, No.2, pp.151–65.

Selmer, J. (2002), 'The Chinese Connection? Adjustment of Western vs. Overseas Chinese Expatriate Managers in China', *Journal of Business Research*, Vol.55, pp.41–50.

Selmer, J. and Lee, S. (1994), 'International Transfer and Assignment of Australian and European Business Executives', *Asia Pacific Journal of Human Resources*, Vol.32, No.3, pp.1–12.

Selmer, J. and. Shiu, L.S.C (1999), 'Coming Home? Adjustment of Hong Kong Chinese Expatriate Business Managers Assigned to the People's Republic of China', *International Journal of Intercultural Relations*, Vol.23, No.3, pp.447–65.

Shaffer, M.A., Harrison, D.A. and Gilley, K.M. (1999), 'Dimensions, Determinants, and Differences in the Expatriate Adjustment Process', *Journal of International Business Studies*, Vol.30, No.3, pp.557–81.

Thompson, J.E. and Thompson, H.O. (1990), 'Values: Directional Signals for Life Choices', *Neonatal Network*, Vol.8, pp.77–9.

Torbiörn, I. (1982), *Living Abroad: Personal Adjustment and Personnel Policy in the Overseas Setting*, Chichester: John Wiley and Sons.

Tung, R. (1981), 'Selecting and Training of Personnel for Overseas Assignments', *Columbia Journal of World Business*, Vol.16, pp.68–78.

Tung, R.L. (1982), 'Selection and Training Procedures of US, European and Japanese Multinationals', *California Management Review*, Vol.25, No.1, pp.57–71.

Tung, R.L. (1988), *The New Expatriates: Managing Human Resources Abroad*, Cambridge, MA: Ballinger.

Wang, X. and Ralston, D. (2000), 'Strategies for Small and Medium-Sized US Businesses Investing in China: Lessons From Taiwanese Companies', *Thunderbird International Business Review*, Vol.6, pp.677–701.

Ward, C. and Kennedy, A. (1992), 'Locus of Control, Mood Disturbance and Social Difficulty During Cross-Cultural Transitions', *International Journal of Intercultural Relations*, Vol.16, pp.175–94.

Ward, C. and Kennedy, A. (1996), 'Crossing Cultures: The Relationship Between Psychological and Socio-Cultural Dimensions of Cross-Cultural Adjustment' in J. Pandey, D. Sinha, and D.P.S. Bhawuk (eds.), *Asian Contributions to Cross-Cultural Psychology*, New Delhi: Sage Publications.

Ward, C., Okura, Y., Kennedy, A.and Kojima, T. (1998), 'The U-Curve on Trial: A Longitudinal Study of Psychological and Sociocultural Adjustment During Cross-Cultural Transition', *International Journal of Intercultural Relations*, Vol.22, No.3, pp.277–91.

Ward, C. and Searle, W. (1991), 'The Impact of Value Discrepancies and Cultural Identity on Psychological and Socio-Cultural Adjustment of Sojourners', *International Journal of Intercultural Relations*, Vol.15, pp.209–25.

Wee, V. (1988), 'What Does 'Chinese' Mean? An Exploratory Essay', Working Paper No. 90, Singapore: Department of Sociology, National University of Singapore.

Wu, Y.-l. and Wu, C.-h. (1980), *Economic Development in Southeast Asia: The Chinese Dimension*, Stanford: Hoover Institution Press.

Zeira, Y. (1975), 'Overlooked Personnel Problems of Multinational Corporations', *Columbia Journal of World Business*, Vol.10, No.2, pp.98–103.

The Supervisory Board in Chinese Listed Companies: Problems, Causes, Consequences and Remedies

JAY DAHYA, YUSUF KARBHARI and
JASON ZEZONG XIAO

Company law in China requires Chinese listed companies to adopt a two-tier board structure, consisting of a Board of Directors (BoD) and a Supervisory Board. Both the BoD and the Supervisory Board are appointed by, and report to, shareholders. This study examines how Supervisory Boards function in Chinese listed companies. Particular attention is paid to the problems that the Supervisory Board is facing and to the likely causes and consequences of these problems. The results will be useful for investors in their future understanding of the risks of Chinese listed companies, and for Chinese listed companies and regulators in finding ways to improve the working of the Supervisory Board.

To date, little study has been undertaken which investigates the operation of China's unique two-tier board structure. The Supervisory Board has attracted even less attention partly because the Supervisory Board is regarded as being ineffective (Tam, 1999). Because of its ineffectiveness, the Chinese board structure is seen as an Anglo-Saxon type one-tier board (Tam, 1995; Tian, 2001). However, if the Chinese Supervisory Board is deemed to be ineffective, there is then a strong case to subject it to rigorous examination. Such research could uncover the reasons why the Supervisory Board is considered to be ineffective. Research in this area could also point to ways to improve the functioning of corporate governance in general and the Supervisory Board in particular. Moreover in several recent cases, the Supervisory Board was reported to have played a crucial role in monitoring the BoD and senior managers in Chinese listed companies. This suggests that some Supervisory Boards do fulfil a certain monitory role and thus this corporate governance mechanism can be improved. Therefore, the task should not be to ignore the Supervisory Board, but find ways to improve it in the future.

After all, it was as recent as the early 1990s that the Supervisory Board and BoD began to be adopted in China. The transitional nature of the Chinese economy implies that market-oriented institutions are emerging and the influence of the traditional planned economic system continues. Therefore, we hypothesize that the transitional nature of the Chinese corporate sector creates problems and difficulties which inhibit the effectiveness of the Supervisory Board in Chinese listed companies. To assess this hypothesis, we undertook face-to-face semi-structured interviews with directors, supervisors, and senior executives in 16 Chinese listed companies. We also interviewed four separate expert panels comprising financial analysts, academics and securities regulatory officials in Beijing, Shanghai and Shenzhen.

The remainder of this study proceeds as follows. Section 2 presents a brief review of the literature. Section 3 outlines the two-tier board structure in China. Section 4 describes the research methodology and data collection. Section 5 gives an overview of the working of the Supervisory Board. The next section discusses the problems facing the Supervisory Board, and more importantly highlights their causes and consequences. This is followed by Section 7 that discusses the findings and their implications. The final section concludes the analysis with a summary and suggestions for future research.

LITERATURE REVIEW

There has been much heated debate over the 'pros' and 'cons' of the unitary board model adopted in the Anglo-American world vis-à-vis the two-tier board structure as practised in Germany and in other continental European countries (such as the Netherlands and France). Proponents of the two-tier board structure maintain that transparency and separation between managerial decision-makers and management monitoring help avoid direct conflicts of interest between owners and managers (Davidson, 1994). The critics of the unitary board system, however, point to its inherent concentration of power and conflict of interest, which could lead to corporate corruption in market-led economies (Turnbull, 1994). Advocates of the unitary system vehemently argue that the Supervisory Board is unnecessary when the company is doing well and that it cannot help either when the company is performing badly (Schneider-Lenne, 1992).

Advocates of each model can point out failures of the other model. The Maxwell scandal (Clarke, 1993) and the Barings Bank fiasco (Hogan, 1997) are examples of the failure of the unitary board, whereas the case of Metallgesellschaft is representative of the problems of the two tier-board structure (Tricker, 1994). Although these cases exist, neither school has produced systematic comparative empirical evidence. Nor is there convincing theoretical comparative analysis of the two models.

Separately, however, extensive research has been undertaken of the unitary board structure (for a review, see Donaldson and Davis, 1994; Shleifer and Vishny, 1997). By contrast, much less attention has been paid to the two-tier board structure. Nevertheless, two recent studies have examined the two-tier board structure in Dutch companies. Van Hamel *et al.* (1998) investigated the relationship between the Supervisory Board and the Managing Board, whilst Massen and Den Bosch (1999) compared the formal structure of the two-tier board with board practices, casting doubts about the supposed independence of the two boards.

In a Chinese setting, Aoki and Qian (1995) examined the phenomenon of insider control in Chinese enterprises and the role of the banking sector in corporate governance, whilst Clarke and Du (1998) drew attention to the emerging patterns of ownership in China. Interestingly, the *Asia Pacific Business Review* devoted a special issue to managerial change in China during the course of economic reform, but this special issue did not pay specific attention to corporate governance (Warner, 1999). Corporate governance did attract the attention of Goodall and Warner (2000) who focus on Sino–foreign joint ventures. Through the perceptions of Chinese board directors, they found that the number of foreign partners serving on boards correlates with the monitoring role of the board as well as with transfer price setting. The study also revealed that share of decision-making is not simply seen as a function of equity shares, that informal interaction is more important and that board meetings are an inappropriate venue for resolving conflict. Tam (1995) also surveyed corporate governance in China, but concentrated on the BoD. The Supervisory Board was not the subject of his study because the evidence available to him suggested that the function of the Supervisory Board was only nominal. Perhaps because of the perceived ineffectiveness of the Supervisory Board, Tam (1999) and Tian (2001) rightly conclude that the Anglo-Saxon unitary board rather than the two-tier board characterize corporate governance in China. However, if the Supervisory Board is deemed to be ineffective and weak, the case then for studying the Supervisory Board would be stronger than when it was perceived to be effective and strong. Such research would help ascertain the likely causes and consequences of the ineffectiveness of the Supervisory Board. Besides, such research would help improve overall corporate governance in China.

THE TWO-TIER BOARD STRUCTURE IN CHINESE LISTED COMPANIES

When China's economic reform began in the late 1970s, all the firms were either state-owned or collectively owned. In reality, firms were mere sub-units of the government and were under tight control of the Communist Party. Three principal organs typically governed firms: the Party Committee, the Workers' Council and the Trade Union (now commonly referred to as the 'old three boards'). During the 1980s, a handful of joint-stock companies emerged and private ownership coexisted with state and collective ownership. Nevertheless, corporate governance in these companies did not change.

The establishment of the Shanghai and Shenzhen Stock Exchanges in the early 1990s split the Chinese corporate sector into listed and non-listed companies. This study focuses on listed companies. There are over 1,100 companies listed on these two exchanges with over 100 listed in Hong Kong, Singapore, New York, Tokyo and other overseas Stock Exchanges. The market valuation of these companies was RMB 43,522 billion which is approximately 45 per cent of China's GDP (CSRC, 2002). In listed companies, there are as many as nine categories of owners. These owners include the state, promoter legal person, foreign legal person, internal employees and other owners of non-tradable shares, holders of A-shares (domestic owners), holders of B-shares (foreign investors) and holders of H-shares listed in HK Stock Exchange and shares listed in other foreign exchanges. The percentages for these nine owners were 34.25, 20.9, 1.42, 6.03, 2.05, 1.25, 24.6, 5.3 and 4.75 respectively of the total Chinese equity capital at the end of 1998 (Fa, 1999).

Essentially, the Chinese Company Law 1993 requires all listed companies as well as non-listed joint-stock companies to adopt a two-tier board structure, consisting of a BoD and a Supervisory Board. The BoD is defined as a decision-making unit and the Supervisory Board a monitoring device. According to the Company Law both should be appointed by, and report to, shareholders. This corporate governance system is markedly different from the Anglo-American unitary board model. Nor is it the same as the German two-tier board. Unlike German supervisors, Chinese supervisors are not empowered to appoint and dismiss directors and executives.

Consistent with our hypothesis stated in the Introduction, we expect that the 'three old boards' and strong state-ownership in listed companies affect the working and effectiveness of the Supervisory Board.

TABLE 1

DESCRIPTION OF COMPANIES AND PANEL DISCUSSIONS

	Location	Industry ('000 RMB)	Total Assets	Exchange	Year Listed	BOD Size	SB Size	Year Founded	Participant
A	Beijing	Properties	6,784,850	HK	1997	12	3	1997	Board director/BoD secretary and BoD office staff
B*	Beijing	Tourism	352,830	SH (A)	1997	9	3	1997	Financial controller
C*	Beijing	Beverage	2,400,621	SH (A)	1997	13	3	1997	BoD secretary /board director
D*	Beijing	Trade	755,143	SH (A)	1997	10	6	1952	BoD secretary
E*	Beijing	Trade	434,518	SH (A)	1998	9	5	1998	Deputy head of finance, and BoD secretary/ chairman of Supervisory Board
F*	Beijing	Pharmacy	741,017	SH (A)	1997	14	5	1997	Finance director, Supervisor, and BoD secretary
G*	Beijing	Trade	1,958,500	SH (A)	1994	16	8	1992	Board director/chief accountant and two senior managers
H	Shanghai	Car rentals	1,336,580	SH (A/B)	1992	14	3	1988	Head of development and strategies
I	Shanghai	Variety	1,099,902	SH (A)	1990	11	5	1986	BoD office staff
J*	Shanghai	Properties	7,718,957	SH (A/B)	1992/94	7	3	1992	Secretary to the BoD
K*	Shanghai	Airlines	27,032,820	SH, HK, and NY			3		Secretary to the BoD and BoD office staff
L*	Shanghai	Trade	672,414	SH (A)	1997	12	3	1987	Supervisor and BoD office staff
M*	Shenzhen	Construction	2,899,550	SZ (A)	1992	11	7	1989	Chairman of the BoD, Board Director, BoD secretary, and Head of auditing and law
N	Shenzhen	Electronic		SZ (B)	1994	7	4	1985	Deputy head of finance and Head of logistics
O*	Shenzhen	Properties and tourism	368,040	SZ (B)	1997			1997	Deputy CEO
P	Shenzhen	Electronic	5,385,980	SZ (A/B)	1992	7	3	1980	Head of personnel
	Shenzhen	Panel discussion A							Head of investment bank and Researcher at a securities firm
	Beijing	Panel discussion B							Three investment consultants, one security broker and an associate professor
	Shanghai	Panel discussion C							Four security analysts
	Beijing	Panel discussion D							A government official, one professor, and one company head of finance

Note: * Companies transformed from one or more state-owned companies.

METHODOLOGY AND DATA COLLECTION

We interviewed a total of 28 directors, supervisors, and executives in 16 Chinese Listed companies. In addition, we undertook interviews with four panels of experts. These included financial analysts, academics and governmental officials (see Table 1). The listed companies in our sample were drawn from different industries in three cities: Beijing, Shanghai, and Shenzhen. The companies in our sample issue A-shares, B-shares, H-shares and NY-shares. They varied in size, with the amount of total assets ranging from 352 million to 27,032 million RMB. The average size of the BoD is 10.5 directors, whilst the figure for the Supervisory Board is 3.78.

Our interviews were undertaken in April and June 1999. The interviews were semi-structured. A checklist of the main questions asked is provided in Appendix 1. Notes were taken during each interview and these were then analysed. No attempt was made to record the interviews as this is not acceptable practice in Chinese culture.

THE FUNCTIONING OF THE SUPERVISORY BOARD

The functioning of the Supervisory Board in China varies. Two mini cases illustrate the extremes. The first case is that of Congqing Department Store Ltd. The company's 1998 annual report did not have a Supervisory Board report although such a report is required (Shen, 1999). This has been the only case of this nature. In 1998, the Supervisory Board in the company consisted of a chairman, a deputy chairman and three other supervisors. The chairman was the party chief and director of the Municipal Bureau of Commerce and the deputy chairwoman had been the deputy party chief in the company. The deputy chairwoman left the company in 1998 and the chairman had retired from his governmental position and had not resumed duties as chairman of the Supervisory Board. Thus the Supervisory Board was unable to carry out its duties and consequently failed to issue a report.

The second case concerns Kaidi Silk Co. Ltd which had recorded poor financial performance. At the 1999 annual general meeting of shareholders (AGM), the Supervisory Board proposed a motion to remove a director who was also a deputy chief executive officer and the proposal was approved (Sheng, 2000). This again is the first instance of this nature. The company had encountered major problems in recent years leading to trading of its shares to be suspended. The director who was removed was responsible for many problems, for instance, the accumulation of bad debts totalling RMB 7 million.

Between the two extremes, our interview data enabled us to categorize Chinese Supervisory Boards into four main groups. In some companies, the Supervisory Board plays only a minor role and is considered as only a nominal unit. For example, supervisors meet twice a year and the meeting is only regarded as a formality. In another group of companies, the supervisors play a slightly greater role and attend BoD and executive meetings. They voice opinions at meetings, but do not enjoy the right to vote. They merely provide advice or offer suggestions, but seldom challenge the BoD or executives. In a third group, supervisors diligently carry out their monitoring duties and do challenge the BoD and executives. However, the BoD censors their external report. The final type of Supervisory Board not only monitors the Supervisory Board and the executives on a daily basis, but also independently reports to the AGM and to the wider public. Among the 16 companies that participated in our study, most Supervisory Boards fall into the first two categories. The next section investigates the reasons for this pattern.

THE PROBLEMS FACING THE SUPERVISORY BOARD

Lack of Legal Power and Responsibilities

We discussed earlier that the Company Law (1993) defines the Supervisory Board as an organ monitoring directors and executives of the firm. Legally, the Supervisory Board and the BoD are on the same hierarchical level in the organization since both report to shareholders. Also, the legal power of the Supervisory Board is limited to requesting directors and managers to alter and rectify any personal action if there is conflict with the firm's objectives. In addition, the Supervisory Board by law does not have the power to hire and fire directors and executives.

The overwhelming majority of our interview respondents agreed that the Supervisory Board lacked authority and power. Some vehemently argued that additional power needs to be bestowed on the Supervisory Board. The usual comment received was that 'the Supervisory Board is like a tiger without teeth'. Interestingly, several of our interviewees revealed that a German-type Supervisory Board should be put in place, that is, the Supervisory Board be given the power to hire and fire directors and executives. Our analysis suggests that it is this lack of power that has caused the Supervisory Board to be commonly regarded as a supplementary or nominal device or even a new version of the traditional trade union.

The Company Law (1993) also fails to prescribe legal liability for supervisors. Thus, in several well-known financial scandals, whilst directors and/or auditors were prosecuted, supervisors escaped any legal prosecution or penalty. Supervisors were not sued by shareholders or for that matter by any other interested party. This was clearly borne out in the case of Hainan Minyuan Modern Agricultural Development Co. Ltd where management had created a false profit of RMB 0.5 billion (£3.8 million) and a false reserve of RMB 0.6 billion (£4.6 million) to boost the firm's share price. Consequently, the share price had increased sixteen-fold over a period of eight months between 1996 and 1997. The BoD resigned in 1997 and the chairman was prosecuted, but the supervisors went 'scot-free'. In another case, Hong Guang Industrial Ltd suffered a huge loss in the first year after listing in 1997. The Chinese Securities Regulatory Commission found that the company had falsified profit figures to obtain a stock market listing. After listing, the firm had used shareholders' funds to make up the losses and employed shareholders' funds to speculate in equity markets. A private shareholder sued the company and the courts charged the BoD with fraud and deception. However, the supervisors again went 'scot-free'.

In general, because of this lenient legal environment, supervisors are under no pressure to treat their job seriously. This is also evident from the case of Congqing Department Store Ltd, which is listed on the Shanghai Stock Exchange. This was the first case of its kind where the 1998 annual report of the company did not even contain a mandatory Supervisory Board report. In this case, the supervisors failed to meet before the firm's annual report was released and thus failed to produce a report.

Lack of Independence

The Supervisory Board should be independent of external forces in carrying out their duties. Without independence, supervisors would compromise and be incapable of protecting shareholders' interests. However, many Supervisory Boards are far less than independent. This is particular true in four situations.

First, in many listed companies that are transformed from state-owned companies, the Supervisory Board is likely to be influenced by the Party/government. Although it is the aim of economic reforms to separate the responsibilities between the Party and the government, and between the government and the firm, there is inevitable inertia at least during the transitional period. This is evident from the fact that in many companies such as Congqing Department Store Ltd, Party/government officials are supervisors or directors. In most of the listed companies that are transformed from state-owned companies, there is still a Party Committee within the newly formed company and the Party chiefs also serve as chairman and/or deputy chairman of the BoD or the Supervisory Board.

The Party/government influence is clear from the following remark made by a director and deputy CEO of Firm A:

> Our listed company remains a state-owned company and is run that way. The Party and the government control the personnel. The chairman of the BoD or Supervisory Board, CEO and their deputies are given a certain governmental rank. We are Party and government officials. We are not measured so much by economic indicators, as we are by political indicators. The Party's organizational division will send a team to the company and talk to various representatives. But the team members seldom look at the financial statements. They actually do not understand financial statements.... All they consider is whether or not the company is socially stable; whether employees complain about the directors and managers; and whether the directors and managers are democratic in their work.

Our discussions with the interviewees suggest that the Party/government can in several ways affect or influence the function of the Supervisory Board. First, if supervisors are Party/government officials, they may display loyalty to the Party by protecting state interest at the expense of other stakeholders. Second, the Supervisory Board may be evaluated against political rather than economic or financial criteria. If the BoD chairman, deputy chairman and directors or executives are Party/government officials, even if supervisors themselves are not, the supervisors may feel they have a duty to protect rather than offend the Party/government officials. Finally, monitoring by the Supervisory Board may be replaced by Party/government monitoring and evaluations of the BoD and executives. Of course the Supervisory Board in some companies may not be subject to the same influence of the Party/government. These companies tend to be Sino–foreign joint ventures and other non-state-controlled listed companies.

In the main, Party/government control is implemented through two main mechanisms. The first is through personnel control. The Party/government still effectively hires and fires the main corporate leaders (such as the chairman, deputy chairman of the BoD and Supervisory Board, and CEO and deputy CEO). In many large transformed listed firms, key individuals continue to enjoy the status of Party/government official by maintaining specific bureaucratic rank (for example, the rank equivalent to a government minister). Their appointments have to be reviewed and approved by the Party/government and are rubber-stamped at the AGM. The second important control device is the fundamental principles and policies of the Party/government such as 'one centre and two basic points'.[1] These principles establish the boundaries outside which activities are unacceptable. Therefore they can be regarded as guidelines for companies, their BoD and Supervisory Board. At present, the maintenance of social and political stability is a basic state policy. It would be unacceptable for the BoD and the Supervisory Board to cause any political unrest in their work. Therefore several financial analysts and a professor we interviewed commented that it was primarily due to the influence of the Party/government that many listed firms were not profit oriented. In many cases, listed companies were forced to take over loss-making state-owned enterprises. In these circumstances, the Supervisory Board could do nothing.

Second, where there is a dominant BoD or an autocratic chairman of the BoD, the functioning of the Supervisory Board is suppressed or censored. In Firm I, which is a non-state-controlled company, the chairman of the BoD is the founder. Although he is not the largest shareholder, he appeared to have absolute control of the BoD, shareholder meetings and the Supervisory Board. In fact, supervisors were all his close friends. The Supervisory Board only had a physical existence. It did nothing to monitor the chairman of the BoD and others. Likewise, in Firm F, the BoD rejected the Supervisory Board report when it was submitted for inclusion in the annual report. Even after the Supervisory Board revised its report, the Supervisory Board report was still abridged by the secretary to the BoD when it was published. A supervisor in this company revealed:

> This year's report was accepted straight, with no single amendment. This report is *weixinde* (that is, against my will) … The BoD wanted me to write a statement that there were no illegal acts in the company. To protect myself, I wrote, 'No illegal acts were discovered in the firm.'

Third, in cases where all the supervisors are wholly insiders, supervisors tend to identify themselves as close friends and associates of directors or executives. They are paid a salary and hold senior managerial positions. Eight out of the ten companies whose detailed information about supervisor background was available to us have between 33 per cent and 100 per cent of supervisors as insiders. This is quite common among Chinese listed companies. Thus they may have incentives not to act professionally as supervisors. As insiders, supervisors are under pressure from the BoD and executives not to rock the boat, or in Chinese, *jiacou buke waiyang* ('family scandals should not be exposed to outsiders' or as in the UK 'dirty linen should not be washed in public'). Therefore, it is not surprising that an insider supervisor of

Firm F highlighted, 'You are a member of the company. You sometimes have to open an eye and close the other (i.e. not be strict).'

Finally, being a shareholder of the company can also undermine supervisor independence. Of the 12 companies whose information on the Supervisory Board is available to us, all supervisors in four companies held shares; 50–75 per cent of supervisors in six other firms were also shareholders; and only in two companies were supervisors not shareholders. Although being a shareholder provides some incentive for supervisors to carry out their duties diligently this may, in theory, create a compromising situation where shareholder supervisors' own interests are in conflict with those of other shareholders. In practice, however, the effect on supervisors of being a shareholder is small because the number of shares that they hold is generally very small, and by law, these shares are not tradable publicly.

Technical Incompetence

Among other duties, the Supervisory Board is required to perform a financial review, to monitor whether directors and executives have complied with the law and the company's by-law, and to explain anomalies in the company's financial and operating performance. These and other duties are technical in nature. For the Supervisory Board to discharge its responsibilities, it is imperative that supervisors have technical expertise in accounting, finance, law and other related disciplines.[2] The Supervisory Board may use the company's internal auditors and legal experts. But supervisors themselves still have to make a judgement and to form a conclusion.

Among the companies that participated in our study, at least three companies reported not to have technical experts on their supervisory board. In most other companies, although supervisors had some technical knowledge, they were generally individuals who were retired and whose skills were likely to be outdated in today's fast changing environment.

Where there was a lack of technical expertise, the Supervisory Board could be misled or were incapable of undertaking any serious activity. This is illustrated well in the comment provided by the financial controller of company B who stated that:

> The Supervisory Board generally does nothing. Even with the annual report, I was the one who briefed them. They don't understand anything. The Supervisory Board meets twice a year, one before the interim report is issued and the other before the annual report is published. Each meeting lasts about half an hour. It is basically a formality. They

cannot discuss serious issues. Our Secretary to the BoD, after all, drafts the Supervisory Board report.

Partly due to the lack of expertise of supervisors, there were other individuals who echoed similar sentiments regarding the Supervisory Board report being wholly written by the Secretary to the BoD rather than the Supervisory Board.

Low Status

Although the Company Law (1993) places the Supervisory Board at the same organizational hierarchy level as the BoD, the Supervisory Board is widely perceived as having lower status than the BoD and senior executive officers. It was often mentioned to us that the lower position of the supervisors in fact restricts the role of the Supervisory Board.

This perception exists for several reasons. First, the law provides the Supervisory Board with neither real power nor legal responsibility. This makes people think that the Supervisory Board is just another traditional trade union which is there to give fading political figures or retired or retiring cadres a position. Second, the previous and other current positions held by supervisors are lower than those of directors and senior executives. In addition, if they happen to be insiders, they are paid less than senior executives and insider directors. The director and chief accountant of Firm G described the close relations between the Supervisory Board and the BoD by highlighting:

> The chairman of the Supervisory Board was nominated by the chairman of the BoD who in turn was nominated by the largest shareholder. Directors are more competent than supervisors and directors occupy higher positions than supervisors.

Finally, the BoD may become more powerful than its statutory status when a company has a concentrated shareholding structure. In such circumstances, both the BoD and shareholders general meetings are dominated by the largest shareholder(s). Essentially, the Supervisory Board reports to the BoD rather than to shareholders. This situation is quite common in China and was confirmed by the chairman of the Supervisory Board of Firm E who stated that:

> The AGM and BoD in China is effectively the same thing. As a result, proposals made by executives will not meet questions from the BoD and the BoD's proposals are accepted without any problems at the AGM.

Information Shortage

Supervisors should have access to all information about their firm in order to fulfil monitoring duties. The Company Law (1993) does not bestow on the Supervisory Board power to access company information, nor does it prescribe how the Supervisory Board should obtain information. In reality, the Supervisory Board in many companies is kept in the dark. This is especially true for outside supervisors. For instance, the Supervisory Board of Firm E consists of all outside supervisors. The financial controller of this company pointed out that he 'only discloses what he should say to supervisors and never discloses what he should not'.

Interestingly, in companies where the Supervisory Board does include insiders, the Supervisory Board still remains relatively uninformed. The following dialogue that took place between a supervisor and a director (who was also company chief finance officer) during one of our interviews illustrates this particularly well:

> *Supervisor*: In practice, Supervisory Board members attend the BoD meetings. They can speak but cannot vote. They don't know the behind-the-scenes operations.... You cannot improve Supervisory Board's work because you are not informed.
>
> *Director*: Yes, we inform the Supervisory Board. Sometimes we tell you, but sometimes we tell another member of the Supervisory Board. Overall, we've kept you informed.
>
> *Supervisor:* In some cases, we are told about a transaction beforehand and nothing when the transaction was complete. You do not tell us about the process.

Our interviews revealed the existence of a trade-off between being independent and being informed. It appears difficult to resolve the dilemma. For example, the Secretary to the BoD at Firm D highlighted this:

> It is necessary to improve the Supervisory Board's independence. However, once the Supervisory Board becomes more independent, supervisors will be treated as outsiders and they will not be given inside information.

Lack of Incentives

The Company Law (1993) intends to make the Supervisory Board an opposing force to the BoD and executives. However, the Supervisory Board is not well motivated to accomplish its legal role. First, The

Supervisory Board is not entirely independent of the BoD and executives and is, in many cases, influenced heavily by the Party/government. Second, as discussed above, many supervisors are insiders and are thus reluctant to blow the whistle. In addition, the market for human resources in general and for supervisors is not well developed. Thus, there is little market pressure for supervisors to perform well. Neither is there a market reward if they do a good job. More specifically, the under-developed human capital market – combined with the fact that the law does not prescribe penalty rules, the reputation of doing either a good or bad job does not affect a supervisor's market value. This is quite different from independent auditors who can earn an above average fee if they enjoy a good reputation and who may be sued for negligence if they fail to discover material fraud. Finally, supervisors in China do not belong to an organized profession, again different from independent auditors. They are, therefore, neither subject to the monitoring of the profession nor are they required to protect the integrity of a profession.

Although, in theory, supervisors are subject to hiring and firing by shareholders, they are safe in that regard because shareholders in China are hardly conscious of their rights. As already pointed out, shareholders are not so concerned about performance as they are highly speculative and opportunistic towards investment.

DISCUSSION

Several conditions make the Supervisory Board important in the governance of Chinese listed companies. First, as market-orientated economic reforms push further ahead, traditional central planning and government direct intervention into corporate affairs become increasingly contradictory to the spirit of economic reform. The existence of state shares may mean that the influence of the government will still continue, but the dilution of corporate capital necessitates the separation of the two functions of the state as an investor and as a government. As an investor, the government is equal to other investors. Second, for historical reasons, 'insiders' control many listed companies. There is therefore a need for an independent force to balance the power of the insiders.

Furthermore, although the market is rapidly growing, the market for corporate control through mergers and acquisitions (M&A) is only emerging. Many M&A are at least partly arranged or even forced by local governments. Market-led M&A are not effective because of the administrative and bureaucratic barriers created by the traditional macro-economic management system which divides the economy into industries and geographic areas controlled by ministries and local governments. It is, therefore, not surprising that China is not a huge market but one that consists of many artificially divided smaller markets. Finally, although an auditing profession exists, the audit profession is far less than independent, and the quality of audit, although improving, is still somewhat dubious (De Fond *et al.*, 2000). In China, auditors' independence is severely impaired by two factors – government influence and economic dependence on the auditee (Xiao *et al.*, 2000). Besides, a professional audit is an external monitoring mechanism that focuses on financial reporting. Corporate governance requires monitoring and directing a broader spectrum of issues than financial reporting. In addition, to make external auditing effective, there should be an internal mechanism to co-ordinate with it. This internal mechanism could be an audit committee under the BoD as suggested by the National Association of Corporate Directors (NACD, 2000), or the Supervisory Board.

Therefore, the Supervisory Board should be an important monitoring mechanism in China. We contend that if the working of the Supervisory Board is improved, corporate governance will inevitably improve. Not only does our analysis reveal the main problems, but it also identifies the main sources of the problems. These problems and their causes suggest the following measures for enhancing the future role of the Supervisory Board.

First, there appears to be a need to reduce the control of the Party/government in order to increase the Supervisory Board's independence. Some of our interviewees suggest that the problems in corporate governance and with the Supervisory Board in China are political. These problems identify the limits of economic reform and call for political reform. In particular, companies should operate as companies and should not be run by the Party/government. However, we do recognize that political reform is a sensitive issue. The need for enhancing the role of the Supervisory Board and for perfecting corporate governance is not necessarily a sufficient reason for political reform.

There is also a need to improve Company Law. Some of our interviewees suggest that the Supervisory Board should be empowered by law to hire and fire directors. This will certainly improve supervisors' status both within and outside the company. While monitoring may be improved, the holding of excessive power by the Supervisory Board may diminish the BoD's ability to innovate and to make timely decisions. Furthermore, when most shareholders are less concerned with the company's affairs, as is the case at present, the Supervisory Board may become uncontrollable; for instance, who will monitor the Supervisory Board? However, it may be necessary for Company Law to clearly empower the Supervisory Board to recommend the removal of directors and senior executives under special circumstances.

In addition, Company Law should clearly prescribe legal responsibilities of the Supervisory Board so that supervisors will be under legal pressure to undertake their duties diligently. Moreover, Company Law should clearly make it an obligation of the BoD and executives to provide the Supervisory Board with timely company information so that the Supervisory Board can effectively exercise its function of monitoring. Also, there is a need to improve the Supervisory Board's technical competence. The professionalization of supervisors, like that of auditors, may be a way to increase the overall competence of supervisors, as well as improve monitoring of supervisors themselves. Finally, China may replace the two-tier board with a unitary BoD or incorporate some of its elements into the two-tier board structure. This model is particularly commendable for its dynamism due to its ability to drive the business forward without undue bureaucratic interference, fear of litigation, or fear of displacement (Charkham, 1995). Appointing independent directors and establishing special committees (such as audit committees) can enhance the accountability of the BoD and senior executives. Its adoption can also alleviate some existing problems of the Supervisory Board in Chinese listed companies such as low status and information shortage.

CONCLUSIONS

Our study has uncovered four different types of Supervisory Board in China. These are:

1. A board that does nothing;
2. A board that merely provides advice;
3. A board that monitors but does not reveal material facts; and
4. A board that both monitors and reveals material facts.

In most of the companies in our sample, the Supervisory Board falls into the first or second type. This is because of one or more of the following reasons:

- Lack of legal power and clearly defined legal responsibilities
- Lack of independence
- Lack of technical expertise
- Perceived low status
- Information shortage and
- Lack of incentives

These findings are generally consistent with our hypothesis that the transitional nature of the Chinese economy creates problems and difficulties that reduce the effectiveness of the Supervisory Board. They confirm that market-oriented systems (including the two-tier board structure in listed companies) are still experimental, while old mechanisms associated with the traditional planned economy (such as Communist Party Committees in listed companies) still exercise influence which are at times very strong.

Although these findings should be interpreted with a degree of caution since our study is only based on a sample of 16 listed companies, the problems identified do have policy implications concerning how to enhance corporate governance and improve the effectiveness of the Supervisory Board. These findings suggest the need for future political reform, revision of corporate law and professionalization of supervisors.

Our findings also point to future research into issues relating to the Supervisory Board. Many of the issues discussed above require further consideration, especially the relationship between political reform and the functioning of the Supervisory Board, the feasibility of empowering the Supervisory Board to hire and fire directors and senior executives, and the best ways to raise professional standards for supervisors. In addition, it would also be interesting and important to undertake research into the impact of supervisors as insiders and shareholders on the performance of the Supervisory Board. There is also a need to investigate the relationship between the Supervisory Board and independent directors whose appointment is encouraged by the Chinese Securities Regulatory Commission (The CSRC, 2001).[3] Also, in light of Goodall and Warner's (2002) study, it would be interesting to examine systematically the ways that foreign investors affect the working of the Supervisory Board and BoD in B-Share and H-Share companies. Finally, it would be worthwhile to evaluate the impact of the recent reductions of state-owned shares on the composition and working of the Supervisory Board (The State Council of China, 2001).[4]

APPENDIX 1
INTERVIEW QUESTIONS

1. Background information
    (1)   Date of first listing
    (2)   Industry
    (3)   History
    (4)   Types of shares (A, B, or H shares)
    (5)   Shareholding structure
    (6)   Largest shareholder
2. Board of Directors (BoD)
    (1)   How many directors are there on the BoD?
    (2)   Who are on the BoD?
    (3)   How does the BoD work?
    (4)   What does the BoD do?
    (5)   Is there any dominant influence within the BoD?
3. Supervisory Board (SB)
    (1)   How many supervisors are there on the SB?
    (2)   Who are on the SB?
    (3)   How does the SB work?
    (4)   What does the SB do?
    (5)   How to improve the work of the SB?
    (6)   How do you describe the relationship between the SB and the BoD, and that between the SB and AGM?
    (7)   How is the SB report prepared?
4. AGM
    (1)   Who attends the AGM?
    (2)   What issues are discussed at the AGM?
5. The executives
    (1)   Who are the executives?
    (2)   Is the CEO the same person for the Chairman of the BoD?
6. How are small and/or individual shareholders' interests protected?
7. What are the roles of the Communist Party, the trade union and the employees' council in corporate governance?

ACKNOWLEDGEMENTS

The authors wish to acknowledge the financial support provided by Cardiff University. We are also extremely grateful to Jane Xiujuan Gu, Lunan Li, Guliang Tang, Bin Wang, Harrison Huacheng Wang, Wenbo Wang, Zhihua Xie, and Youhong Yang for their valuable assistance in arranging interviews on which this paper is based.

NOTES

1.   The 'centre' is economic development. The first basic point is the reform and open door policy and the second is the 'four principles', i.e., adherence to the leadership of the Communist Party, Marxism and Mao Zedong thought, Proletarian Dictatorship, and Socialism.
2.   The Blue Ribbon Report on Audit Committees (NACD, 2000), for example, requires each audit committee member to be financially literate or become financially literate within a reasonable period of time after becoming a committee member.
3.   The China Securities Regulatory Commission issued 'Standard on Corporate Governance' (trial) on 11 September 2001. This standard requires listed companies to appoint independent directors to the BoD.
4.   The State Council of China issued 'Tentative Regulation on Reducing State-Owned

Shares to Raise Funds for Social Welfare' on 12 June 2001. This regulation requires joint-stock companies owned by the state to sell 10 per cent of state shares in any initial public offering or subsequent public offering and the proceeds from sale will go to the State Social Welfare Fund.

REFERENCES

Aoki, M. and Qian, Y. (1995), *Corporate Governance in Transitional Economies, Insider Control and the Role of the Banks*. Beijing: Chinese Economic Press.

Charkham, J. (1995), *Keeping Good Company: A Study of Corporate Governance in Five Countries*. Oxford: Oxford University Press.

China Securities Regulatory Commission (CSRC) (2001), *Standard on Corporate Governance* (Trial). Beijing: CSRC. 11 Sept. 2001.

China Securities Regulatory Commission (CSRC) (2002), *Statistics*. www.csrc.gov.cn (visited in April 2002).

Clarke, T. (1993), 'Case Study: Robert Maxwell: Master of Corporate Malfeasance', *Corporate Governance: An International Review*, Vol.1, No.3, pp.141–51.

Clarke, T. and Du, Y. (1998), 'Corporate Governance in China: Explosive Growth and New Patterns of Ownership', *Long Range Planning*, Vol.31, No.2, pp.239–51.

Davidson, I.H. (1994), 'On the Government of Companies', *Corporate Governance: An International Review*, Vol.2, No.1, pp.5–7.

DeFond, M., Wong, T.J. and Li, S. (2000), 'The Impact of Improved Auditor Independence on Audit Market Concentration in China', *Journal of Accounting and Economics*, Dec. pp.113–27.

Donaldson, L. and Davis, J.H. (1994), 'Boards and Company Performance – Research Challenges the Conventional Wisdom', *Corporate Governance – An International Review*, Vol.2, No.3, pp.151–60.

Fa, M. (1999), 'An Analysis of the Categories of Listed Companies and their Shares', *China Securities Daily*, 10 May, p.10.

Goodall, K. and Warner, M. (2002), 'Corporate Governance in Sino–Foreign Joint Ventures in the PRC: The View of Chinese Directors', *Journal of General Management*, Vol.27, No.3, pp.77–92.

Hogan, W.P. (1997), 'Corporate Governance: Lessons from Barings', *Abacus*, Vol.33, No.1, pp.26–48.

Massen, G. and van den Bosch, F. (1999), 'On the Supposed Independence of Two-tier Boards: Formal Structure and Reality in the Netherlands', *Corporate Governance: An International Review*, Vol.7, No.1, pp.31–7.

NACD (2000), *Report of the NACD Blue Ribbon Commission on Audit Committees*, Washington: National Association of Audit Committees.

Schneider-Lenne, E.R. (1992), 'Corporate Governance in Germany', *Oxford Economic Policy*, Vol.8, No.3, pp.11–23.

Shen, Y. (1999), An Incomplete Annual Report, *China Securities Daily*, 15 April.

Sheng, G.L. (2000), *The Supervisory Board Proposed to Fire a Director at Kedi*, accessed April 2002 at www.cs.com.cn/enp.

Shleifer, A. and Vishny, R. (1997), 'A Survey of Corporate Governance,' *Journal of Finance*, Vol.52, No.2, pp.737–82.

State Council of China (2001), *Tentative Regulation on Reducing State-Owned Shares to Raise Funds for Social Welfare*. Beijing: The State Council of China.

Tam, O.K. (1995), 'Corporate Governance in China's Listed Companies', *Corporate Governance – An International Review*, Vol.3, No.1, 21–9.

Tam, O.K. (1999), *The Development of Corporate Governance in China*. Cheltenham: Edward Elgar.

Tang, Y. (2000), 'Bumpy Road Leading to Internationalization: A Review of Accounting Development', *Accounting Horizons*, Vol.14, No.1, pp.93–102.

Tian, G. (2001), *State Shareholding and the Value of China's Firms*. Working paper: London Business School.

Tricker, B. (1994), 'Editorial: German Two Tier Boards and Bank Share Holdings: The Case of Metallgesellschaft', *Corporate Governance: An International Review*, Vol.2, No.3, pp.123–24.

Turnbull, S. (1994), 'Competitiveness and Corporate Governance', *Corporate Governance: An International Review*, Vol.2, No.2, pp.80–6.

Van Hamel, J., van Wijk, H., de Rooij, A. and Bruel, M. (1998), 'Boardroom Dynamics – Lessons in Governance', *Corporate Governance: An International Review*, Vol.6, No.3, pp.193–201; and Vol.6, No.4, 284–88.

Warner, M. (1999), 'China's Managerial Revolution', *Asia Pacific Business Review*, Special Issue. Vol.5, No.3/4, pp.1–246.

Xiao, J.Z., Zhang, Y. and Xie, Z. (2000), 'The Making of Independent Auditing Standards in China', Vol.14, No.1, pp.69–89.

Which Managers Trust Employees?
Ownership Variation in
China's Transnational Economy

The Chinese economy was one of the world's fastest growing during the 1990s. By the end of 2000, China had attracted a total of US$474.3 billion in capital investment from foreign direct investment since opening the door to the world in the late 1970s (China State Statistics Bureau, 2001). China's entrance into the World Trade Organization is accelerating this phenomenon. More and more multinational corporations (MNCs) seek strategic alliances among Chinese enterprises. A challenge for them is to understand changing and complicated operating systems under China's economy reforms both now and in the near future. Currently, state-owned, collectively owned, privately owned and joint venture forms coexist in China.

The emergence of multiple forms of ownership in China poses some central organizational research questions regarding future management. Have managers of various forms of ownership enterprises developed different levels of trust in their employees? This may substantially influence their managerial practice when facing divergent operational conditions. Do Chinese managers in international joint ventures (IJVs), who are originally from state-owned enterprises (SOEs), trust their employees in a context where managers need to adapt to new hybrid Chinese/Western management practices? Do Chinese managers in privately owned enterprises (POEs) place more trust in employees and invite more employee participation than Chinese managers in collectively owned enterprises (COEs)?

There is an increasing necessity for foreign investors to understand the beliefs and behaviour of Chinese staff at the management level in specific ownership contexts, as localization of foreign-invested companies has become a crucial issue. Previous studies of China's enterprise ownership focused on 'organizational hardware' such as human resource policies, strategy orientations, performance and alliances between international business partners (Defilippo, 1997;

Luo and Chen, 1997; Zhu and Dowling, 2000; White and Liu, 2001). However, much less attention has been given to organizational 'software' such as operation-related managerial beliefs and attitudes. These psychological factors may also be crucial for successful business outcomes, once substantial operations have been established. Theoretically and practically, patterns of ownership are assumed to shape managers' perceptions, beliefs, attitudes and related behaviour (Mascarenhas, 1989). Ownership factors have been identified as a determinant for trust development (Chan 1997; Whitener *et al.*, 1998). Prior work on China's management has stressed differences in cross-cultural values (Hofstede, 1993; Ralston *et al.*, 1993; Schwartz and Sagiv, 1995; Holt, 1997), but beliefs at management level have been under-explored. Studies propose that managerial values have an influence on the development of trust (Chan 1997; Whitener *et al.*, 1998; Armstrong and Yee, 2001). Interpersonal trust is found to correlate negatively with power distance (Shane, 1993; Porta *et al.*, 1997). Chen and his colleagues (1998) argue that cognitive-based trust is enhanced by individualism, while development of affect-based trust is promoted by collectivism.

This study not only conjectures that different forms of ownership in China will be associated with variations on the issues of trust, but also assumes that managerial values of power distance and individualism–collectivism will affect the development of trust. In the empirical investigation, the focus is first on the extent to which managerial beliefs of trust vary in divergent ownership models, including COE, POE and IJV forms; and second, on the extent to which managerial values of power distance and collectivism affect management trust in the context of these ownership forms.

THEORETICAL BACKGROUND AND HYPOTHESES

Development of Trust

Managers' values and beliefs have a complex impact on the practice of management and leadership (Szabo *et al.*, 2001). Managerial behaviour concerning the dimensions of beliefs about trust initiates mutual trust between leader and followers and enhances organizational commitment (Ray, 1994; Shaw, 1997). Trust has been studied from several disciplinary perspectives, such as economics, psychology, sociology, social psychology and political science, with differing methods (Bhattacharya and Devinney, 1998). This research looks at management trust more from perspectives of psychology and social psychology. Building trust is a sophisticated psychological process, which involves the truster in multiple processes of calculation, predication and perception about the trusted's intentions and capacity (Butler and Centrell, 1984; Doney et al., 1998). Rempel and his colleagues (1985) argue that trust in the targeted person's dependability, predictability and good faith reflects key aspects in the trust-building process.

Based on the quality and attributions of the target's current behaviour, investors in trust increase their *trust in the target's dependability*. Trust is an exchange relationship in which risk or vulnerability is involved (Rousseau et al., 1998). Both Shapiro and colleagues (1992) and Adler (2001) suggest that trust in business relationships develops on a calculative basis, as parties try to determine the nature of their interdependence, what benefit they will obtain from the relationship and give to it, and to what risks and vulnerabilities they are likely to be exposed. The competence and responsibility of the person in whom trust is being vested, therefore, are central for the other person to invest in trust building (Barber, 1983; Shapiro, 1987; McAllister, 1995; Chen et al., 1998).

It is also argued that, based on previous experience of the target's stability and consistency of behavioural patterns, investors in trust develop *trust on the basis of predictability*. The investment of trust is positively developed further when the trusted consistently interact benevolently in prior encounters (Stack, 1978; Adler, 2001). Trust in predictability emerges when the person vesting trust gains confidence in his or her ability to predict the target's future behaviour with accuracy (Rempel et al., 1985; Doney et al., 1998).

Feelings of security about the target *foster trust on the basis of an expectation of good faith*, a trust that goes beyond the available evidence and which is rooted in expectations of confidence (Rempel et al., 1985). Trust requires one party to believe that it is important to depend on the other party and to have positive, confident expectations that they will behave competently and honestly in achieving common goals (Das and Teng, 1998).

Likewise, management trust in subordinates' dependability, predictability and faith is related to the degree to which a manager believes that subordinates are capable of carrying out and willing to carry out their jobs independently, and are also capable of sharing responsibility in work (Graen and Uhl-Bien, 1995; Wang and Clegg, 2002). Research on leader–member exchange suggests that high quality exchange relationships involve showing mutual respect and sharing decision control (Dienesch and Liden, 1986; Liden and Maslyn, 1993). To obtain true employee involvement and loyalty, managers must send a clear message to employees that they are trusted and their participation is valued (Marcus and House, 1973; Graen and

Scandura, 1987; Kelly and Weber, 1995; Lindsay, 1996). In this study, in the context of a vertical interaction of management processes, trust is defined as the belief of managers in the importance of depending on employees and having positive, confident expectations and faith of competent behaviour and honesty in achieving common goals, with a predictable outcome, even in the face of uncertain circumstances.

Patterns of Ownership and Trust in China

China is transforming from a centrally planned economy into one that is more market oriented, with three types of economic ownership characterizing the present conjuncture: state, collective and private ownership coexist and compete with Sino–foreign joint ventures and fully foreign-owned enterprises. These heterogeneous ownership types vary significantly in their degree of government administrative intervention. Ownership is found to lead directly to particular autonomy with respect to human resource practices and subordination policies in China (Zhu and Dowling, 1998; Jefferson, 1999). Consequently, these divergent forms of ownership may possess different demographic characteristics and qualities of employees. The management of these different types of ownership enterprise is likely to develop dimensions of trust in dependability, predictability and good faith to various degrees.

COEs are established and supported by local governments rather than by the central government. Compared with the central government, local governments usually have limited resources to offer COEs. Typically, COEs find it difficult to attract and maintain sufficient quality employees for their operation, especially in managerial positions. Graduates of university and colleges rarely choose or are officially appointed to join COEs, which are believed to have low profile status and limited welfare (Sun, 2000), ranking, in most cases, the lowest among ownership enterprises. Under the mandates of the local government, COEs cannot select employees against their own preferred criteria in terms of loyalty and quality. The employees of COEs are mainly composed of local residents of variable quality, who are desirous of other jobs in better workplaces. There would be unjustified risk from a management point of view in developing trust through power sharing with subordinates. COEs usually develop a simple, centralized organizational structure (Tan, 1999; Jiang and Hall, 1996), which may indicate management's deep concern about their employees' quality and the high business risks that they face. As a result, managers in COEs are less likely to trust in employee dependability, good faith and predictability than those in IJVs and POEs.

Almost all POEs in China start up in a highly competitive environment with neither central nor local government support. With respect to human resource management, POEs in China are the only type of ownership that has complete autonomy to recruit employees. Nepotism and favouritism in filling the management structure (Lau *et al.*, 1999) are used to avoid extremely high uncertainty. Although managers in private enterprises have been identified as higher risk takers compared with managers of SOEs and IJVs (Holt, 1997), they have been seen to justify the need to reduce their risk. They believe that friends and relatives are trustworthy, even though their competence is sometimes questionable, and that, in an extremely uncertain and tough environment, one reduces business risk by hiring such people as managers (Lau *et al.*, 1999). Managers believe they can predict such followers' behaviour patterns and maintain their good faith by virtue of knowing and trusting them for a long time. In a Chinese cultural context, prevailing social values of reciprocity strengthen such perceptions and belief. Managers are likely to believe that people who are selected for tough conditions through particular criteria of *guanxi* should think that they have been given trust, and therefore should show their allegiance to management in return. POE management also uses competency criteria when selecting unfamiliar new employees who are not from their network. Consequently, managers in private enterprises are likely to have the strongest trust in employees' good faith and predictability, while amongst the three types of ownership, they may have only a reasonable level of trust in dependability compared with those in IJVs.

IJVs in the Chinese context invariably comprise a domestic firm and a foreign partner. The ownership form of the domestic partner is usually that of a state-owned enterprise (Goodall and Warner, 1999), though this may vary across the other types. To ensure business success and attract more foreign direct investment, various levels of the Chinese government always select the best SOEs of industries to be one partner in Sino–foreign joint ventures. These selected enterprises not only have better equipment but also have relatively high quality employees for that particular industry. IJVs, with higher salaries in comparison with local companies (Leung *et al.*, 1996) and knowledge/learning advantages, are strongly attractive for young qualified people to join. These enterprises thus have a better chance of selecting the best qualified people. Therefore, managers in IJVs are likely to have more grounds for trusting in employees' dependability than ones in other types of enterprise. However, a special report indicates that the young qualified people employed are 'frequent fliers' who have a very high rate of turnover in IJVs (Ahlstrom *et al.*, 2001).

This is most likely to lower the extent of management trust in employee predictability and faith in IJVs, compared with managers in the private and collective enterprises. The present study, thus, hypothesizes that:

1a: Managers in joint ventures will have the highest trust in employees' dependability, followed, in descending order, by those in privately owned and collectively owned enterprises.

1b: Managers in privately owned enterprises will have the highest trust in employee predictability, followed, in descending order, by those in joint ventures and those in collectively owned enterprises.

1c: Managers in privately owned enterprises will have the highest trust in employees' faith, followed, in descending order, by those in joint ventures and managers in collectively owned enterprises.

Managerial Values and Trust

Managerial values have been identified as a useful tool for understanding people's perceptions and behaviour in respect of trust (Jones and George, 1998; Armstrong and Yee, 2001). It is proposed that individualism/collectivism and power distance through cognitive processes have an impact on trust-building processes (Shane, 1993; Mente, 1994; Porta et al., 1997; Chen et al., 1998; Doney et al., 1998; Adler, 2001). Individualism/collectivism refers to the relationship between the individual and the collectivity that prevails in society: a self versus a group orientation. Power distance addresses ideological orientation and behavioural adaptation to authority.

Chen and colleagues (1998) argue that cognitive-based trust, which is based on other's performance behaviour – similar to trust in dependability – is enhanced by individualism; while development of affect-based trust, which goes beyond regular business professional relationship –trust in good faith – is promoted by collectivism. A social group with the prevailing value of collectivism has a propensity to lay down norms to curb deviant behaviour within the group. Accordingly, behaviour and attitudes of members toward the group are expected to favour conformity within the group. Managers with high collectivism, therefore, are likely to believe that the behaviour of employees is trustworthy with respect to predictability and good faith, and prefer to develop trust via prediction and faith processes (Doney et al., 1998). Such managers are encouraged to engage in trust relationships of collective–group orientation. In contrast, a manager whose managerial values are more individualistic may find it difficult to initiate interpersonal trust (Chen et al., 1998; Whitener et al., 1998; Hewett and Bearden, 2001). People highlighting individualism prefer to achieve personal success with independence and distinctiveness from others.

Power distance is found to relate negatively to trust, in cross-cultural studies (Williams *et al.*, 1966; Negandhi and Prasad, 1971; Hofstede, 1980; Shane, 1993). Hofstede (1980) argues that shorter power distance leads to a control system based on trust in subordinates, whilst such trust does not exist in longer power distance countries. This indicates that people placing a high value on allegiance to authority are likely to show low levels of trust with lower status employees and expect those subordinates to follow whatever they require. In the power–dependency relationships, trust is not a key element in developing and maintaining these relationships; instead, control plays a significant role (Reed, 2001). The expectation of conformity to authority is likely to reduce the perception for the necessity of trust in the leader–follower relationship, although Doney and colleagues (1998) propose that managers with large power distance are believed to prefer to develop trust via capacity and predication processes. Studies also find that the presence of hierarchical values leads to a climate of non-trust in Chinese organizations in China (Mente, 1994; Wang and Clegg, 2002). Control is believed to be an effective way to run the organizations.

Doney and colleagues (1998) argue that context may play a role in determining the relationship between managerial preferences and practice. Therefore, it would be helpful to gain a deeper understanding of trust by looking at the effect of individualism/collectivism and power distance in relation to the different forms of ownership and trust. Chinese employees, in general, are believed to devalue vertical job involvement because of high power distance (Mente, 1994; Pelled and Xin, 1997). Additionally, demographic characteristics are found to be related to managerial values in China's context (Birnbaum-More *et al.*, 1995; Ralston *et al.*, 1999). This study focuses on testing the effect of collectivism and power distance on trust related to these characteristics within the three forms of ownership. It, thus, is hypothesized that:

2a: Managerial values of power distance are negatively related to the managers' trust (in predictability, dependability and good faith) through the demographic characteristics of China's private and collective enterprises and joint ventures.

2b: Managerial values of collectivism are positively related to the managers' trust (in predictability, dependability and good faith) through the demographic characteristics of China's private and collective enterprises and joint ventures.

METHODS

Sample and Procedure

The sample for this study consisted of 310 managers, randomly sampled from the three enterprise forms, in a hierarchical range stretching from top and middle management to first-line management. These managers were drawn from Beijing and cities and counties of Hebei province, covering a large area of Northern China. A questionnaire survey was conducted between September 2000 and July 2001. In the first stage, COEs and POEs from Beijing and Hebei province were contacted. Enterprise size was chosen between 200 and 2000 full-time employees. Enterprises were selected at random from industry groups of textile, real estate, equipment manufacturing, consumer product manufacturing, and information services to business and consumers.

Three POEs in Beijing and five in cities and counties of Hebei province were chosen. Three COEs in Beijing and seven in cities and counties in Hebei province were also chosen. All questionnaires were distributed and collected with the support of local officials and enterprise authorities. Although the response rate is 75 per cent, only 80 per cent of these returned questionnaires are usable. In the second stage, four IJVs were drawn from Sino–foreign joint ventures in Hebei province. The Chinese partners of these IJVs were SOEs. With the

TABLE 1

DEMOGRAPHIC CHARACTERISTICS FOR MANAGERS IN THREE TYPES OF OWNERSHIP ENTERPRISES IN CHINA

Number in group	COE 86		POE 135		IJV 89	
	Mean	SD	Mean	SD	Mean	SD
Age[a]	1.67	0.96	1.76	0.79	2.40	0.86
Education[b]	2.36	0.65	3.03	0.50	2.93	0.45
M. Position[c]	3.05	0.92	30.13	0.92	2.83	0.75
Years in M.[d]	2.13	1.06	2.27	1.18	3.11	1.12
Gender						
Male	52 (64.3%)		92 (60.3%)		71 (80.2%)	
Female	34 (35.7%)		61 (39.7%)		18 (19.8%)	

Notes
[a] Age was coded as: 1 = 20–29; 2 = 30–39; 3 = 40–49; 4 = 50 or over
[b] Education level was coded as: 1 = primary school; 2= secondary school; 3 = bachelor degree; 4 = postgraduate degree.
[c] Management position was coded as: 1 = top management; 2 = senior management; 3 = middle management; 4 = first line management.
[d] Years in management was coded as: 1 = less than 2 years; 2 = 2 – 5 years; 3 = 6–10 years; 4 = 11–20 years; and 5 = over 20 years.

same administrative procedure, the response rate was 70 per cent. The total sample consisted of responses from 86 managers of COEs, 135 managers in POEs and 89 managers from Sino–foreign joint ventures (see Table 1).

Survey Design and Measures

The survey instrument was developed by conducting literature reviews and adopting standard validation measurements. First, existing measurement scales were identified through a review of prior research. All the items used in the survey were adopted and modified from the literature. Second, because the survey was of managers' trust, the perspective of the scales was shifted from a peer interpersonal relationship to the views of a manager.

Dependent Variables

Trust was measured using three scales modified from the trust survey questionnaire of Rempel and colleagues (1985). Trust Scale 1 – trust in predictability – tested a manager's belief that subordinates were consistent, stable and predictable in terms of past patterns of behaviour. Trust Scale 2 – trust in dependability – tested the extent to which a manager believed that subordinates were dependable and reliable, and able to act competently and responsibly, rather than tending to take advantage. Trust Scale 3 – trust in good faith – tested the extent to which a manager believed that subordinates would be trustworthy in the future, beyond the available evidence.

Independent and Control Variables

Power distance was measured using Robertson and Hoffman's (2000) measurement. Collectivism was measured using a scale 'vertical collectivism', which tests a view of relationship between interests of an individual and the whole group, from Chen and Menidl (1997) 'Vertical and Horizontal Collectivism Questionnaire'. Demographic data consisted of gender, age, the level of position, the education level, the length of experience in management, and current managerial position. Such data are controlled for the potential effects on trust through the independent variables of power distance and collectivism. The questionnaire was translated from an English version, as the original items were all derived from the English-language literature. The versions in Mandarin and English were made equivalent in meaning, refining the questions through backwards/forwards translation as the process of validation.

Analyses

The main analysis of this study involves a comparison among the three types of ownership enterprises (COEs, POEs and IJVs) and regression on trust dimensions with scales: *Trust in Faith* (Cronbach alpha = 0.84), *Trust in Dependability* (Cronbach alpha = 0.71), and *Trust in Predictability* (Cronbach alpha = 0.70) as dependent variables, and managerial values of *Power Distance* (Cronbach alpha = 0.78) and *Vertical Collectivism* (Cronbach alpha = 0.70) as independent variables. For these tested items, subjects expressed their level of agreement with a given statement via a seven-point, Likert-type scale – strongly agree to strongly disagree – with higher means representing a higher level of preference on the scale. Prior to statistical analysis, the responses to a number of items were reverse coded, so that all items measured with a higher score representing the construct to a greater extent.

A one-way ANOVA and the *post hoc* analysis were conducted to identify specifically differences on trust variables between managers of these ownership types by comparing means. An ownership dummy variable was formed based on IJVs, POEs and COEs respectively, with codes 1 and 0. In the hierarchical regression analysis, trust in good faith, trust in dependability, and trust in predictability were regressed on demographic variables (Step 1), managerial values of power distance and collectivism (Step 2) and the ownership dummy variable (Step 3), which tested the effect of managerial values on trust and whether there is a significant difference on trust variables amongst ownerships.

RESULTS

The results of ANOVA and the *post hoc* analysis reported in Table 2 demonstrate mean comparisons of demographic, dependent and independent variables to assess ownership-level differences in effect. The results of ANOVA indicate that there are statistically significant associations with organizational ownership for *trust in predictability* (F value = 8.30; $p < 0.001$), *collectivism* (F value = 3.35; $p < 0.05$) and *all demographic variables*. There is no significant difference amongst the managers of the three types of ownership enterprises on the managerial value of power distance.

The results of the *post hoc* analysis further indicate that the extent of managers' trust in predictability is highest in POEs ($p < 0.001$ and $p < 0.05$), followed, in descending order, by those in IJVs and those in collectively owned enterprises. Hypothesis 1b is thus strongly supported. However, there are no significant differences among the managers of the three types of ownership enterprises on trust in

TABLE 2
ANOVA ON TRUST, NATIONAL VALUES AND DEMOGRAPHIC
FOR COEs, POEs AND IJVs IN CHINA

Variable	COE 86		POE 135		IJV 89		F value
	Mean	SD	Mean	SD	Mean	SD	
Gender	1.36^a	0.48	1.40^u	0.49	1.19^{a,u}	0.40	5.80**
Age	1.67^a	0.96	1.76^u	0.79	2.40^{a,u}	0.86	20.66***
Education	2.36^{u,v}	0.65	3.03^u	0.50	2.93^v	0.45	45.13***
M. Years	2.13^u	1.06	2.27^v	1.18	3.11^{u,v}	1.12	20.49***
Position	3.05	0.92	3.13^a	0.92	2.84^a	0.75	3.22*
Power Distance	3.34	1.66	3.28	1.14	3.06	1.13	1.20
Collectivism	4.85^{a,b}	1.20	5.14^a	1.07	5.26^b	1.04	3.35*
Trust in predictability	4.42^{u,a}	0.45	5.13^u	1.19	4.84^a	1.29	8.30***
Trust in dependability	4.81	1.23	5.07	1.18	5.15	1.13	2.08
Trust in faith	4.83^a	1.13	5.16^a	1.01	5.10	0.94	2.83

Notes
The last column gives the F value and its level of significance for ANOVA test of equality of means for the three types of ownership organizations.
*$p<0.05$; **$p<0.001$; *** $p<0.000$.
Differences between means with the same letter, 'a' or 'b', indicate statistical significance at the 0.05 level between two types of enterprises, and likewise those with the letters 'u' or 'v', indicate significant difference at the 0.001 level.

dependability. There is only a significant difference between the managers of private and collective enterprises on trust in faith, with a higher extent of trust from managers in private enterprises. Hypotheses 1a and 1c, therefore, are basically rejected.

The means and standard deviations, and the Pearson correlations for demographic variables, trust variables (faith, dependability, predictability), power distance and collectivism presented in Table 3. The results of correlations indicate that there are negative relations between the value of power distance and two trust variables (with *trust in predictability*, $r = -0.32$, $p<0.001$; with *trust in dependability*, $r = -0.12$) and positive relationships between collectivism and all trust variables ($r = 0.22$, $p<0.001$; $r = 0.41$, $p<0.001$; $r = 0.22$, $p<0.001$)

The results of hierarchical regression in Table 4 report effects for dependent variables of trust. The demographic variables accounted for relatively little variance in the dependent variables of trust, except for the length of experience in management which has both positive direct and indirect effects on *trust in predictability* ($p<0.05$). The managerial values of power distance and collectivism mediate the relationship between the length of experience in management and trust in predictability. The direct effect for collectivism was significantly

TABLE 3

MEANS, STANDARD DEVIATIONS, AND PEARSON CORRELATIONSA FOR VARIABLES

Variable	M	SD	1	2	3	4	5	6	7	8	9	10
1. Age[b]	1.92	0.90	—									
2. Education[c]	2.83	0.60	0.08	—								
3. Years in management[d]	2.48	1.20	0.74**	0.06	—							
4. Managerial Position[c]	3.06	0.85	-0.37**	-0.30**	-0.34**	—						
5. Gender	1.33	0.47	-0.25**	-0.02	-0.17**	0.04	—					
6. Trust: faith	5.04	1.17	0.12*	0.05	0.13*	-0.05	-0.04	—				
7. Trust: predictability	4.83	1.31	0.03	0.06	0.08	0.00	-0.03	0.28**	—			
8. Trust: dependability	5.08	0.98	0.05	0.09	0.10	-0.09	-0.03	0.59**	0.21**	—		
9. Collectivism	5.10	1.11	-0.01	-0.01	-0.00	0.14*	0.03	0.24**	0.43**	23**	—	
10. Power distance	3.26	1.28	0.12*	0.10	0.12*	-0.15**	-0.02	-0.08	-0.33**	-0.16**	-.41**	—

a   *p <0.05, ** p< 0.001 (2-tailed).
b   Age was coded as: 1= 20–29; 2=30–39; 3= 40–49; 4=50 or over
c   Education level was coded as: 1 = primary school; 2= secondary school; 3 = bachelor degree; 4 = postgraduate degree.
d   Management Position was coded as: 1 = top management; 2 = senior management; 3 = middle management; and 4 = first line management.
e   Years in management was coded as: 1 = less than 2 years; 2 = 2–5 years; 3 = 6–10 years; 4 = 11–20 years; and 5 = over 20 years.

TABLE 4

HIERARCHICAL REGRESSION ANALYSIS OF TRUST FOR COEs, IJVs AND POEsS
IN CHINAa

Variable	Trust in Predictability			Trust in Dependability			Trust in Faith		
	Model 1	Model 2	Model 3	Model 1	Model 2	Model 3	Model 1	Model 2	Model 3
Gender	−0.03	−0.03	−0.05	−0.02	−0.02	−0.02	−0.01	−0.01	−0.02
Age	−0.11	−0.10	−0.09	−0.09	−0.09	−0.10	0.05	0.05	0.05
Education	0.06	0.07	−0.02	0.08	0.08	0.04	0.05	0.05	0.05
Years in mgt.	0.15	0.16*	0.17*	0.15	0.15	0.14	0.10	0.15	0.14
Mgt. Position	0.01	−0.06	−0.10	−0.05	−0.09	0.10	−0.01	−0.08	−0.10
Power distance	−0.22**		−0.23**		−0.11	−0.11	−0.01	−0.01	
Collectivism	0.33**	0.32**			0.20**	0.20**		0.24**	0.24**
Ownershipb									
COE			−00.20**			−00.08			−00.06
IJV			−0.17**			0.02			0.03
R^2	0.11	0.22	0.26	0.02	0.10	0.12	0.03	0.10	0.16
Adjust R^2	0.02	0.21	0.24	0.01	0.08	0.10	0.01	0.10	0.15
F	0.90	13**	12.1**	1.27	3.78**	3.01*	1.48	4.62*	3.77**
Observation number:	320			320			320		

Notes
a   Standardized coefficients are reported.
   * $p<0.05$; ** $p<0.001$
b   Dummy variables of ownership include POE, COE and IJV

related to all the three trust variables. However, there were only the negative indirect and direct effects for power distance related to managers' trust in employee predictability. The results of regression also indicate that the types of ownership were significantly different on the dependent variable *trust in predictability* via the effect of power distance and collectivism (*p*coe <0.001 and *p*jiv <0.001). Hypothesis 2a is partially but weakly supported and H2b is partially but strongly supported.

DISCUSSION

The purpose of the present study is to compare managers' beliefs related to trust at the management operation level across three types of ownership enterprises in China, in order to understand better China's management. The results of the present study are also helpful in getting knowledge of how managerial values have effects on trust within the context of their reform.

Theoretical Implications

First, the findings of this study suggest that managers' beliefs about trust in some aspects do vary across different types of ownership in China. The results indicate that the different types of ownership, which are characterized by varying averages of employee quality and autonomy of human resource management, provide references to managers' trust-building strategies with respect to employee predictability. This may indicate that although business conditions are extremely competitive, managers trust their employees as predictable, as long as they can influence recruitment.

Secondly, the research provides some support for the proposition that managerial values have an effect on the development of trust. The findings of this study suggest that power distance has a negative effect on managers' trust in employee predictability, providing empirical evidence for a specific aspect of trust to support previous research that people placing a high value on allegiance to authority are likely to show low levels of trust with lower status (Shane, 1993). Trust is usually initiated through rational perceptions rather than through emotions (Lewicki and Bunker, 1996). It brings about possibilities of co-operation and delegation, instead of control. Large power distance, which reflects the inequality of hierarchical relationships, may lead to an emphasis on obedience in the leader–follower relationships, without the development of trust as a rational justification. As a result, the higher magnitude of power distance preferred by managers, the less trust in employees they develop. They prefer towards the direction of control in the trust– control spectrum.

The findings of this study also suggest that the value of collectivism is positively related to trust in predictability, dependability and good faith, especially to trust in predictability. These findings support the proposition of Chen and colleagues (1998) that collectivism promotes such an aspect of trust. Trust in predictability and good faith is formed as a social bond between managers and subordinates beyond regular work relationships. Conformity with group collectivism may lay the groundwork for managers to believe in the predictability of employee behaviours and attitudes. Collectivism, which emphasizes an individual's contribution to the whole group, may facilitate managers' belief of trust in the dependability of such eligible members. The belief that an individual should put group interest above individual interest, even when there is conflict between the two values, may enhance the belief that employees/group members could be trusted in good faith.

Finally, the findings of the study do not provide strong support for the propositions of the relationship between demographic characteristics and trust variables via power distance and collectivism in China's current context. Only the number of years which managers have been in management correlate significantly with their trust in employee predictability. The longer in management, the more managers trust in employee predictability.

Practical Implications

The results of the study provide distinct profiles of managers in COEs, POEs and IJVs in China on managerial beliefs related to trust. Managers in POEs hold the highest level of trust in employees' predictability and faith. Managers in this type of enterprise have, on average in this sample, the highest level of education and the highest level of managerial position. Managers in COEs have the lowest levels for all dependent variables of trust. Of the three types of enterprise, on average, COE managers have the shortest period of experience in management and the lowest level of education. Managers in IJVs develop the second highest level of trust in employees' faith and predictability amongst the survey sample groups.

Interestingly, there is no statistically significant difference between the three types of ownership enterprise on the value of power distance. This result is not consistent with the findings of Holt's study (1997), which found that there was significant difference between managers in private enterprise and a group composed of managers from IJVs and SOEs on this dimension by using an instrument of the Schwarz Value Survey. This may need further study to verify the results.

The findings of the present study indicate that Chinese managers in IJVs are developing some positive managerial beliefs and attitudes in operation. They are favourable to trust in employees and collectivism. This positive picture of managerial values and beliefs may indicate that managers of IJVs are moving in the direction of more effective management for the future.

Holding an autonomous right to recruit employees, managers in POEs develop a strong sense of trust in the predictability of their subordinates, compared with managers in the other two types of ownership, both of which to some extent remain under government control. Trust in faith and predictability is developed from feelings of confidence and security in the caring responses of others and the strength of a relationship. Selection criteria of recruitment in POEs are based on either the quality of the person or their potential trustworthiness; sometimes the latter is more important than the former. This emphasis may provide conditions for managers to believe that their subordinates are loyal and predictable in the long term.

COEs have played a unique role in China's economic transformation since the early stages of economy reform, sometimes as a bridge of transformation between state-owned enterprise domination and the development of privatization. Their performance in the market has been an impressive phenomenon of the 1980s and early 1990s (Sun, 2000). However, China's acceleration of marketization in the late 1990s requires that all types of enterprise develop effective management systems. Managers in COEs seem not fully equipped to handle rapid change and increasingly acute competition. Many COEs easily became fragile and failed after a few years of high performance (Xiang, 2001). The findings of the present study, to an extent, provide an explanation for this. Managers in COEs have not shown a strong preference for trust in the predictability and good faith of employees, which in turn favour effective motivation. This may be an indication that they need to foster positive managerial beliefs so that increased long-term growth becomes sustainable.

LIMITATIONS AND FUTURE RESEARCH DIRECTIONS

This study sheds light, through the differences shown in the data, on the trust that varies by ownership in China but with certain limitations. First, the present study only uses the quality of the employees as the source for understanding how managers in different types of ownership in China build trust. However, building trust is a sophisticated psychological process, in which managers are also influenced by other important elements, such as organizational culture, business nature and personalities, to develop trust in employees. These factors definitely need to be explored further in order to understand the development of management trust in China comprehensively. Second, the sample of the present study was limited geographically to regions of Northern China. Although those cities and counties provide quite a wide coverage, additional data collected from Southern China, and other areas, would make the findings more generally applicable across all of China.

Finally, we only measured relationships between managerial values and trust within the ownership context of China, but did not tap other specific variables in relation to form of ownership. For instance, various factors including access to financial resources, the degree of managers' risk sentiment and government support in relation to ownership were not investigated.

The results of this study suggest several avenues for future research within international studies of values and ownership. There is a need for research into the pivotal role that trust plays in managing the uncertain business environment and enterprise performance. Exploring other factors such as organizational cultures, business environment and personalities, even historical influence (Reed, 2001) in China, would provide a comprehensive understanding of the development of management trust.

It would be meaningful for further research to study how Chinese employees develop their trust in management. The development of trust within organizations not only depends on the mentality of managers, but it is also an outcome of interaction between managers and employees in their working relationships.

We may note that investigation of wider regions of China is necessary, as China is a large heterogeneous country (except at the most central level) with provinces, regions and cities which vary greatly in subcultures, industrialization and degrees of economic development and enterprise reform.

CONCLUSION

To understand future organizational behaviour better and to avoid wrongly specified models, it is important to examine the context in which behaviour occurs (House *et al.*, 1995). The present study suggests that managerial beliefs of trust and the managerial value of collectivism vary across the ownership context, even where all managers share the same Chinese 'national culture'. More significantly, the findings of the investigation indicate that the development of management trust not only depends on their perceptions of employee behaviour and attitudes, but also is affected by their managerial values.

The present research provides a practical reference for both Chinese reformers, who want to improve continuously the effectiveness of Chinese enterprises, and foreign investors, who need to make future investment decisions with respect to China. Both need to decide which type of ownership enterprises should be chosen as partners to fit their business and how best to operate business in China. The performance of multinational corporations is largely affected by the ability to manage human resources in complex contexts. Insights into specific beliefs of trust pertaining to enterprise ownership in China make possible the prediction of managers' future work-related behaviour and thus increase the chances of collaborative success between foreign and Chinese management.

REFERENCES

Adler, P.S. (2001), 'Market, Hierarchy, and Trust: the Knowledge Economy and the Future of Capitalism', *Organization Science*, Vol.12, No.2, pp.215–34.

Armstrong, R.W. and Yee, S.M. (2001), 'Do Chinese trust Chinese? A study of Chinese buyers and sellers in Malaysia', *Journal of International Marketing*, Vol.9, No.3, pp.24–64.

Ahlstrom, D., Bruton, G. and Chan, E.S. (2001), 'HRM of Foreign Firms in China: The Challenge of Managing Host Country Personnel', *Business Horizons*, Vol.44, No.1, pp.59–71

Barber, B. (1983), *The Logic and Limits of Trust*. New Brunswick NJ: Rutgers University Press.

Bhattacharya, R. and Devinney, T.M. (1998), 'A Formal Model of Trust Based on Outcomes', *Academy of Management Review*, Vol.2, No.3, pp.459–73.

Birnbaum-More, P.H., Wong, G.Y.Y. and Olver, N. (1995), 'Acquisition of Managerial Values in the Peoples' Republic of China and Hong Kong', *Journal of Cross-Cultural Psychology*, Vol.26, No.3, pp.255–75.

Butler Jr., J.K. and Centrell, R.S. (1984), 'A Behavioral Decision Theory Approach to Modelling Dyadic Trust in Superiors and Subordinates', *Psychological Reports*, Vol.55, pp.19–38.

China State Statistics Bureau (2001), Annual Report.

Chan, M.K. (1997), 'Some Theoretical Propositions Pertaining to the Context of Trust', *International Journal of Organizational Analysis*, Vol.5 No.3, pp.227–48.

Chen, C.C. and Menidl, J.R. (1997), 'Testing the Effects of Vertical and Horizontal Collectivism: A Study of Reward Allocation Preferences in China', *Journal of Cross-Cultural Psychology*, Vol.28, No.1, pp.44–70.

Chen, C.C., Chen, X. and Menidl, J.R. (1998), 'How can Cooperation be Fostered? The Cultural Effects of Individualism–Collectivism', *Academy of Management Review*, Vol.23, No.2, pp.285–304.

Das, T.K. and Teng, B.S. (1998), 'Between Trust and Control: Developing Confidence in Partner Cooperation in Alliances', *Academy of Management Review*, Vol.23, No.3, pp.491–512.

Defilippo, J.S. (1997), 'World-class Manufacturing in Chengdu: A Case Study on China's First Aviation Joint Venture', *International Journal Technology Management*, Vol.13, No.5, pp.681–94.

Dienesch, R.M. and Liden, R.C. (1986), 'Leader–Member Exchange Model of Leadership: A Critique and Further Development', *Academy of Management Review*, Vol.11, pp.617–34.

Doney, P.M., Cannon, J.P. and Mullen, M.R. (1998), 'Understanding the Influence of National Culture on the Development of Trust', *Academy of Management Review*, Vol.23, No.3, pp.601–20.

Goodall, K. and Warner, M. (1999), 'Enterprise Reform, Labor–Management Relations, and Human Resource Management in a Multinational Context', *International Studies of Management and Organization*, Vol.29, No.3, pp.21–36.

Graen, G.B. and Scandura, T.A. (1987), 'Toward a Psychology of Dyadic Organizing' in L.L. Cummings and B.M. Staw (eds.), *Research in Organizational Behavior*. Greenwich CT: JAI Press, Vol.9, pp.175–208

Graen, G.B. and Uhl-Bien, M. (1995), 'Relationship-Based Approach to Leadership: Development of Leader-Member Exchange (LMX) Theory of Leadership over 25 Years: Applying a Multi-Level Multi-Domain Perspective', *Leadership Quarterly*, Vol.6, pp.219–247.

Hewett, Kelly and Bearden, William O. (2001), 'Dependence, Trust, and Relational Behavior on the Part of Foreign Subsidiary Marketing Operations: Implications for Managing Global Marketing Operations', *Journal of Marketing*, Vol.10, No.1, pp.51–66.

Hofstede, G. (1980), *Culture's Consequences: International Differences in Work-Related Values*. Beverly Hills CA: Sage.

Hofstede, G. (1993), 'Cultural Constraints in Management Theories', *Academy of Management Executive*, Vol.7, pp.81–94.

Holt, D.H. (1997), 'A Comparative Study of Values among Chinese and U.S. Entrepreneurs: Pragmatic Convergence between Contrasting Cultures', *Journal of Business Venturing*, Vol.12, pp.483–505.

House, R., Rousseau, M. and Thomas-Hunt, M. (1995), 'The Meso Paradigm: A Framework for the Integration of Micro and Macro Organizational Behaviour' in L.L. Cummings and B.M. Staw (eds), *Research in Organizational Behaviour*. Greenwich CT: JAI Press, Vol.17, pp.71–114.

Jefferson, G.H. (1999), 'Are China's Rural Enterprises Outperforming State Enterprises? Estimating the Pure Ownership Effect' in G.H. Jefferson and I. Singh (eds.), *Enterprise Reform in China: Ownership, Transition, and Performance*. New York: Oxford University Press, pp.159–70

Jiang, S. and Hall, R.H. (1996), 'Local Corporatism and Rural Enterprises in China's Reform', *Organizational Studies*, Vol.17, No.6, pp.929–52.

Jones, G.R. and George, J.M. (1998), 'The Experience and Evolution of Trust: Implications for Cooperation and Teamwork', *Academy of Management Journal*, Vol.23, No.3, pp.531–47.

Kelly, D. and Weber, D. (1995), 'Creating an Environment for Participation in Healthcare', *Journal for Quality and Participation*, Vol.18, No.7, pp.38–43.

Lau, C.M., Ngo, H.Y. and Chow, C.K. (1999), 'Private businesses in China: Emerging Environment and Managerial Behaviour' in L. Kelley and Y. Luo (eds), *China 2000: Emerging Business Issues*. London: Sage Publications, pp.25–48

Leung, K., Smith, P.B., Wang, Z.M. and Sun, H. (1996), 'Job Satisfaction in Joint Venture Hotels in China: An Organizational Justice Analysis', *Journal of International Business Studies*, Vol.27, No.5, pp.947–62, Special Issue Supplement.

Lewicki, R.J. and Bunker, B.B. (1996), 'Developing and Maintaining Trust in Work Relationships' in M. Kramer, M. Roderick and T.R. Tyler (eds.), *Trust in Organizations: Frontiers of Theory and Research*. London: Sage Publications, pp.114–37.

Liden, R.C. and Maslyn, J.M. (1993), LMX-MDM: Scale Develops.

Lindsay, J. (1996), 'Respect and Trust in Management a Necessity', *Canadian Manager*, Vol.21, No.1, pp.26–9.

Luo, Y. and Chen, M. (1997), 'Does *guanxi* Influence Firm Performance?', *Asia Pacific Journal of Management*, Vol.14, pp.1–16.

Mascarenhas, B. (1989), 'Domains of State-owned, Privately Held, and Publicly Traded Firms in International Competition', *Administrative Science Quarterly*, Vol.34, pp.582–97.

Marcus, P.M. and House, J.S. (1973), 'Exchange between Superiors and Subordinates in Large Organizations', *Administrative Science Quarterly*, Vol.18, pp.209–22.

McAllister, D.J. (1995), 'Affect- and Cognition-Based Trust Formations for Interpersonal Cooperation in Organizations', *Academy of Management Journal*, Vol.38, No.1, pp.24–39.

Mente, B.L.D. (1994), *Chinese Etiquette and Ethics in Business*. Illinois: NTC Business Books.

Negandhi, A. and Prasad, S. (1971), *Comparative Management*. New York : Appleton-Century-Crofts.

Pelled, L.H. and Xin, K.R. (1997), 'Work Values and their Human Resource Management Implications: A Theoretical Comparison of China, Mexico, and the United States', *Journal of Applied Management Studies*, Vol.6, No.2, pp.185–99.

Porta, R.L., Lopez-de-Silanes, F., Shleifer, A. and Vishny, R.W. (1997), 'Trust in Large Organizations', *American Economic Review*, Vol.87, No.2, pp.333–8.

Ralston, D.A., Gustafson, D.J., Cheung F. and Terpstra, R.H. (1993), 'Differences in Managerial Values: A Study of US, Hong Kong and PRC Managers', *Journal of International Business Studies*, Vol.24, No.2, pp.249–75.

Ralston, D.A., Egri, C.P., Stewart, S., Terpstra, R.H. and Kaicheng, H. (1999), 'Doing Business in the 21st Century with the New Generation of Chinese Managers: A Study of Generational Shifts in Work Values in China', *Journal of International Business Studies*, Vol.30, No.2, pp.415–28.

Ray, D.W. (1994), 'The Missing T in TQM ... Trust', *Journal for Quality and Participation*, Vol.17, No.3, pp.64–7.

Reed, M.I. (2001), 'Organization, Trust and Control: A Realist Analysis', *Organizational Studies*, Vol.22, No.2, pp.201–30.

Rempel, J.K., Holmes, J.G. and Zanna, M.P. (1985), 'Trust in Close Relationships', *Journal of Personality and Social Psychology*, Vol.49, No.1, pp.95–112.

Robertson, C. and Hoffman, J. (2000), 'How Different Are We? An Investigation of Confucian Values in the United States', *Journal of Managerial Issues*, Vol.12, No.1, pp.34–47.

Rousseau, D.S., Sitkin, R.B. and Camerer, C. (1998), 'Not So Different After All: A Cross-discipline View of Trust', *Academy of Management Review*, Vol.23, pp.393–404.

Schwatz, S. and Sagiv, L. (1995), 'Identifying Culture-specifics in the Content and Structure of Values', *Journal of Cross-Cultural Psychology*, Vol.26, No.1, pp.92–116.

Shane, S.A. (1993), 'The Effects of Cultural Differences in Perceptions of Transactions Costs on National Differences in the Preference for International Joint Ventures', *Asia Pacific Journal of Management*, Vol.10, No.1, pp.57–69.

Shapiro, D., Sheppard, B.H. and Cheraskin, L. (1992), 'Business on a Handshake', *Negotiation Journal*, Vol.8, pp.365–77.

Shapiro, S.P. (1987), 'The Social Control of Impersonal Trust', *American Journal of Sociology*, Vol. 93, pp. 623–658.

Shaw, R.B. (1997), *Trust in the Balance*. San Francisco: Jossey-Bass Publishers.

Stack, L. (1978), 'Trust' in H. Lonon and J.E. Exner Jr (eds.), *Dimensions of Personality*. New York: Wiley, pp.561–99.

Sun, L. (2000), 'Anticipatory Ownership Reform Driven by Competition: China's Township-Village and Private Enterprises in the 1990s', *Comparative Economic Studies*, Vol.42, No.3, pp.49–7.

Szabo, E.R., Weibler, G., Brodbeck, F.C. and Wunderer, R. (2001), 'Value and Behaviour Orientation in Leadership Studies: Reflections based on Findings in Three German-speaking Countries', *The Leadership Quarterly*, Vol.12, No.2, pp.219–44.

Tan, J.J. (1999), 'Environment-strategy Configurations among Ownership Types' in L. Kelley and Y. Luo (eds). *China 2000: Emerging Business Issues*. London: Sage Publications, pp.49–72.

Wang, K.Y. and Clegg, S. (2002), 'Trust and Decision Making: Are Managers Different in the People's Republic of China and in Australia?', *International Journal of Cross Cultural Management*, Vol.9, No.1, pp.30–45.

White, S., and Liu, Y. (2001), 'Transition Trajectories for Market Structure and Firm Strategy in China', *Journal of Management*, Vol.38, No.1, pp.103–24.

Whitener, E.M., Brodt, S.E. and Korsgaard, W.J.M. (1998), 'Managers as Initiators of Trust: An Exchange Relationship Framework for Understanding Managerial Trustworthy Behaviour', *Academy of Management Review*, Vol.23, No.3, pp.513–30.

Williams, L., Whyte, K. and Green, C S. (1966), 'Do Cultural Differences Affect Workers' Attitudes?', *Industrial Relations*, Vol.5, pp.105–17.

Xiang, R. (2001), 'Six Keys of Chinese Enterprises' Development', *Journal of Business World*, Supplement, pp.14–17, in Chinese.

Zhu, C. and Dowling, P. (2000), 'Managing People during Economic Transition: The Development of HR Practices in China', *Asia Pacific Journal of Human Resources*, Vol.38, No.2, pp.101–23.

Zhu, C. and Dowling, P. (1998), 'Employment Systems and Practices in China's Industrial Sector during and after Mao's Regime', Working Paper 81/98, Department of Management, Monash University.

WTO Accession and the Managerial Challenges for Manufacturing Sectors in China

GODFREY YEUNG and VINCENT MOK

After the Chinese delegate signed the World Trade Organization (WTO) accord in November 2001, China formally agreed to the accession treaties after 15 years of on-and-off negotiations.[1] It has been widely recognized that China will become the 'factory of the world' in the twenty-first century. Most analysts regarded this as a golden opportunity for foreign entrepreneurs to 'jump on the bandwagon' by investing in China in future years.

LITERATURE REVIEWS AND RESEARCH HYPOTHESE

Apart from general studies (e.g. Kong, 2000; Woo, 2001), much of the literature about WTO accession by China has focused on three themes. First, some examined the impact of WTO accession on the vitality of state-owned enterprises (SOEs) in China, e.g. Blumental (1999), Liu and Woo (2001). Second, some studied the implications of WTO accession for foreign direct investment (FDI) and international trade between China and other developed countries (DCs), for example, Wang (1999), Ianchovichina and Martin (2001). Third, some identified the competitiveness of specific industries in China, such as agriculture (Yamamoto, 2000; Thiers, 2002), textile and clothing (Zhong and Yang, 2000; Yeung and Mok, forthcoming) automobiles (Sun, 2000; Harwitt, 2001), pharmaceuticals (Yeung, 2002a), banking and finance (Langlois, 2001; Bottelier, 2002) and the telecommunications sector (Shen, 2000; DeWoskin, 2001), etc. All the above studies are able to illustrate the future impact of WTO accession on the Chinese economy in one way or another.

For company management in China, previous research has typically emphasized the general practice of human resource management (Ng and Warner, 2000; Björkman and Lu, 2000), the specialized study of employee motivation system in Sino–foreign joint ventures (JVs)

(Goodall and Warner, 1997; Braun and Warner, 2002), and the difficulties in managing transnational corporations (TNCs) in China (Child, 1999, 2000; Tsang, 2001). Other studies have examined the characteristics of strategic decision-making by Chinese managers of SOEs and privately owned enterprises. As a limited number of managers in China have experience of competing in a market-based economy (Björkman and Lu, 1999), Nolan (2001a, 2001b) argued that the innovativeness of managers has significant implications for the competitiveness of Chinese industry during the transitional period of industrial deregulation. Tan (2001) also found that proactive entrepreneurs (often described as risk takers and innovators) have high chances of survival in an evolving and changing environment. All these studies analyse the managerial problems in Chinese manufacturers in different perspectives. However, there are virtually no published papers on the managerial challenges for Chinese manufacturers with regard to WTO accession.

To fill this gap in the literature, this study investigates the major managerial challenges for manufacturers in China after WTO accession.[2] China is one of the largest global manufacturers, and its accession to the WTO has tremendous implications for the management and development of the manufacturing sectors in China. Based on the WTO accession treaties and the existing nature of Chinese manufacturers, in the following , we develop four hypotheses on the managerial challenges for manufacturers in China.

WTO accession will eliminate the uncertainty surrounding the annual renewal of Permanent Normal Trade Relations (PNTR) by the USA, but it will not reduce the possibility of trade disputes between China and other countries for at least another 14 years, since the USA/EU can still use its current anti-dumping methodology, special safeguard and product-specific safeguard mechanisms during this transitional period (see section under WTO Accession) (Dong *et al.*, 1998; Potter, 2001).[3] Therefore, we would expect that:

Hypothesis 1

China's accession to the WTO will drive Chinese manufacturers to develop contingency plans for handling the potential trade disputes with international trading partners.

Low prices and a quality product are necessary, but no longer sufficient, for success in China during the post-accession era. Intense competition for market share is expected, partly due to the elimination of local content and foreign exchange balancing requirements for foreign-financed firms, as well as the reduction of import tariffs and the opening up of distribution channels in China (Adhikari and Yang,

2002). Foreign-financed firms in China are no longer constrained by their production contracts and other Customs documentation and thus are able to sell their products locally and at competitive prices.[4] The subsidiaries of TNCs can also expand their retail chains in China and import their brand name products without paying for high tariffs (Yeung and Mok, forthcoming). Furthermore, Sino–foreign JVs in China may have to compete with parallel imports of the same brand products (see under Managerial Challenges). We would therefore expect that:

Hypothesis 2

China's accession to the WTO will drive Chinese manufacturers to upgrade the value-added chain of their products and to diversify their markets.

While Chinese firms are expecting to achieve advanced managerial and technical know-how by hiring expatriates, there are three possible drawbacks for firms top-heavy with expatriates, for example the mismatch between expatriates' generous remuneration packages and their job responsibilities, their lesser contact with the international market, and cultural conflicts (Li and Kleiner, 2001; Legewie, 2002). Chinese manufacturers may have to accelerate their localization process to address these challenges. We would thus expect that:

Hypothesis 3

China's accession to the WTO will drive Chinese manufacturers to accelerate the localization of management.

Hypothesis 3a

The mismatch between expatriates' generous remuneration packages and their job responsibilities will have negative impact on Chinese manufacturers.

Hypothesis 3b

Less contact with the international market by expatriates will lead to conflicts in Chinese manufacturers.

Hypothesis 3c

Cultural differences between expatriates and locals will have negative impact on working relationships in Chinese manufacturers.

In international business, it is pivotal for management to consider the compliance with international standards, given that the consumers in importing countries are increasingly concerned with the impact of trade liberalization on the environment and on societies (Martinsons *et al.*, 1997). To improve the competitiveness of their products, international buyers are increasingly requesting their suppliers to comply with international standards (Yeung and Mok, forthcoming). As the WTO accession is expected to nurture further trade liberalization, in order to enhance the competitiveness of their products, Chinese manufacturers have to be aware of compliance with international standards. Therefore, we would expect that:

Hypothesis 4

China's accession to the WTO will catalyse Chinese manufacturers into becoming aware of the need for compliance with international standards.

METHODOLOGY

To examine these issues, informal interviews with government officials and semi-structured interviews with 36 owners and managers of 31 manufacturing firms located in Guangdong and Zhejiang provinces and in the municipality of Beijing were conducted by the authors in April–May of 2000 and August of 2001.[5] The interviews and company visits were conducted with the facilitation of various institutes in China, especially the Management Commission of the Hangzhou Economic and Technology Development Zone in Zhejiang, the Bureau for Foreign Economic Relations and Trade and the Guangdong Provincial Research Centre for Economic Development in Guangdong. It is a well-known fact that securing appropriate personal connections is probably the most important precondition for conducting visits to firms in China. This explains why the majority of firms investigated are either located in Guangdong (16 cases) or Zhejiang (13 cases). Unsurprisingly, most of the firms located in Guangdong are financed by Hong Kong-based entrepreneurs, whilst most firms interviewed in Zhejiang are financed by the Taiwanese or Japanese (partly due to their locations and historical ties).

Each interview and company visit lasted for at least an hour and the questions were focused on empirical evidence related to the hypothesis test of this study, that is, about trade disputes, product and market development, localization, and international standards. Field survey co-ordinators (including several government officials) accompanied the researchers during the interviews and visits to companies, but they never intervened in the interviews. On several occasions, interviewees were willing to express their opinions in front of government officials on issues related to WTO accession, including criticisms against the government for being secretive and for being unprepared for WTO accession (see the following).

The sample firms ranged across various investment formats – wholly foreign-owned ventures (WFVs) (10 cases), equity joint ventures (EJVs) (11 cases), processing and assembling (P&As) (6 cases) and locally-funded (4 cases) firms.[6] They also ranged across manufacturing sectors: textiles and clothing (15 cases), electrical and power appliances (5 cases), beverages and food ingredients (3 cases), plastics products (including toys, 2 cases), telecommunications, automobile components, petrochemicals, medical equipment, electronic products and packaging materials. With the exception of three smaller firms (two P&A clothing firms in Guangdong and another locally-funded clothing firm in Zhejiang), all the other sample textile and clothing firms are large-scale with registered capital of at least several million $US and employing several hundreds to thousands of workers. The examples of textile and clothing firms incorporate mainly the subsidiaries of transnational corporations (TNCs), major sub-contractors for designer brand clothing or major department stores in the USA and Europe, for example Kellwood (USA), Macy's Department Store, J.C. Penny, K-mart, etc. Other TNCs in the sample include Motorola, Siemens and Nestlé. The sample size is relatively small but representative of the manufacturing firms in southern and south-eastern China, especially the foreign-financed ones.

Chinese manufacturing and the WTO accession treaties will be reviewed briefly in the following, before we investigate the major managerial challenges to Chinese manufacturers after WTO accession. The analysis will be based on the testing of the four hypotheses outlined earlier: trade disputes, product and market development, localization, and international standards. The major findings of this study will be summarized in the conclusion.

BACKGROUND

Chinese Manufacturing

China has been the second most popular destination for foreign direct investment (FDI) in the past nine consecutive years, behind the USA. At the end of 2001, the total FDI in China was US$ 393.5 billion, averaging US$43.4 billion per annum during 1996–2001 (NBS, 2002). The value of FDI is expected to reach US$50 billion in 2002 (The Standard (TS), 4 Oct. 2002). With such a large amount of FDI and a large proportion of it invested in manufacturing (66 per cent in 2001), it is not surprising that China ranked fourth as a global manufacturing power by producing US$400 billion of goods in 2000. This is equivalent to 34 per cent of GDP in China. Manufacturing is the second largest employer (81 million workers) in China and it accounts for a significant proportion of the exports (82 per cent in 2001) (National Bureau of Statistics, 2002). In terms of output, China ranks first in the world on 80 products in ten manufacturing sectors, for example, 60 per cent of toys, sporting goods and footwear imported by the USA were made in China (TS, 12 April 2002; China Economic Information (CEI), 5 Aug. 2002).

Accession Treaties

According to the WTO accord signed in November 2001, the major areas of liberalization related to manufacturing sectors are as follows (White House, 2001; MOFTEC, 2001).

Export quotas, safeguard mechanism and anti-dumping

• The deal incorporates the Agreement on Textiles and Clothing (ATC), signed in 1995, under which the Multilateral Fibre Agreement (MFA) restrictions (export quotas) on textile and clothing sector will be phased out by 1 January 2005.[7]
• The special safeguard mechanism to prevent a surge of imports will remain in effect until 31 December 2008. The product-specific safeguard which determines the 'market disruption' caused by a specific product will remain in force for 12 years after Chinese accession.
• Overseas markets maintain their current anti-dumping methodology (treating China as a 'non-market economy') in future anti-dumping and countervailing cases for 15 years after China's accession.[8]

Import tariffs, import quotas and licences

• Tariffs will be reduced from an average of 24.6 per cent in 2001 to an average of 9.4 per cent (7.1 per cent on US priority products) by 1 January 2005.
• China will reduce the tariffs on automobiles from the current 80–100 per cent to 25 per cent, and automobile parts from an average of 23.4 per cent to 10 per cent by 1 July 2006, respectively.
• China will participate in the Information Technology Agreement (ITA) and eliminate all tariffs on computers and computer equipment, telecommunications equipment, semi-conductors and other high-technology products by 1 January 2005.
• Import quotas and other quantitative restrictions will increase from the current trade level of 15 per cent per annum and be phased out no later than 2005.

Trading and distribution rights

• Foreign-financed firms will have comprehensive trading and

distribution rights in China for the first time, including goods made in China.
• The rights will be phased in progressively over three years.

TRIPS and TRIMs
• China will implement the Agreement on Trade-Related Aspect of Intellectual Property Rights (TRIPS) of the Uruguay Round upon accession.[9]
• China will implement the *Agreement on Trade-Related Investment Measures* (TRIMs). China will eliminate foreign exchange balancing and local content requirements upon accession and not enforce provisions in existing (JV) contracts that impose these requirements.

SOEs, taxes and fees
• China will ensure that the sale and purchase of SOEs and state-invested enterprises (SIEs) are based solely on commercial considerations rather than on 'government procurement'.
• The SOEs and SIEs are regulated under the *WTO Agreement on Subsidies and Countervailing Measures*, for example, no export subsidies, no soft loans, etc.
• China will apply uniform taxes and fees to domestic-funded and foreign-financed firms.

WTO ACCESSION AND MANAGERIAL CHALLENGES

Based on empirical information collected from the field survey, we shall test the validity of the four hypotheses on the managerial challenges for manufacturers in China.

Preparation for Trade Disputes
Due to the potential disputes between the WTO accession treaties and the realities of the transitional economy in China, managers of Chinese manufacturers have to develop contingency plans for handling international trade disputes. This is especially the case when the current anti-dumping methodology treats China as a *'non-market economy'*. USA/EU regulatory authorities can use third country reference prices to determine the existence of state subsidies or of the dumping of Chinese exports.[10] Moreover, the US/EU's *'special safeguard'* and *'product-specific safeguard'* mechanisms to prevent a surge of imports will not be phased out until 2008 and 2014, respectively.

The fact that China ranked first in the world on anti-dumping suits filed by her trading partners (about 490 suits covering 4,000 products, involving 30 countries and worth US$15 billion in 2002) exemplifies the urgency for managers to develop contingency measures for trade disputes (*China Daily* (CD), 9 July 2002).[11] But managers were not well informed, as the Chinese central government did not distribute documents relating to WTO treaties before their delegates signed the agreement in November 2001. Moreover, most managers in SMEs have limited or no experience in dealing with international trade disputes. This resulted in their reluctance to counter the anti-dumping charges by releasing sensitive cost and pricing information to the relevant authorities (field survey, 2001). A survey revealed that more than half of the Chinese firms involved in anti-dumping charges had been reluctant to participate in foreign anti-dumping procedures. Subsequently, the Chinese firm was the loser in 80 per cent of the cases (Hong Kong Economic Journal (HKEJ), 18 Dec. 2001: 21).

It must however be emphasized that potential trade disputes do not just proliferate between China and the DCs, but also between China and less developed countries (LDCs), for example India has filed 51 anti-dumping suits against Chinese products (Bureau of Industrial Damage Investigations (BIDI), 27 Sept. 2002). This is partly because some LDCs relying on the exports of low value-added products are unable to beat the bargain-basement prices charged by Chinese firms. For instance, Mexican manufactures make T-shirts for US$1/each and tennis shoes for US$38/pair, while their Chinese counterparts offer more value for money by charging US$0.20/each and US$13/pair, respectively (South China Morning Post (SCMP), 23 Aug. 2001). Moreover, some LDCs complain of illegal shipments of Chinese goods attempting to evade import tariffs. It is estimated that up to half of all garments sold in Mexico are contraband. Some unscrupulous firms import finished garments into Mexico (but claim in the documents that they are partly finished) and then sell them locally or export them to the USA (SCMP, 2 May 2001). In fact, some LDCs may want an extension of export quotas to protect their industries from Chinese imports, for example in September 2002 Turkey imposed three-year quotas on imports of Chinese electric fans, spectacles frames and glasses (BIDI, 29 Sept. 2002).

Since the Chinese government may *not* be well-prepared for WTO accession, managers of Chinese manufacturing firms face an uphill battle in any future trade disputes. China had not established any specific department to deal with potential trade disputes before November 2001, and the Ministry of Foreign Trade and Economic Co-operation (MOFTEC)'s legal team remains understaffed (SCMP, 2 Nov. 2001; CD, 8 Oct. 2002). The lack of co-ordination within, and between, different bureaux to administer foreign trade policies efficiently, further undermines preparations to counter anti-dumping cases (Potter, 2001: 600–601). For instance, there are no Customs officers to follow up a case when the officer in charge is on annual or sick leave. Worse still, it is not uncommon for two or more bureaux in the local government to have their senior officers on annual leave simultaneously (especially during the Chinese New Year). In arbitration cases, managers only meet a 'wall of silence', receiving advice such as 'I don't deal with this; come back in two weeks when Mr X is back!' (field survey, 2001). This can cost Chinese-based firms dearly as managers are unable to deal with trade disputes without the full support of the corresponding government bureau.

Furthermore, some managers simply do not have the resources to counter anti-dumping charges. In fact, the cash flow of small and medium-scale enterprises (SMEs) is so tight that their managers simply cannot wait for the outcome of the arbitration of a trade dispute (Yeung, 2002b). Generally, most managers in large-scale foreign-financed firms know how to navigate through the minefield of anti-dumping allegations (field survey, 2001). Individual companies can apply for 'market economy' treatment from the importing country's regulatory authorities. But the transaction cost of doing so is very high, as it demands on-site inspection by the regulatory authorities. Thus, only 16 Chinese firms have been granted 'market economy' treatment by the European Commission (CD, 11 Oct. 2002). The two recent instances in which Chinese firms successfully countered charges of anti-dumping illustrate the high costs of fighting such disputes. After the Canadian authorities imposed a 57 per cent anti-dumping duty on Fuyao Glass Industry Group's automotive replacement windscreen in February 2002, the company set up an anti-dumping office and hired US-based lawyers to prepare for the appeal. The Canadian International Trade Tribunal eventually rejected the anti-dumping charge, saying that the higher selling price in China was part of the original equipment manufacturer's (OEMs) contract, and their lower selling prices in Canada represented the market price for the replacement market. Despite the fact that this case was resolved quickly, Fuyao spent more than 3 million *yuan* in legal expenses alone (CD, 10 Sept. 2002). The second instance involves TV manufacturers in China. In 2002, the EU eventually agreed to lift the 44.6 per cent anti-dumping duty on seven major TV makers in China after 15 years of on-and-off investigation. But the Chinese Chamber of Commerce must keep track of exports on a daily basis and submit a fortnightly report to the EU to ensure that the products are selling at the minimum prices and not exceeding the quotas (CEI, 13 Sept. 2002). Without support from the domestic market, it is likely that most of the TV makers will be unable to survive the 15-year-long anti-dumping investigation. No matter how efficient the WTO resolution mechanism is, the involvement of trade disputes will definitely divert a firm's valuable resources from other priorities, for example product and market development. This will obviously tests the skills (in keeping up the morale of the workforce) and patience of managers to their limits.

The above discussions support the hypothesis on trade disputes. Due to the current anti-dumping methodology and the safeguard mechanisms that can be initiated by trading partners, and the lack of proactive preparation by the Chinese government to engage in potential trade disputes, Chinese manufacturers have to develop contingency plans for handling the potential disputes with international trading partners after the accession of WTO.

Product and Market Development

To minimize the effects of trade disputes and to pre-empt the expected increase in non-trade barriers against Chinese exports, Chinese manufacturers are tooling their products to climb up the value-added chain and diversifying their markets. Managers are investing more resources on improving productivity and quality control, developing new products and markets, and so forth. To boost productivity, most managers are introducing some form of incentive package for their staff, for example the 'production contract' where management teams can earn a bonus if they are able to delivery shipments on time and within the pre-determined costs. Others invest in new equipment to improve productivity. For instance, the Tianhai Decorative Warpknitted Fabric Co. in Guangdong has imported 30 computerized multi-bar raschel machines for the newly developed 44-inch wide lace fabric, and became the largest specialized lace manufacturer in China. In cellular phone manufacturing, Motorola's EJV in Hangzhou went from complete reliance on imported components to sourcing half its components locally, reducing costs and facilitating 'Just in Time' (JIT) production. Most well-funded textile firms in China are focusing their R&D resources on producing higher value-added products, such as waterproof and ventilated fibres, dirt-repellent fibres, silk-like fibres, suede-like fibres, etc. (field survey, 2000, 2001).

In the beverage industry, the Wahaha Group is an example of a firm that is developing new brand names and building its own distribution channels. It was established by three managers from a SOE with 140,000 *yuan* who built up the brand name through children's drinks 15 years ago. A number of EJVs were subsequently formed and the group now has 55 bottling plants (employing 30,000 workers) and accounts for 30 per cent of the Chinese beverage market. The group has diversified into fruit drinks, tea, mineral water, etc. In 1998, it launched the 'Special Coke' (*Feichang Kele*) and it now ranks third in the coke market in China, achieving a 'comparable market share with that of Pepsi Cola' (Coca Cola ranked first) (field survey, 2001).[12] In the automobile components sector, the privately-funded Qianjian Spring Factory in Hangzhou is an example of a firm developing a niche market by strictly controlling quality and integrating into the supply chain of automobile assemblers. It was established by Mr Yong-sen Zhang in 1988 with the tiny sum of 800 *yuan*. By 1996, the firm was securing OEM contracts on suspension and engine springs from major automobile assembly plants in China, including Shanghai Volkswagen, Guangzhou Honda, First Automobile, etc. In 2000, the firm was employing 120 workers and recorded sales value of 28 million *yuan* (field survey, 2000, 2001).

No matter how hard managers try to develop their products, they cannot avoid the fact that there is still a big gap between TNCs and Chinese firms in R&D capabilities. The president of TCL, one of the biggest TV manufacturers in China, frankly admitted that their cost efficiency is still well behind that of the TNCs and many of their products use patents and technology belonging to TNCs (SCMP, 30 Oct. 2001). Moreover, Chinese manufacturers do not have the capital reserves to endure a prolonged period of heavy losses when attempting to conquer a new market, compared with the deep-pocketed TNCs. These points have already been meticulously documented by Nolan (2001a, 2001b) and Yeung (2002a).

Instead of being constrained by limited R&D capabilities, when trying to persuade decision-makers at a TNC's headquarters that China is not just a manufacturing base for labour-intensive and low value-added projects, managers of JVs in China are encountering issues of intellectual property rights (IPRs) related to product development. The crux of the issue is with *which* JV(s) should the TNC invest the capital and technology to develop the new products. Being the minority owner (with 40 per cent of the equity), Motorola (US) is reluctant to invest capital and transfer the latest manufacturing technology on CDMA phones to the EJV in Hangzhou. Moreover, Motorola worries that its IPRs will be infringed, should it use the EJV as the launch pad for its latest products. As the EJV's Deputy General Manager commented, 'The product can be pirated even before it is launched officially!' (Field survey, 2001). The uncertainty surrounding new product development not only affects the long-term development strategy of the EJV, but also the retention of the managerial and technical staff (field survey, 2001).

The above discussions lend support to the hypothesis on product and market development. To minimize the effects of potential trade disputes and to improve the product competitiveness, Chinese manufacturers are upgrading the value-added chain of their products to diversify their markets.

In reality, the drive of manufacturers for product development may lead to other managerial issues at company level. The experience of Siemens' EJV in Hangzhou illustrates what can happen when senior managers differ over product development strategy. Being the majority owner holding 51 per cent of the equity, Siemens appointed a German engineer as the General Manager when the EJV was established in 1995. The (Chinese) Deputy General Manager realized there was a golden opportunity for the firm to introduce the GIS high voltage electric circuit-breaker to China. Despite gaining approval from headquarters for the adoption of Siemens' technological 'crown jewel', the General Manager in Hangzhou refused to adopt the technology. In 2000, Siemens established another EJV in Shanghai using the GIS manufacturing process. The new EJV has already recorded sales of 150 million *yuan* in the first nine months of its operation. It is expected the new EJV in Shanghai will soon become the most profitable of Siemens' 54 JVs in China (field survey, 2001).

As the head of what is currently the most profitable Siemens' JV in China, with 550 million *yuan* of sales and 100 million *yuan* of profits in 2000, it can be argued that the (German) General Manager is behaving relatively 'conservatively' by focusing on the cost efficiency of the existing production line (by regarding China as a low-cost manufacturing base for uniform products) rather than by taking the 'unnecessary risk' of introducing new products without a strong existing market demand (field survey, 2001). Paradoxically, the 'production-oriented' managerial approach undertaken by the General Manager implies that he may be detached from the potentialities of market demand due to the lack of a harmonious and well co-ordinated working relationship with his Chinese colleagues (see below). In stark contrast, the (Chinese) Deputy General Manager understands that the long-term competitiveness of the firm is based on its ability to introduce innovative and higher value-added products to target a niche market. This is especially the case after China's entry into the WTO, where the firm is facing intense competition locally (including other Siemens' JVs) and internationally (including the parallel import of Siemens' products). The bottom line is that he has little to lose but everything to gain, by staying in Siemens or joining other companies, should his plan succeed. Nonetheless, this may not be the case for the General Manager. Despite his international experience and technical expertise, his job opportunities are more limited than those of his Chinese counterparts because of the increasing tendency by foreign firms to localize their management in China (see below).

'Globalized' Versus 'Localized' Localization

The localization of management after WTO accession is receiving greater attention from owners and general managers of Chinese manufacturing firms. While expatriates can bring advanced managerial and technical know-how to a firm, there are three possible drawbacks for firms with a high ratio of expatriates on their payrolls.

First, firms with higher ratios of expatriates may have difficulty localizing their senior managers. Expatriate staff in China often enjoy much more favourable remuneration packages than those of their local counterparts with similar qualifications and job responsibilities, for example the remuneration package of an American expatriate (US$ 300,000/year) is six times higher than that of a Chinese executive (Li and Kleiner, 2001: 51). The perceived lack of promotion opportunities, 'discriminatory' remuneration packages, and the abundance of job opportunities in the market all contribute to the high turnover rates of mid-ranking local managers in JVs (Lasserre and Chin, 1997: 94; Goodall and Burgers, 1998).[13] As the average tenure for mid- to high-level Chinese managerial staff was 8–12 months, the lack of continuity of the management team interrupts the firms' daily production (field survey, 2001; Chan and Cui, 2002: 15). This finding is consistent with hypothesis 3a.

Second, expatriate managers stationed in China may have less contact with the market. They may not have the incentive or ability to follow the most up-to-date market information, partly because of their 'temporary' job assignments in China (Li and Kleiner, 2001: 52). Quite often, this leads to conflicts between managers of the marketing department (who are on the front line of the market) and other operational departments when their information about the (international) market demand differs. This is demonstrated by the refusal of the General Manager in Siemens' EJV to adopt the advanced manufacturing technology that was mentioned previously (field survey, 2001). The above evidence supports hypothesis 3b.

Third, cultural differences and language barriers may contribute to the lack of a harmonious working relationship between expatriates and locals. Some expatriates (including overseas Chinese) may be rather self-centred and even arrogant in dealing with their local counterparts, in thinking that they need to 'teach' their Chinese colleagues everything from day one, and so on. Expatriates also tend to sack workers who either under-perform or violate company rules, on the spot and in front of other workers, whilst the local managers tend to talk to the workers concerned privately (to 'save their face') and either give them a 'second chance' or ask them to resign.[14] This is illustrated by the experience of a European-based TNC's EJV in China, where the wife of an expatriate 'scolded the Chinese workers and threatened to sack them publicly, despite the fact that she is not a staff member of the JV or of the European-based firm' (field survey, 2001). Due to the cultural conflicts between the expatriates and the locals, six of the seven local engineers left the US-financed manufacturing firm after they had helped it to acquire ISO 9002 qualification (Li and Kleiner, 2001: 53). This finding validates hypothesis 3c.

The above discussions provide a *prima facie* case in support of the hypothesis on localization: foreign-financed firms are accelerating their localization of management in China, especially after WTO accession.[15] It must be emphasized that localization in China is more complicated than simply being a case of replacing expatriates with local talent.[16] In practice, localization in China can be generalized into at least two categories, according to the work experience and educational background of managers: *'globalized localization'*, where expatriates are replaced by overseas Chinese or Mainland Chinese with overseas experience, and *'localized localization'*, where expatriates are replaced by mainland Chinese who have worked their way through the ranks but who possess limited or no overseas experience. This complex situation can be illustrated by the experience of two JVs in China.

The experience of the Siemens' EJV exemplifies the need for 'globalized localization', due to the detached market information of the expatriate General Manager. Partly due to cultural differences, the General Manager questioned the validity of his Deputy (who is a mainland Chinese with extensive overseas experience) because he spent so much time visiting and dining with potential customers all over China. Yet the Deputy General Manager complained that his European superior did not understand the way of doing business in China: 'He expected that I only have to cultivate *guanxi* with the people who are in charge and with whom we are doing business, but not with my other 'old friends'.' (field survey, 2001). In other words, there is a need to cultivate personal connections, *guanxi*, with potential as well as with existing customers. This is vital for the future competitiveness for the EJV after WTO accession as 'there are few differences in terms of technicality between the products manufactured by this EJV and other TNCs, so the established customer network can make a difference' (field survey, 2001).[17]

The experience of a US-financed EJV demonstrates the need for 'localized localization' due to the lack of a harmonious working relationship between overseas Chinese and local managers. During our visit to the firm, the (Chinese) Deputy General Manager openly criticized the present trend of recruiting young Chinese with freshly minted overseas MBAs: 'Their senior positions and high salaries are based on their university diplomas rather than on their proven job performance' (field survey, 2001). This phenomenon suggests that the existing trend of recruiting foreign-educated or overseas Chinese without working experience in China may backfire, as this will lead to resentment and infighting rather than co-operation between managers. Freshly minted overseas MBAs or those with years of international experience may have fresh outlook and ambition, but their lack of practical working experience in China may also lead to direct conflict with the conservative 'old guards', who have risen through the ranks after decades of working. This is especially the case when the localization process is implemented too quickly, as illustrated by the food and beverage processing EJV of Nestlé in Guangdong. After implementing the localization policy in 1997, the new management team took over the firm too quickly, and the lack of trust between the (new) top and (old) mid-ranking managers subsequently resulted in a number of internal wrangles and even allegations of graft, nepotism, etc. (field survey, 2000). If this phenomenon of infighting is widespread in China, it may have tremendous implications for the recent drive by Chinese firms (including private and state-owned) to recruit overseas Chinese to improve their competitiveness.

The excess demand for experienced local managers in China is expected to increase after WTO accession. A survey revealed that 40 per cent of JVs in manufacturing, retailing, banking and telecommunications sectors intend to localize their senior executives in China (The Straits Times (TST), 20 April 2002). The use of head-hunters to poach experienced managers from competitors has already contributed to wage inflation (specifically, inflation of the remuneration package). With the expected rush among foreign investors to gain a foothold in China, 'bidding war' for experienced and qualified local managers will heat up. If this 'bidding war' goes unchecked, it may lead to a vicious circle of 'wage inflation and job-hopping'. This would not only partially offset the cost advantages of localization, but also disrupt the long-term development strategies of firms in China. This may also be of importance if the firms have to comply with international standards audits in the future years.

Compliance with International and Regional Standards

Apart from issues outlined explicitly in the WTO accession treaties, the proliferation of international and regional standards in the global manufacturing sectors has far-reaching implications for the management of Chinese manufacturing firms (Yeung and Mok, forthcoming). In addition to the International Organization for Standards (ISO), which is normally (though wrongly) regarded as the benchmark for quality and environmental friendliness, managers of Chinese manufacturers also have to be aware of the SA 8000 and other regional standards that may be required by importing countries.[18]

Securing ISO certification is a challenge for managers. As of 2001, only seven out of 31 firms interviewed were in compliance with ISO 9000. All certified firms are either publicly listed companies or subsidiaries of TNCs. Even Motorola's EJV was only certified as ISO 9000 compliant in 1999, three years after its establishment (field survey, 2000, 2001). This can probably be explained by the fact that the implementation of ISO standards demands a new outlook from managers and workers. Despite the managerial challenges, most managers are willing to train their workforce to achieve ISO 9000 certification, partly to fulfil their customers' requirements and partly to improve quality control processes. The systematic documentation demanded by ISO 9000 assists firms in maintaining the quality of their products at a pre-determined level (field survey, 2000, 2001).

As with ISO 9000, ISO 14000 not only demands detailed and systematic documentation but also focuses on environmental management. Many managers are reluctant to implement the ISO 14000 standard as it demands tremendous investment in environmentally friendly equipment, and on monitoring and measurement devices to ensure that the emission of pollutants etc. is minimal. The investment can be prohibitively high for some managers. This is illustrated by the Qianjian Spring Factory mentioned previously. To keep the OEMs contracts, the firm not only has to invest heavily on environmentally friendly equipment, but also has to retrain its workers to document each batch of product systematically. This will however impose tremendous pressure on the cash flow of this SME, in addition to the competitive pressure of the significant reduction in import tariffs for foreign springs. In the case of Motorola's EJV, it was not yet ISO 14000 compliant as of 2001 (but the manager planned to get the certification 'soon') (field survey, 2000, 2001).

Regarding social accountability, *SA 8000* covers the International Labour Organization's Conventions on Labour Rights, the Universal Declaration of Human Rights, and the United Nations Convention on the Rights of the Child (*Social Accountability International* (SAI), 1997: 4–8). Even if the manager is willing to adopt the system wholeheartedly, it is very costly to fully implement the SA 8000. To pacify customers and ensure that 'scandals' on child labour and 'sweatshop' will not be publicized by labour rights groups, a number of major US/EU department stores have insisted that their suppliers and subcontractors adopt SA8000 or acquire similar certification. For instance, Macy's Department Store (USA) has a special Asia–China Division to scrutinize the working environment of its clothing subcontractors in Asia. The director of a sub-contractor privately admitted that 'it is impossible to fully fulfil all the requirements laid out by the SA 8000 certification. The production costs are simply too high to remain competitive while doing so.' (field survey, 2001). This is especially the case for overtime work, where the standard imposes a limit of 12 hours of overtime per week on top of a maximum 48 hours of regular shifts (SAI 1997: 6). Due to the short product cycle of the clothing, footwear and toys markets, it is very costly for sub-contractors to employ and train more workers during the period of peak market demand and sack them during the period of low demand. This explains why overtime work is very common in China in firms producing clothing, toys and shoes, regardless of their size. This is exemplified by the experience of Taiwanese-financed Chung Hoo Shoes Factory in Guangdong, the sub-contractor for Converse and Skechers. The firm was stripped by SAI from its approved lists of certified factories in 2000 after their 3,000 workers were found to have regularly exceeded the working limit of 60 hours per week.[19] The Marketing Manager for C.D. Star, which owns the factory, complained that 'being SAI-certified … has made us a target.' (*Far Eastern Economic Review* (FEER), 10 May 2001: 40–1).

Moreover, it is very difficult, if not impossible, for the firm to ensure that it employs no child labour, partly due to the fact that a large number of workers are involved, most of them are migrant workers about whose dates of birth the local Public Security Bureau lacks accurate information. The widespread availability of false identity cards in China further hampers the process of verification. Probably the most difficult item of SA 8000 to achieve is the demand faced by certified firms to ensure that their suppliers and sub-contractors are conforming to the same standards of social accountability (SAI, 1997: 7). In reality, it is too costly to demand that all suppliers implement SA 8000, as there are dozens of major suppliers for a single firm. Managers of large-scale firms may be able to use their market power as leverage on their major suppliers. Managers of SMEs however simply do not have the market power to impose any control over their suppliers, other than on product requirements.

The above discussions support the hypothesis on international standards. In reality, Chinese manufacturers not only have to be aware of compliance with international standards, but also have to be aware that some importing countries may apply other regional standards, which may impose more stringent requirements. This is especially the case for the so-called 'green' standards or even the more broadly defined 'Technical Barriers to Trade' (TBT) (WTO, 2002c).[20] In China, only 17 out of 21,000 textile and clothing firms have received the 'green certificate', which allows their products to be exempt from stringent inspections. Other firms without the relevant certificates may have their products returned, as in December 2001, when 300,000 jackets were returned to China from Europe because the metal in the zip did not meet the EU's safety standards. It is estimated that about 15 per cent of textile and clothing products in China did not fulfil the 'green standards' and this affected about US$8 billion of exports (CEI, 14 Jan. 2002; SCMP, 7 Jan. 2002). For those factories without the relevant certificates, the buyers of their products will have to budget for the higher transaction costs of stringent inspections by importing countries. This is equivalent to reducing a firm's competitiveness. Another challenge for managers is the common existence of counterfeit 'green' products. They have to ensure that when purchasing equipment, they will really be able to fulfil the stringent requirements outlined by the ISO 14000 or other 'green' standards. They also have to 'fight' counterfeits of their own products, which may sabotage their hard-earned reputation for investment in expensive, environmentally friendly equipment and retraining of workers; the Chinese government discovered, for example, that 90 per cent of 250 products in Shanghai and Guangdong, proclaimed to meet environmental requirements, were counterfeit (SCMP, 7 Jan. 2002).

CONCLUSIONS

While we acknowledge the firm-specific limitations of our study, the empirical evidence presented above can provide a *prima facie* case to support the four research hypotheses on the managerial challenges for Chinese manufacturing. The tentative conclusions are summarized in Table 1.

The first hypothesis – *China's accession to the WTO will drive Chinese manufacturers to develop contingency plans for handling the potential trade disputes with international trading partners* – is verified. WTO accession will not reduce the possibility of trade disputes between China and other countries for at least another 14 years, where importing countries can still use their current anti-dumping methodology (treating China as a 'non-market

TABLE 1
WTO ACCESSION AND MAJOR CHALLENGES
FOR CHINESE MANUFACTURING SECTORS

Managerial challenges	Remarks
Preparing for trade disputes	• To become familiar with the procedures on dealing with allegations of dumping and other trade disputes with DCs or LDCs under the WTO resolution mechanism • To develop contingency measures for trade disputes • To maintain cash flow and production while the firm is appealing against dumping duties imposed by importing countries • To co-ordinate with local and central governments on investigations and to lobby for their support
Developing products and markets	*For OEMs or sub-contractors:* • To upgrade and localize the value-added chain of their products, given limited capital and R&D capability • To develop one's own brand name • To develop niche markets, either locally or internationally *For JVs:* • To persuade headquarters to transfer advanced technology and the latest products to the JVs • To protect the IPRs (manufacturing processes and technologies associated with the new products) from piracy • To compete with imported products (from other TNCs), including parallel imports of products of the same brand
Choosing the best localization strategy	• To maintain a harmonious working relationship between expatriates and locals, i.e. to minimize potential conflicts due to differences in culture, language, or management style • To maintain the loyalty and motivation of the local mid-ranking managers and the continuity of the management team • To decide on the localization strategy ('globalized localization' Vs 'localized localization') and the pace of its implementation (the transitional period between the new and old management teams) • To prevent the vicious circle of 'wage inflation and job-hopping'
Complying with international and regional standards	• To strike a balance between fulfilling international standards and maintaining a product's competitiveness, including to re-train workers to handle new work practices complying with international standards and yet to keep costs down • To secure existing OEMs / sub-contracting deals while preparing for certification • To persuade major customers that it may not be possible to fully implement certain international standards (SA8000) without corresponding complementary government policies • To be aware of and prepare for contingency measures in importing countries using regional or national standards (e.g. TBT or the 'green standard') as non-trade barriers

Source: Authors.

economy'), special safeguards and product-specific safeguard mechanisms during the transitional period. As a number of LDCs are relying on low value-added exports, in which Chinese manufacturers are more competitive, managers will have to develop contingency measures for trade disputes with DCs and LDCs (Table 1). Apart from accepting the hypothesis on trade disputes, this study suggests that managers are likely to encounter an uphill battle in any future trade disputes, since neither they nor the Chinese government are well prepared for the accession. No matter how efficient the WTO resolution mechanism for trade disputes, the reality is that managers are either without the capital to fight allegations of dumping, or will have to divert valuable resources from product and market development, which will have significant implications for the long-term competitiveness of a firm.

The second hypothesis – *China's accession to the WTO will drive Chinese manufacturers to upgrade the value-added chain of their products and to diversify their markets* – is supported. Managers are upgrading and localizing the value-added chain of their products and diversifying their markets to minimize the potential effects of trade disputes and improve companies' competitiveness from the onslaught of competitive products manufactured or imported directly by TNCs and their subsidiaries. Such threats will arise due to the lowering of import tariffs and the opening up of distribution channels in China (Table 1). In addition to the competition from direct and parallel imports, managers of Sino-foreign JVs will have to persuade their bosses at headquarters to transfer advanced manufacturing technology for the latest products to the JVs, as China is not just a cost-effective manufacturing base for labour-intensive, low value-added products alone. Moreover, they have to guard the transferred technologies from piracy, and thus their competitive advantage over their competitors.

There is support for the third hypothesis: *China's accession to the WTO will drive Chinese manufacturers to accelerate the localization of management.* In fact, WTO accession not only accelerates the processes of management localization, but also highlights the importance of 'getting the strategy right' – to decide on the appropriate localization strategy and the pace of its implementation. For general managers and human resources managers, the goals are to maintain a harmonious working relationship between expatriates and locals, and between overseas Chinese and mainland Chinese, and to retain the motivation and loyalty of the existing mid-ranking managers and prevent them from being headhunted by competitors (Table 1). Due to wage inflation caused by the 'bidding war' for experienced local managers, they also have to be aware that localization will not necessarily lead to reductions in executive labour costs.

The fourth hypothesis – *China's accession to the WTO will catalyse Chinese manufacturers to be aware of the need for the compliance with international standards* – is confirmed. Moreover, this study suggests that managers have to strike a balance between fulfilling international standards and maintaining a product's competitiveness (Table 1). This not only involves retraining the workforce, but also requires implementation of corresponding complementary policies by the government, such as regulations on migrant workers. Apart from the high cost of implementing international standards (which partially offset the low nominal labour costs), some importing countries may use these standards as non-trade barriers to protect their local industries from 'hollowing out' by Chinese products. This is especially the case for the TBT or 'green standards', where each importing country or region can have its own regulations and standards and pursue the 'necessary measures' to enforce them. The transaction costs for managers to comply with these national standards are even higher than for international standards.

All in all, managers of manufacturing firms in China have to strike a delicate balance in dealing with these challenges under the constraints of time and available resources. It must be emphasized that these four categories of challenges are *interrelated*, and one should not focus on one challenge without paying attention to the possible implications for others. For example, the policy for product development and the policy for localization may not complement each other. The drive for localization demands cutting labour costs, while the drive for R&D demands engineers and product designers with innovative ideas. This is one of the reasons why a number of firms are recruiting overseas Chinese – 'globalized localization'. With their overseas experience, 'overseas Chinese' are presumed to be more innovative than the local talent, but are also more expensive. Partly because of the 'overseas' experience of the newly recruited Chinese engineers, general managers are encountering another potential challenge in the form of trade disputes. Sometimes, a 'big hitter' in the international market may invite 'tactical' lawsuits filed by competitors.[21] Other foreign competitors may also persuade their countries' regulatory authorities to adopt a new set of national standards to forbid the import of a newly developed product. Obviously, the managerial skills of managers of manufacturing firms in China will be severely tested after China's entry into the WTO and in the decades to come.

ACKNOWLEDGEMENT

The authors are grateful for financial support from the Hong Kong Polytechnic University Research Grant (A/C no. GT301). The helpful assistance of various people (especially Mr Bilai Zhang and his colleagues at the Hangzhou Economic and Technology Development Zone, the staff of the Guangdong Provincial Research Centre for Economic Development, and a number of other officials in Guangdong, Hangzhou and Beijing who prefer to remain anonymous) in facilitating the field survey is deeply appreciated.

NOTES

1. For accounts of the historical background to, and the politics surrounding the WTO accession, see Lai (2001) and Fewsmith (2001).
2. In this study 'Chinese firms' or 'Chinese manufacturers' are generic terms referring to both foreign-financed and locally-funded manufacturing firms located in mainland China.
3. The PNTR status entails levying the same tariffs on Chinese imports as on the imports of the USA's other major trading partners. The bilateral deals between China and the USA are 'multi-lateralized' to all WTO members.
4. The bureaucracy associated with production contracts and other import documentation has been discussed by Yeung and Mok (2002).
5. The 36 manufacturers interviewed and their positions are as follows: four Owners, three Presidents, one Vice-President, 13 General Managers, three Deputy General Managers, two Financial Managers, nine Factory/Production Managers and one external Consultant for a textile firm.
6. See Yeung (2001: 3–7) for a detailed classification of FDI in China.
7. China was excluded from the ATC before joining the WTO (Ianchovichina and Martin, 2001: 10).
8. The Agreement on Implementation of Article VI of GATT 1994 (The Anti-Dumping Agreement) allows importing countries to take action against dumping (WTO, 2002a).
9. TRIPS regulates the trading of products with ideas and knowledge involving copyrights, trademarks, patents, undisclosed information (including trade secrets), etc. (WTO, 2002b).
10. Michalopoulos (2001: 189) argues that '[t]he WTO agreements have no explicit requirement for member states to be market economies'. If China is admitted into the WTO with the status of a 'transitional economy', the regulatory authorities should compare the production costs locally (or the representative export price of the product to a third country) when determining whether a firm is guilty of dumping (WTO, 2002a).
11. China drew up its first anti-dumping and anti-subsidy regulation in 1997 (SCMP, 6 Dec. 2001).
12. Readers interested in the business development of Coca-Cola in China can refer to Nolan (1995) and Mok, Dai and Yeung (2002).
13. Li and Kleiner (2001: 53) suggest that the institutionalized differential power often protects expatriates even if they are less competent than the locals. Braun and Warner (2002: 569) reveal that most TNCs in China do not adjust their performance appraisal systems according to Chinese cultural norms.
14. Readers interested on the concept of 'face' (*mianzi*) can refer to Redding (1993) and Chen (1995).
15. Two recent surveys also revealed that there is a global trend of importing fewer expatriates, and that the sky-high remuneration packages and monetary incentives for expatriates could be coming to an end in China (SCMP, 16 Sept. 2002: 4; TST, 20 April 2002).
16. Conventionally, localization is defined as replacing expatriates with local talent, together with the delegation of decision-making authority to local executives in a planned manner to assure continuity, so as to achieve the firm's objectives (Wong and Law, 1999).

17. There is a vast amount of literature on the significance of *guanxi* in doing business in China despite its high transaction costs. Among others, see Yeung (2001) and Davies *et al.* (2003).
18. Developed by the International Organization for Standardization, ISOs are generic management system standards. ISO 9000 is concerned with 'quality management' (i.e. whether the firm has done everything to ensure that its products conform to the customer's requirements), while ISO 14000 is about the 'environmental management system' (i.e. whether the firm has done everything to ensure that a product will have the least harmful impact on the environment during production or disposal) (ISO, 2001). Designed and monitored by the Social Accountability International, Social Accountability 8000 (SA 8000) is focused on the 'social accountability' of the firm's activities (SAI, 1997: 4).
19. By law, workers are not allowed to work more than 11 hours/day. However, it is not uncommon for workers in Guangdong to work up to 18 hours/day between July and September to fulfil Christmas orders from McDonald's, Mattel, Disney, etc. This partly explains the high number of industrial accidents in China (SCMP, 29 Oct. 2001, see also Yeung, 2001: 183–88).
20. 'Green standards' is a set of technical standards to protect the importing country's environment, which should, in principle, be covered by the ISO 14000. TBT is a set of technical regulations and standards that importing countries consider appropriate to protect the health and safety of their citizens, animals, plants and the environment, etc. The WTO *Agreement on Technical Barriers to Trade* aims to ensure that regional technical standards for imports do not create unnecessary obstacles for trade, but it does not prevent member countries from taking 'necessary measures' to ensure their standards are met (WTO, 2002c).
21. The dispute between BYD in Shenzhen (the largest maker of rechargeable batteries in China) and Sanyo Energy (USA) (the subsidiary of Sanyo Electric) serves as an example. Sanyo Energy recently filed a patent infringement lawsuit against BYD. Analysts suggest that this actually reflects a desperate bid by Sanyo Energy to halt the defection of its customers to BYD, after the Shenzhen-based firm became the largest supplier of lithium ion batteries to Motorola and then won contracts from Nokia (TS, 26 Sept. 2002).

REFERENCES

Abbreviations for Newspapers and Magazines
BIDI: Bureau of Industrial Damage Investigations (http://www.cacs.gov.cn) (in Chinese)
CD: *China Daily* (www.chinadaily.com.cn)
CEI: China Economic Information (www1.cei.gov.cn/hottopic/doc/ztbc/) (in Chinese)
FEER: *Far Eastern Economic Review*
HKEJ: *Hong Kong Economic Journal* (in Chinese)
SCMP: *South China Morning Post* (http://www.scmp.com)
TS: *The Standard* (www.thestandard.com.hk)
TST: *The Straits Times* (Singapore)

Adhikari, R. and Yang, Y. (2002), 'What Will WTO Membership Mean for China and its Trading Partners?', *Finance & Development*, Sept., pp.22–5.
Björkman, I. and Lu, Y. (1999), 'The Management of Human Resources in Chinese–Western Joint Ventures', *Journal of World Business*, Vol.34, No.3, pp.306–24.
Björkman, I. and Lu, Y. (2000), 'Local or Global? Human Resource Management in International Joint Ventures in China' in Malcolm Warner (ed.), *Changing Workplace Relations in the Chinese Economy*. Basingstoke: Palgrave, pp.117–38.
Blumental, D.M. (1999), 'Applying GATT to Marketizing Economies: The Dilemma of WTO Accession and Reform of China's State-owned Enterprises (SOEs)', *Journal of International Economic Law*, Vol.2, No.1, March, pp.113–54.
Bottelier, Pieter (2002), 'Implications of WTO Membership for China's State-owned Banks and the Management of Public Finances: Issues and Strategies', *Journal of Contemporary China*, Vol.11, No.32, Aug., pp.397–411.

Braun, Werner H. and Warner, Malcolm (2002), 'Strategic Human Resource Management in Western Multinationals in China: The Differentiation of Practices across Different Ownership Forms', *Personnel Review*, Vol.31, No.5, pp.553–79.

Chan, T.S. and Cui, G. (2002), 'Management Localization and FDI Performance: An Exploratory Study' in *WTO and Global Competition: A New Era for International Business*, AIB Southeast Asia and Australia Regional Conference, 18–20 July 2002, Shanghai, China.

Chen, M. (1995), *Asian Management Systems: Chinese, Japanese and Korean Styles of Business*. London: Routledge.

Child, J. (1999), 'Management in China' in P. Buckley and P. Ghauri (eds.), *The Global Challenge for Multinational Enterprises: Managing Increasing Interdependence*. Amsterdam: Pergamon, pp.444–66.

Child, J. (2000), 'Occupying the Managerial Workplace in Sino–foreign Joint Ventures: A Strategy for Control and Development?' in Malcolm Warner (ed.), *Changing Workplace Relations in the Chinese Economy*. Basingstoke: Palgrave, pp.139–62.

Davies, H., Leung, T., Luk, S. and Wong, Y.H. (2003) '*Guanxi* and Business Practices in The People's Republic of China' in Alon, I. (ed.), *Chinese Culture, Management Challenges and Corporate Strategy*. Greenwood.

DeWoskin, K.J. (2001), 'The WTO and the Telecommunications Sector in China', *The China Quarterly*, No.167, Sept., pp.630–54.

Dong, Y., Xu, H. and Liu, F. (1998), 'Antidumping and the WTO: Implications for China', *Journal of World Trade*, Vol.32, No.1, Feb., pp.19–27.

Fewsmith, J. (2001), 'The Political and Social Implications of China's Accession to the WTO', *The China Quarterly*, No.167, Sept., pp.573–91.

Goodall, K. and Warner, M. (1997), 'Human Resources in Sino–foreign Joint Ventures: Selected Case Studies in Shanghai Compared with Beijing', *Journal of International Human Resource Management*, Vol.8, pp.569–94.

Goodall, K. and Burgers, W. (1998), 'Frequent Fliers: Strong Retention Programs Are the Key to Curbing Chinese Manager Turnover', *China Business Review*, May–June, pp.50–2.

Harwitt, E. (2001), 'The Impact of WTO Membership on the Automobile Industry in China', *The China Quarterly*, No.167, Sept., pp.655–70.

Ianchovichina, E. and Martin, W. (2001), *Trade Liberalization in China's Accession to the World Trade Organization*. World Bank Working Paper No. 2623. (http://econ. worldbank.org/files/2228_wps2623.pdf).

International Organization for Standardization (ISO) (2001), *ISO 9000 and ISO 14000 in Plain Language*, accessed at www.iso.ch/iso/en/iso9000-14000/tour/plain.html.

Kong, Q. (2000), 'China's WTO Accession: Commitments and Implications', *Journal of International Economic Law*, Vol.3, No.4, Dec. pp.655–90.

Lai, H.H. (2001), 'Behind China's World Trade Organization Agreement with the USA', *Third World Quarterly*, Vol.22, No.2, April, pp.237–55.

Langlois, J.D. Jr. (2001), 'The WTO and China's Financial System', *The China Quarterly*, No.167, Sept., pp.610–29.

Lasserre, P. and Chin, P.S. (1997), 'Human Resources Management in China and the Localisation Challenge', *Journal of Asian Business*, Vol.13, No.4, pp.85–99.

Legewie, J. (2002), 'Control and Co-ordination of Japanese Subsidiaries in China: Problems of an Expatriate-based Management', *International Journal of Human Resource Management*, Vol.13, No.13, Sept., pp.901–19.

Li, L. and Kleiner, B.H. (2001), 'Expatriate–local Relationship and Organisational Effectiveness: A Study of Multinational Companies in China', *Management Research News*, Vol.24, No.3/4, pp.49–56.

Liu, G. and Woo, W.T. (2001), 'How Will Ownership in China's Industrial Sector Evolve with WTO Accession', *China Economic Review*, Vol.12, No.2/3, pp.137–61.

Martinsons, M., So, S., Tin, C. and Wong, D. (1997), 'Hong Kong and China: Emerging Markets for Environmental Products and Technologies', *Long Range Planning*, Vol.30, No.2, pp.277–90.

Michalopoulos, C. (2001), *Developing Countries in the WTO*. Basingstoke: Palgrave.

Ministry of Foreign Trade and Economic Cooperation (MOFTEC) (2001), *Compilation of the Legal Instruments on China's Accession to the World Trade Organization*, accessed at www.moftec.gov.cn/moftec_cn/wto/wtolaw.html.

Mok, V., Dai, X. and Yeung, G. (2002), 'An Internalization Approach to Joint Ventures: The Case of Coca-Cola in China', *Asia Pacific Business Review*, Vol.9, No.1, pp.39–59.

National Bureau of Statistics (NBS) (2002), *China Statistical Yearbook 2002*. Beijing: China Statistics Press.

Ng, S.K. and Warner, M. (2000), 'Industrial Relations versus Human Resource Management in the PRC: Collective Bargaining with Chinese Characteristics' in Malclom Warner (ed.), *Changing Workplace Relations in the Chinese Economy*. Basingstoke: Palgrave, pp.110–6.

Nolan, P. (1995), *Joint Ventures and Economic Reform in China: A Case study of the Coca-Cola Business System, with particular Reference to the Tianjin Coca-cola Plant*. ESRC Centre for Business Research, University of Cambridge, Working Paper no. 24.

Nolan, P. (2001a), *China and the Global Economy: National Champions, Industrial Policy and the Big Business Revolution*. Basingstoke: Palgrave.

Nolan, P. (2001b), *China and the Global Business Revolution*. Basingstoke: Palgrave.

Potter, B.P. (2001), 'The Legal Implications of China's Accession to the WTO', *The China Quarterly*, No.167, September, pp.592–609.

Redding, S.G. (1993), *The Spirit of Chinese Capitalism*. Berlin: Walter de Gruytrer.

Shen, J. (2000), 'The Impact of China's Entry into the WTO on the Chinese Telecommunications Industry', *Cambridge Review of International Affairs*, Spring–Summer, Vol.XIII, No.2, pp.121–35.

Social Accountability International (SAI) (1997), *Social Accountability 8000*. New York, accessed at www.cepaa.org/Standardper cent20English.doc.

Sun, J. (2000), 'Report 7: WTO and the Chinese Automobile Industry' in Yongding Yu, Bingwen Zheng and Hong Song (eds.), *Research Reports on the WTO Accession of China: The Analysis of Chinese Industries*. Beijing: Social Sciences Documentation Publishing House, pp. 366–420 (in Chinese).

Tan, J. (2001), 'Innovation and Risk-taking in a Transitional Economy: A Comparative Study of Chinese Managers and Entrepreneurs', *Journal of Business Venturing*, Vol.16, pp.359–76.

Thiers, P. (2002), 'Challenges for WTO Implementation: Lessons from China's Deep Integration into an International Trade Regime', *Journal of Contemporary China*, Vol.11, No.32, August, pp.413–31.

Tsang, E.W. (2001), 'Managerial Learning in Foreign-invested Enterprises of China', *Management International Review*, Vol.41, No.1, pp.26–51.

Wang, Z. (1999), 'The Impact of China's WTO Entry on the World Labour-intensive Export Market: A Recursive Dynamic CGE Analysis', *World Economy*, Vol.22, No.3, May, pp.379–405.

White House. (2001), *White House Factsheets*, accessed at www.uschina.org/public/wto/factsheets.

Wong, C.S. and Law, K. (1999), 'Managing Localization of Human Resources in the PRC: A Practical Model', *Journal of World Business*, Vol.34, No.1, pp.26–40.

Woo, W.T. (2001), 'Recent Claims of China's Economic Exceptionalism: Reflections Inspired by WTO Accession', *China Economic Review*, Vol.12, No.2/3, pp.107–36.

World Trade Organization (WTO) (2002a), *Anti-dumping*, accessed at www.wto.org/english/ thewto_e/ whatis_e/eol /e/wto04/wto4_2.htm).

World Trade Organization (WTO) (2002b), *Intellectual Property: Protection and Enforcement*, accessed at www.wto.org/english/thewto_e/whatis_e/tif_e/agrm6_e.htm.

World Trade Organization (WTO) (2002c), *Technical Barriers to Trade*, accessed at www. wto.org/wto/english/tratop_e/tbt_e/tbt_e.htm).

Yamamoto, H. (2000), 'Marketization of the Chinese Economy and Reform of the Grain Distribution System', *Developing Economies*, Vol.38, No.1, March, pp.11–50.

Yeung, G. (2001), *Foreign Investment and Socio-economic Development in China: The Case of Dongguan*. Basingstoke: Palgrave.

Yeung, G. (2002a), 'The Implications of WTO Accession on the Pharmaceutical Industry in

China', *Journal of Contemporary China*, Vol.11, No.32, August, pp.473–93.

Yeung, G. (2002b), 'WTO Accession, the Changing Competitiveness of Foreign-financed Firms and Regional Development in Guangdong of Southern China', *Regional Studies*, Vol.36, No.6, August, pp.627–42.

Yeung, G. and Mok, V. (2002), 'Chinese Government Policy and the Competitive Advantage of Foreign-financed Firms in the Southern Chinese Province of Guangdong', *Asian Business & Management*, Vol.1, No.2, pp.227–47.

Yeung, G. and Mok, V. (forthcoming), 'Does the WTO Accession Matter for the Chinese Textile and Clothing Industry?', *Cambridge Journal of Economics*.

Zhong, C. and Yang, Y. (2000), 'China's Textile and Clothing Exports in the Post Uruguay Round', in Peter Drysdale and Ligang Song (eds.), *China's Entry to the WTO: Strategic Issues and Quantitative Assessments*. London: Routledge, pp.175–93.

China's Entry to the WTO:
Prospects and Managerial Implications for Foreign Life Insurance Companies

MAN-KWONG LEUNG and TREVOR YOUNG

Despite the strong growth of life insurance premiums since late 1978 when the economic reform programme began in the People's Republic of China (PRC),[1] Chinese life insurance firms have been noted for their low efficiency in operation. In the absence of an open and competitive market, the predominately state-owned domestic firms have monopolized the insurance market. The introduction of foreign life insurance companies is therefore perceived as a policy response to enhance the competitiveness of the market through the transfer of foreign capital, expertise and knowledge in products, risk and investment management. However, in a bid to protect domestic life insurers, operations of foreign life insurers have been confined to selling individual policies denominated in domestic currency (*Renminbi, Rmb*) in a few cities, along with the restriction on ownership. Now that China has been formally accepted as a full member of the World Trade Organization (WTO) on 10 November 2001, it is expected that more foreign insurers will be attracted to the Chinese market, amid the ensuing liberalization in its insurance sector.[2]

Against this background, this study seeks to analyse, within a theoretical framework, the entry of foreign life insurance firms in China. This will serve as a base for assessing future prospects and deriving some managerial implications for them following China's entry to the WTO. An outline of the current insurance reforms in China, with a review of the institutional constraints that have hindered the development of the industry is followed, drawing on Dunning's eclectic framework, by two proposed hypotheses on the attractions offered by the Chinese economy and particular ownership-specific advantages of foreign life insurers, and confronted with available data. The impact of China's accession to the WTO on its domestic industries, including life insurance is then examined. This provides the background to assess the future prospects of and managerial implications for foreign life insurers.

INSURANCE REFORMS IN CHINA

Shortly after the founding of the socialist regime of the PRC in 1949, the fully state-owned People's Insurance Company of China (PICC) was established. It became the only insurance provider and played a significant role in restoring industrial production under the new regime. However, as a result of subsequent political upheavals, all domestic operations of the PICC were suspended between 1959 and 1978 and the company was subsumed under the mono-banking system. The socialist government then was responsible for covering all accidental losses of manufacturing enterprises and domestic households.

The PICC resumed its domestic operations in 1980 following the implementation of the comprehensive reform programme in late 1978. Two years later, life insurance as a business product was also re-introduced in China. The detachment of the PICC from the People's Bank of China, the central bank of the country, in 1984 was another major structural change in the insurance sector. However, it was not until the creation of a shareholding system for life insurance companies that the monolithic structure of the insurance sector finally broke up.[3] Two nation-wide shareholding companies, the Shenzhen-based Ping An and the Shanghai-based China Pacific, were established in 1988 and 1991 respectively (OECD, 2002). They were then followed by another two nation-wide companies, Tai Kang and New China (Xin Hua), and by two regional companies, Xin Jiang and Tian An.[4]

Since the goal of establishing a socialist market economy, albeit with a Chinese character, was adopted in China's constitution in 1993, market-oriented financial reforms have gained momentum. In particular, a legal framework aimed at facilitating transactions in the insurance market was put in place in 1995, with the enactment of the very first nation-wide insurance legislation, the Insurance Law. This law formalized the operational framework for the industry, making it compulsory for all insurance agents to be registered and prohibiting overseas (and domestic) companies from obtaining a single business licence covering both life and non-life insurance. Moreover, the law restricted foreign investors in the life insurance market to joint ventures in two cities, Shanghai and Guangzhou (Allen, Leyssens and Liu, 1999).

The 1997 financial crisis in South-East Asia highlighted the importance of proper risk management to the stability of a country's financial system. China realized that a major focus of the financial reforms should be the improvement of its supervisory and risk management systems. The insurance sector was a case in point. A new insurance regulator, the China Insurance Regulatory Commission (CIRC), was formed, taking over the supervisory role in insurance business from the central bank at the end of 1998. To facilitate effective supervision, the government also officially declared that the PICC's three functional divisions – life insurance, property insurance and re-insurance – were to become independent and autonomous companies: China Life Insurance, PICC (Property) Insurance and China Re-insurance.

Table 1 shows the life premium incomes of both domestic and foreign life insurance companies operating in China in 2000. It can be seen that, despite the presence of eight foreign-funded life insurers,[5] they have had less than 2 per cent of the market share, with domestic companies accounting for more than 98 per cent of the life insurance premiums. Moreover, the fully state-owned China Life, the life insurance spin-off from the PICC, accounted for 68.6 per cent of the total, followed by Ping An (20.2 per cent) and China Pacific (7.5 per cent). Given that the three big Chinese firms have a market share of 96 per cent, the insurance market in China takes the form of oligopoly in structure.[6]

Although enjoying a near monopoly of the rapidly growing life premiums, the insulated Chinese life insurers, when compared with their counterparts in developed market economies, are both

TABLE 1
THE CHINESE MARKET FOR LIFE INSURANCE PREMIUMS IN 2000

Domestic companies	Insurance premiums (Rmb *Yuan* million)
China Life	65,165 (65.1%)
The China Pacific#	8,404 (8.4%)
Ping An	22,435 (22.4%)
Tai Kang	719 (0.7%)
New China (*Xin Hua*)	1,506 (1.5%)
Xianjiang Corporation#	71 (0.1%)
Tian An#	7 (*)
Foreign-funded companies	1,762 (1.8%)
TOTAL	100,069 (100%)

Notes:
Composite insurer
* Less than 0.01%
Source: Yearbook of China's Insurance 2001

technically and organizationally backward in their operations. In addition, the development of the life insurance industry in China is also hampered by the following institutional constraints.

Constraints on the Demand for Insurance

In China the concept of insurance providing cover and compensation for economic loss is still not widely understood beyond a few developed and prosperous cities such as Shanghai, Guangzhou and Shenzhen. Life insurance policies are largely regarded as a savings instrument. Low awareness of commercial life insurance and its related products can also be attributed to the fact that individuals have been covered until recently by a comprehensive state-managed social security system. Moreover, individuals in China, particularly those living in rural areas may not have adequate financial resources to buy life insurance policies. They may also find it difficult to comprehend the rather complex terms and conditions of an insurance contract and there are reportedly cases of frauds and malpractice in the selling of life policies to customers by unauthorized agents. If insurance companies are to exploit the latent demand for insurance, they must gain the trust and confidence of their potential customers.

A Predominately State-Owned Cartel

Insulated from international insurance markets for a long time, Chinese life insurers have found themselves short of the required skills and expertise in product development and risk management in balancing the structure of assets and liabilities. They have therefore experienced difficulties in meeting the growing and varied needs of their customers. Furthermore, undertaking insurance operations on a commercial basis, driven by a profit motive, has been a new challenge for the senior management of the Chinese insurance companies. As noted above, the market is dominated currently by the fully state-owned China Life Insurance. Moreover, the major shareholders of the share-based insurance companies are also large state-owned enterprises.[7] In essence, the Chinese insurance sector can be viewed as a cartel, which in practice is still heavily influenced by the State with a socialist ideology of public ownership. The firms do not have a proper incentive system in place to tie performance with remuneration.

Restricted Investment Channels in Capital Markets

As a potential major source of long-term domestic capital, the Chinese government has been cautious in regulating the flow of premiums. Insurance firms were banned from investing in the highly speculative stock market in 1995 and thereafter they could only invest in deposits with state commercial banks and in government bonds. Insurance companies were subsequently allowed to engage in transactions in the inter-bank market in November 1998 and to invest in selected corporate bonds in April 1999. With a more established stock market, they have further been allowed, since November 1999, to trade listed securities investment funds in stages up to 15 per cent of their assets. They are still, however, unable to trade shares and bonds freely in the domestic capital markets. In July 2001, bank deposits accounted for 40 per cent and listed securities funds only 4.2 per cent of the total assets of all insurance companies.[8]

Underdeveloped Legal and Regulatory Framework

From a legal perspective, Dorfman (1998) defines insurance as a contract arrangement whereby one party agrees to compensate another party for losses. Hence it creates rights and obligations for the insurance company and the insured. A life insurance contract in China was only formalized with the enactment of the Insurance Law in 1995. Contract specifications that are not well established and tried out are open to different interpretations and, in the absence of a civil court system, contract agreements are more difficult to enforce. A regulatory framework only started to emerge in China after the establishment of the CIRC in 1998. Nevertheless, the administrative ties that exist amongst the CIRC, the state-owned insurance companies and other state-owned enterprises may limit the effective enforcement of the Insurance Law.

One of the government's policy responses to these institutional constraints is to allow foreign life insurance firms to operate in China. With active marketing and agency distribution systems, foreign firms have helped to transfer the most up-to-date knowledge and professional insurance practice and through competition to spur Chinese firms to be more efficient. Chinese firms can gain management expertise and acquire risk management systems from foreign firms. CIRC can also draw on the supervisory experience of its counterparts in the home countries of these foreign insurance firms. All these will help to pave the way for Chinese life insurers to enter the international insurance market and China's accession to the WTO will expedite the process.

ENTRY OF FOREIGN LIFE INSURERS

In order to afford domestic firms a measure of protection, the introduction of foreign insurance firms has been a gradual and cautious process. It was not until 1986 that China first allowed foreign insurance firms to set up representative offices to engage in liaison services in selected cities. In 1992, American International Assurance (AIA) was the first foreign life insurer to set up a branch in Shanghai, selling life policies denominated in domestic currency to individual Chinese customers only. Since 1995, foreign life insurers have been able to operate in China as a joint venture with a local Chinese firm in Shanghai and Guangzhou. By the end of 2000, there was a total of eight foreign-funded life insurers from six countries operating three branches and seven joint ventures in Guangzhou, Shanghai and Shenzhen.[9] There were around 30 foreign insurance firms establishing representative offices in China in 2000.[10]

TABLE 2
FOREIGN-FUNDED LIFE INSURERS IN CHINA AS OF END 2000

Name (foreign interests)	Organizational Form	Year of Establishment (location)
AIA (USA)	Branch	1992 (Sha)
AIA (USA)	Branch	1995 (G)
Allianz Dazhong (Germany)	JV	1998 (Sha)
Pacific-Aetna (ING/Netherlands)*	JV	1998(Sha)
AXA-Minmetals (France)	JV	1999 (Sha)
Manulife-Sinochem (Canada)	JV	1999 (Sha)
AIA (USA)	Branch	1999 (She)
China Life CMG (Australia)	JV	2000 (Sha)
John Hancock Tianan Life Insurance (USA)	JV	2000 (Sha)
CITIC-Prudential Life Insurance (UK)	JV	2000 (G)

Notes: JV = joint venture
Sha = Shanghai, She =Shenzhen G = Guangzhou
* In December 2000, ING took over Aetna
Source: Yearbook of China's Insurance, 2001.

Table 2 shows the organizational form, year of establishment and location of foreign-funded life insurance companies operating in China in 2000. It can be seen that, apart from CMG (Australia), the foreign firms were from developed economies with large home insurance markets in either Europe or North America. It has been argued that the Chinese government selectively issued licences to large multinational firms, which signalled its commitment to the internationalization of its insurance sector (OECD, 2002).

Dunning's Eclectic Framework and Hypotheses
The entry of foreign life insurance firms in China can be explained by the 'eclectic approach' first developed by Dunning (1977). This approach distinguishes three forces at work: location-specific

advantages (LSAs), ownership-specific advantages (OSAs) and internalization incentives. OSAs mainly take the form of specialized knowledge, relationships with the host government and customers, whereas LSAs include financial incentives and liberalized regulations of a host economy. As the markets for knowledge and client relationships are imperfect, due to their public good and proprietary nature, an insurance firm has incentives to 'internalize' these OSAs and LSAs through the establishment of an institution, namely a branch and/or a subsidiary, subject to the legal requirements of the host country (Leung and Young, 2002).

Applying this framework in the context of China's insurance market, our first hypothesis is that the LSAs of the Chinese economy include the availability of business opportunities, represented by the growth of the insurance market, and the improving political environment. A priori economic and political conditions in China would be expected to influence the decision of foreign life insurers to enter the market. Specifically, an increasing level of life insurance premium incomes is likely to encourage foreign insurance firms to enter the Chinese market. As a developing country in transition from a socialist planned economy to a market economy, the market in China is inevitably associated with some political risks. A reduction of these risks is expected to have a positive influence on the likelihood of entry of a foreign life insurer.

Our second hypothesis is that the OSAs are represented by the attributes of a foreign life insurer, viz. the size of assets and special links to Hong Kong. These attributes help to lower operational costs, reduce risk and increase the expected returns of operations in China (Hymer, 1976; Kindleberger, 1969; Caves, 1971). A multinational firm with large assets would have lower information costs and would instil confidence in potential customers in China, while its operations in a range of countries would generate scale economies and the benefits associated with international risk diversification. Concurrent operations in the Hong Kong market would enable a foreign firm to reduce the costs of information regarding the Chinese culture, facilitate the deployment of personnel, and permit the selling of similar products across the border.

The ownership-specific advantages must more than offset the various costs associated with operating in China. A foreign-funded life insurer will have to incur costs in building up relationships with key ministries, city governments and potential corporate clients. This helps to minimize red tape, which usually takes the form of large time-costs in obtaining approval for a product. Permission to repatriate profits in foreign currency must also be sought. Given the relatively low awareness of insurance and the absence of well-established institution-alized procedures, enforcement of contractual agreements associated with insurance policies can be time-consuming and costly.

A foreign life insurer can now enter the Chinese market in a joint venture and the foreign partner can hold 50 per cent of the joint venture's shares.[11] The foreign partner will be responsible for making strategic decisions as well as the general administration of the joint venture. This arrangement allows the foreign partner to reduce the time needed to gain the trust of local customers and, more importantly, provides access to nation-wide distribution networks. From the Chinese partner's perspective, the partnership will provide managerial skills, opportunities for technology transfer and training of local staff. The Chinese partners, however, must be approved by the government and some of them are not undertaking insurance as their core business.[12]

We now consider whether the two hypotheses concerning the specific LSAs and OSAs, which would explain the entry of a foreign life insurer (in a branch or a joint venture) into China, are supported by the data.

Verification of the Hypotheses

There has been empirical research on foreign direct investment (FDI) in banks in developed and less developed economies from the early 1980s (Goldberg and Saunders, 1981; Sabi, 1988). In contrast, empirical work on FDI in insurance has been sparse and limited to well developed market economies. Moshirian (1997, 1999) investigates, using quantitative models, the causes of FDI in insurance in the USA and of German and British FDI in insurance abroad. He reports that demand for insurance services, the exchange rate, relative rate of returns, and the size of the insurance sectors of the source country are significant factors.

However, given foreign exchange control and the restriction on the access of insurance companies to the developing capital markets in China, it would not be feasible to apply Moshirian's approach in the context of China's insurance markets. The scope of the econometric analysis is further hampered by the limited number of observations. Hence, a simple linear regression is used to test whether the availability of business opportunities and reducing political risks are responsible for the growth of foreign life insurers in China during the period 1992 to 2000 (Table 3). Specifically, the variables are defined as follows:

Dependent variable:
$ENTERPRC_t$ = number of joint ventures and branches of foreign life insurers in year t
(*Source: Almanac of China's Insurance*)

Independent variables:
$PREMIUM_t$ = amount of life insurance premiums in year t (*Rmb Yuan* 10 billion)
(*Source: Almanac of China's Insurance*)

$POLSTAB_t$ = index of average monthly political stability in year t[13]
(*Source:* Political Risk Services)

Table 3 shows that *PREMIUM* and *POLSTAB* have a positive impact at 1 per cent and 5 per cent significant level respectively. These results provide evidence that the first hypothesis is valid, namely increasing business opportunities and improving political risk environment are significant factors explaining the entry of foreign life insurers in China over the data period.

Figure 1 shows that the growth of foreign life insurers in terms of the total number of branches and joint ventures (Number) is strongly correlated with the flow of life insurance premiums, which has registered an annual increase of 33.8 per cent during the period 1989 to 2000. Despite a rapid growth rate, life insurance premiums as a proportion of gross domestic incomes (Density) have only increased from 0.24 per cent in 1989 to 1.12 per cent in 2000. Taking the comparable figure of 5.66 per cent in Asia in 2000 as a benchmark, it is clear that there is considerable scope for further growth in the life insurance industry in China. In particular, given that foreign life

TABLE 3
RESULTS OF THE LINEAR REGRESSION MODEL

	Coefficient	Standard error	T – ratio
PREMIUM	1.199	0.154	7.766***
POLSTAB	0.437	0.148	2.948**
Constant	−30.32	10.289	−2.947**
	Adjusted R2 = 0.931		
	Durbin-Watson = 2.135		

Notes: ***1% and **5% significance level

FIGURE 1
GROWTH OF FOREIGN LIFE INSURERS IN CHINA FROM 1989 TO 2000

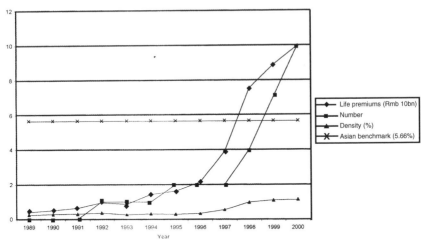

Notes: Number = Number of branches and joint ventures of foreign-funded life insurers
Density (%) = Premium incomes/Gross domestic incomes x 100%
Asian benchmark (5.66%) = The density in Asia, 5.66% in 2000

Sources: Yearbook China's Insurance; China Statistical Yearbook

insurance companies only accounted for 1.8 per cent of the total market in premium incomes, there are vast, untapped opportunities for expansion.[14] With the enactment of the 1995 Insurance Law and the establishment of CIRC in 1998, an additional single branch and five joint ventures were established between 1999 to 2000. This may lend support to the claim that the increase in number of foreign life insurers is associated with the wider market access which China's entry to the WTO is perceived to bring (OECD, 2002). Furthermore, as one of the outcomes of the WTO negotiations, six more life insurance licences were given to EC countries in October 2001.

There have been virtually no quantitative studies of the ownership-specific advantages, which have prompted foreign life insurers to operate outside their home territory. The case in China is no exception. In order to understand the impacts of some attributes of foreign insurance companies on their decision to enter the China market, a binomial logit model has been estimated for the 40 large insurance companies listed in *Fortune,* July 2001. Here it is hypothesized that the foreign firm's decision is determined by the asset size of the company and whether it already has established operations in Hong Kong. Specifically, the variables considered in the model are defined as follows:

Dependent variable:

PRCMARKET = 1 if the insurance firm in 2000 had a joint venture or branch in China;

= 0 otherwise.

(Sources: *Almanac of China's Insurance; Fortune*, July 2001)

Independent variables:

SIZE = asset size in US$ 10 billion.

(Source: *Fortune*, July 2001)

HKLINK = 1 if the insurance firm has operations in Hong Kong; = 0 otherwise.

$$\Pr(PRCMARKET = 1 | X_i) = \frac{\exp(X_i \beta)}{1 + \exp(X_i \beta)}$$

where $X_i \beta = \beta_1 + \beta_2 SIZE_i + \beta_3 HKLINK_i$

$i = 1, .., 40$

Table 4 shows that both *SIZE* and *HKLINK* have a positive impact on the likelihood to enter the China market at 5 per cent significant level. In order to have a deeper insight into the comparative advantages of foreign insurance firms over the Chinese firms, the data presented in Table 5 allows a comparison of the three largest domestic insurance firms and the three largest foreign-funded life insurers (also the three largest global firms) at present operating in China.[15] It can be seen that the three Chinese firms are overwhelmingly outclassed by the three global firms in terms of size, profits and employee productivity. When China Life is compared with AXA, the most marked differences are in

TABLE 4
RESULTS OF THE BINOMIAL LOGIT MODEL

Coefficient		Robust stand. errors	P>|z|	
SIZE	.0.082	.04	0.047	
HKLINK		3.243	1.27	0.011
Constant		−4.753	1.76	0.007

Wald chi2(2)	=	7.33
Prob > chi2	=	0.0257
Log likelihood	=	−9.34
Pseudo R2	=	0.50

TABLE 5
TOP THREE FOREIGN AND DOMESTIC INSURANCE COMPANIES IN CHINA IN 2000

Rank	Institution	Revenue (US$ mn)	Profits (US$ mn)	Assets (US$ mn)	Equity (US$ mn)	Employees	Profits per employee (US$ 000)
G1	AXA (France)	92,782	3,608	445.6	22,835	95,422	37.8
G2	ING (Netherlands)	71,196	11,075	610.4	23,728	92,650	119.5
G3	Allianz (Germany)	71,022	3,198	413.1	33,426	119,683	26.7
D1	China Life	8,201	112	19.3	556	44,334	2.5
D2	China Pacific	2,063	33	3.8	242	12,182	2.7
D3	Ping An	3,306	155	7.9	268	197,192	0.8

Sources: Fortune (31 July 2001); Yearbook of China's Insurance 2001.
Exchange rate for Rmb/US$ was 8.2774 at the end of 2000.

equity (40 times higher in AXA) and profits per employee (15 times greater).

We can infer from these comparisons that foreign firms have comparative advantages over Chinese firms in various aspects of their insurance operations, a point borne out by the following extract from Nolan (2001):

> The relatively small scale of the China's financial services [insurance] sector means large competitive disadvantage with the large global firms [operating in China] in terms of unit costs, expenditure on R&D, IT systems and brand building, risk management, product development and diversification, and ability to attract the best staff and to provide services for global clients. (p.826).

In addition, these companies have all undertaken life insurance business in Hong Kong for a long time.[16] All of these observations tend to further support the second hypothesis that a foreign life insurer with specific attributes will enable them to more than offset the set-up costs and so be motivated to enter the Chinese market.

IMPACT ON CHINESE INDUSTRIES OF ACCESSION TO THE WTO

The future impact of China's WTO accession in terms of the survival of domestic firms and employment opportunities will depend on the interaction of two factors.[17] The first is the extent to which the large Chinese firms are engaged in domestic sales or export-oriented

TABLE 6
THE IMPACT OF CHINA'S WTO ACCESSION ON ITS INDUSTRIES

Industry	Efficiency Differentials (Df–Ff)	Market barriers in China after WTO	Impact on survival of Chinese firms	Impact on employment opportunities
Agriculture (wheat, cotton and rice – DS)	Negative	Small	Large negative	Negative
Light industry (textiles and wearing apparels – DS, EO)	Positive	Small	Large positive	Positive
Heavy industry (car manufacturers – DS)	Negative	Small	Large negative	Negative
Financial services (life insurance – DS)	Negative	Large	Mixed	Positive

Notes:
Df – Domestic firms; Ff – Foreign firms
DS – Domestic sales; EO – Export-oriented.

production and how far they have lagged behind the large global firms in respect of organizational and production efficiencies. Other things being equal, the larger the gap, the more vulnerable the domestic firms and the greater the job losses will be in the increasingly competitive markets upon WTO accession. The second factor is the level of explicit and implicit market barriers in the post-WTO entry period which will increase the costs and risks of operations of foreign firms. Explicit barriers may include open restrictions on foreign ownership and foreign exchange control, whereas implicit barriers can cover consumer loyalty and awareness, and slack enforcement of laws and regulations. It follows that the greater these barriers and the longer they are maintained, the more likely that domestic firms will be able to survive and to continue to provide job opportunities.

Table 6 presents a classification of the impact of China's accession to the WTO on its domestic industries, including life insurance. Firstly, the labour-intensive Chinese agricultural sector (principally, wheat, cotton and rice) is currently protected from foreign competition, notably from the large-scale mechanized farming in North America, by high tariffs. After WTO entry, China's tariffs on agricultural products will fall within five years from an average level of 22 per cent to 17 per cent.[18] American farmers could flood the Chinese markets with cheaper exports and, as a result, 13 million people in Chinese farm households could lose their livelihoods.[19] Secondly, in similar fashion, the domestic market of China's car industry will face competition from the mass, high technology production of global firms from Japan and the USA when tariffs are reduced from the current level of 70–80 per cent to 25 per cent and import quotas are lifted by 2006.[20] It is estimated that, of the present number of 136 domestic car manufacturers, only four or five will be able to survive. This means that a large number of Chinese car workers will be displaced. Thirdly, China has a comparative advantage in the production of light industrial goods such as textiles and wearing apparel for export by highly competitive, small and medium-sized local firms and joint ventures. With the reduction in tariffs and removal of quotas, textile exports are expected to rise by 20 per cent and those of apparel by 200 per cent.[21] This will offer greater profit opportunities for domestic firms and more employment in these sectors.

On 22 November 2001, China formally released its commitments to the WTO in its insurance sector. Access to the Chinese markets will be much expanded for foreign life insurers, as most restrictions on entry, operations and location in the market in China will be lifted within five years after China's accession.[22] Firstly, administrative control over the entry of foreign life insurers will be replaced by prudent licensing. Foreign insurers will qualify for a licence if they have more than 30 years of experience in a WTO member country and possess global assets of over US$ 5 billion. They can also choose their own partners in joint ventures with 50 per cent share of equity immediately upon accession. Secondly, foreign life insurers will be permitted to provide group, health and pension insurance to foreign and local clients within three years of accession. Thirdly, more cities are opened to foreign life insurers on China's accession, and all geographical restrictions will be lifted within three years of China's WTO entry.

The impact of China's accession to the WTO on the life insurance industry is, however, less clear-cut than that expected of Chinese agriculture and the car industry. This is because, despite a remarkable increase in the life premium incomes of Chinese firms, there still exists a large gap between them and the large foreign firms in terms of organizational and economic efficiency, as shown in Table 3. However, it is unlikely that domestic firms will be completely wiped out by their larger foreign counterparts.

Foreign life insurers will be faced with explicit and implicit market barriers even after China has entered the WTO. Chinese firms will be able to take shelter, albeit on a temporary basis, behind these barriers. Firstly, restrictions on ownership will enable a Chinese partner to capture a large share of the profits of joint venture operations. Secondly, inconvertibility of the *Rmb* on capital account and restricted investment opportunities in the capital market will undermine the comparative advantages of foreign firms in investment management. Thirdly, Chinese insurance companies have long term commercial and social relationships with their corporate and individual customers, which foreign firms will not be able to establish within a short period of time. There are also operational risks originating from the low ethical standards of some insurance agents and consumers, and the changing insurance laws and regulations. Finally, the segregation of the markets for insurance, banking, and securities in China will also apply to foreign life insurers whose parent companies are financial conglomerates from Europe and the USA.[23] In fact, much to the disadvantage of foreign firms, some Chinese life insurers have managed to team up with the large domestic banks and have made use of their large branch network to sell life policies. Given these high market barriers (which are expected to exist in the post-WTO entry period for some time), it is not surprising to find that the assets per employee for the joint venture, AXA-Minmetal, Shanghai was US$ 0.19 million in 2000, compared to US$ 0.43 million for China Life over the same period.[24] In fact, it appears that no branches and joint ventures have been able to report operating profits in recent years.

The WTO impacts on Chinese insurance firms are therefore rather mixed. Domestic firms will benefit from the transfer of expertise and knowledge about insurance operations, and the continuing growth of the market will generate more job opportunities in the insurance sector. At the same time, Ping An, Taikang and New China have introduced foreign shareholders, with a maximum holding of 5 per cent for a single investor.[25] The foreign capital and advice that an international strategic investor can provide may help to increase the competitiveness of Chinese insurance firms. Although Chinese firms are expected to grow in size, their market shares in the big cities may decline. This is because foreign firms are particularly appealing to some wealthy educated Chinese customers in those cities.

PROSPECTS AND MANAGERIAL IMPLICATIONS

Despite the high market barriers and the subsequent mixed impact on Chinese life insurance firms, the WTO agreements are sure to offer a much wider set of business opportunities for foreign life insurers. The institutional constraints that have prevailed in the Chinese insurance market will also become much less binding and the prospects for foreign life insurers in China are therefore promising for the future.

Increase in Demand

Since the 1997 financial crisis, the government has engaged in expansionary fiscal and monetary policies to sustain the country's growth momentum. As a result, China has achieved a respectable real economic growth rate of 7.1 per cent in 1999 and 8.0 per cent in 2000. Moreover, both trade and direct investments in China are expected to increase after its entry to the WTO. This will help to sustain the growth momentum of the Chinese economy. The average income level of households is expected to rise accordingly. At the same time, the state's exclusive funding role is being withdrawn and replaced by a contributory old age insurance system and a medical insurance system. Increasingly, individuals must plan for their own future and retirement, making use of commercial life insurance (Lauffs, 1999). All these factors will lead to an increase in the underlying demand for life insurance and its related products.[26]

Increase in Competitiveness

The market liberalizations and other benefits associated with WTO accession have already attracted the entry of large multinational insurance firms. Lifting restrictions on the location and scope of business activities of foreign-funded life insurance firms will encourage further competition and the transfer of expertise and management skills from foreign companies to local companies. In fact, domestic insurance firms have already acquired international practices such as actuarial skills and strategies, which until recently were seen as foreign concepts. Chinese companies have copied the highly successful direct selling and agency distribution system pioneered by AIA in 1992, with the result that they are claiming market share from AIA (Langlois, Jr., 2001). Permitting holding of equity by an international investor in domestic insurance firms and the proposed listing of Chinese insurance firms on the stock exchanges in future will help to further improve the future corporate governance and the competitiveness of domestic insurance firms.

Improving the Risk Environment

China's WTO membership will involve commitments to liberalization as well as effective supervision in its protected sector (Kong, 2000). The financial services sector is no exception. To prepare the Chinese insurance sector for the WTO, the CIRC has increasingly played a more active supervisory role in the market by tightening regulations and standardizing the rules governing the development of new insurance products. In addition, insurance law has been regularly reviewed to cope with the rapidly changing insurance sector.[27]

Furthermore, to boost public confidence in the life insurance market, CIRC has increased the number of routine investigations carried out and cracked down on unauthorized agents. At the same time, associations of insurers have been established in major cities in China in order to promote self-regulation.[28] WTO accession will require domestic laws and regulations to become more transparent and to conform to international standards and practices. All these developments will improve the risk environment for the operation of foreign life insurers.

Rapid Growth of Stocks and Liberalization of the Capital Market

The number of 'A' shares for Chinese residents on two exchanges in Shanghai and Shenzhen increased more than threefold in 1995 to 1088 in 2000, and the market capitalisation by nearly 15 times to *Rmb* 4806 billion in the corresponding period. However, the turnover in the secondary market has essentially been driven by a large number of individual investors.[29] The fund management business is also very limited, with a total of 33 closed-end stock funds run by ten domestic fund management companies in 2000. In this regard, China seeks to increase the number of institutional investors and permit the formation of joint venture fund management companies upon China's entry to the WTO. By 2006, foreign investors might be able to invest directly in China's domestic capital markets.[30] It is expected foreign insurance companies are likely to benefit from these liberalizations on the capital market and be able to export their comparative advantage in investment management.

Given these projections, and consistency and continuity of government policies in implementing China's commitments under the WTO agreement, the prospects of foreign life insurers in China should be promising. However, although many foreign firms will be attracted to this market, not all will be able to make profits. Only those which are able to make sound managerial decisions, drawing on the very attributes which facilitated their entry to the market, are likely to be commercially viable.

Unlike foreign firms, Chinese life insurers can provide life insurance and related products across the whole country and they also have a large agency force and a well-established pool of customers. Foreign-funded firms therefore need to offset these disadvantages by capitalizing on their ownership-specific advantages. The managerial implications for business policy that can be drawn for them are as follows.

A Market Niche and the Right Chinese Partner

The rising demand for insurance comes almost entirely from the residents of the major cities in China. In 2000, for example, life premium expenditures per head were substantially higher in Shanghai (*Rmb* 699), Beijing (*Rmb* 552), Shenzhen (*Rmb* 415) than the national average (*Rmb* 79). Foreign life insurers therefore need to focus on these cities and others with a strong growth potential. Moreover, following the withdrawal of state provision, demand for commercial, personal medical insurance and pension retirement schemes will increase. As the markets for these products are still at the infant stage, this certainly presents a large, untapped opportunity for those foreign life insurers with specific expertise in these areas. Moreover, multinational insurers with large asset size and equity base will have a strong bargaining position to secure a market niche and to choose a Chinese partner in a joint venture.

A Well-Planned Long Term Strategy

China has cut its interest rates seven times since May 1996. The interest rate for one-year fixed individual deposits dropped from 9.18 per cent in 1996 to 2.25 per cent at present. This has caused considerable financial difficulty for insurance firms selling fixed rate life products in China. With restricted access to insurance markets and capital markets, all foreign-funded life insurers in China incurred losses between 1998 and 2000.[31] This reinforces the fact that operating in the life insurance market in China is an investment decision with a long payback period for the foreign firm. A foreign firm with a modern governance structure and a large capital base will be better placed to absorb losses due to short-term fluctuations, and the significant start-up costs and overheads. A large capital base will also allow the firm more flexibility in the formulation of its long term strategic planning of the size of its sales force, the design and marketing of products, and future investment in the Chinese stock markets.

Effective Utilization of Links with Hong Kong

Foreign-funded insurance firms with active operations in Hong Kong can market the same or similar products to their customers on the mainland. The deployment of Chinese personnel from Hong Kong to the mainland will further help to reduce operating costs as the problems of language and cultural barriers can largely be overcome. The extensive links between Hong Kong and the mainland can also be an important source of business connections and income. This is especially significant when foreign life insurance companies are allowed to sell group policies to the new breed of Chinese enterprises which have emerged following the economic reforms. The accumulated expertise and business connections of the Chinese staff can facilitate the management of local staff, product design, marketing and underwriting of insurance policies.

It is then important for foreign life insurance firms to examine whether they have the appropriate attributes before they enter the Chinese markets, and, where they do, to build on these advantages. As human capital in the form of expertise and local connections is embodied in personnel staff, those trying to become more established in the market may need to attract senior and experienced staff from large domestic firms and other foreign insurance firms operating in China.[32] This will help to build up their local networks and expertise and will enhance their chances of survival in the increasingly liberalized markets. Foreign insurance firms which do not develop these attributes may have to consider the option of making a financial investment of up to 5 per cent in the equities of a Chinese insurance firm.

CONCLUSIONS

The attractions of the Chinese economy, such as its large market potential and the improving political environment, have motivated the entry of foreign firms. In particular, a foreign insurance firm with specific attributes, viz. large assets and special links to Hong Kong, is also more likely to enter the Chinese market, although the incidence of SARS may be a short-term complication. As the institutional constraints on demand, market competitiveness and legal framework will become less binding on China's entry to the WTO, the prospects for foreign life insurers, albeit via joint ventures, are promising. However, to become profitable, a foreign life insurer has to exploit the attributes facilitating its entry effectively. It has to make sound managerial decisions in its choice of market niche and a Chinese partner, as well as its long-term business strategy, and product and personnel management. Expertise in investment will only become a crucial factor to future profitability when there is full access to capital markets.

NOTES

1. In China life insurance premiums include those from the related products of personal accident insurance and health insurance. They altogether accounted for 41.8 per cent of the total insurance premiums in 1996. The share of life insurance premiums rose to 63.7 per cent of the total in July 2001. (China Insurance Regulatory Commission)
2. After a 15-year exhaustive negotiation process, China was formally admitted as a full member of the WTO during the Fourth Ministerial Conference held in Doha of Qatar on 10 Nov. 2001.

3. Insurance reforms in China have lagged behind banking reforms in respect of the number of establishments of diversified ownership and of the opening up to foreign financial institutions. This could be attributed to the Chinese government's preoccupation with the macroeconomic control and improvements over enterprise's production efficiency through banking reforms. (Leung, 2000).

4. China Pacific, Ping An, Xinjiang, Tian An are composite insurers selling both life and property insurance products in China.

5. In China foreign life insurance firms which have set up branches or joint ventures are called foreign-funded insurance companies. See Table 2 for the list of foreign-funded insurance companies in China at the end of 2000.

6. These data do not reflect the increasingly larger role played by the Shenzhen-based Ping An in recent years. With the adoption of a market-based corporate governance, it has been active in promoting new products and has even captured a larger market share than China Pacific in Shanghai. [Source: Personal interviews with Chinese financial institutions in Shanghai in May 2002].

7. For example, the shareholders of New China (*Xin Hua*) insurance include Shanghai-based Baoshan Iron & Steel and 14 other large and medium-sized state-owned enterprises.

8. China Insurance Regulatory Commission website: http://www.circ.gov.cn. [8 November 2001]

9. Under the provisions of the November 1999 bilateral Sino–American agreements, the two branches of AIA in Shanghai and Guangzhou would be 'grandfathered' into China's WTO obligations.

10. Foreign companies must have had a representative office in Beijing, Shanghai and Guangdong province for two years before they can apply for a licence to operate life insurance business.

11. The foreign partners, the AXA group and the Aetna group, hold 51 per cent and 50 per cent of their joint ventures' shares respectively.

12. The Chinese partners for Manulife-Sinochem and AXA-Minmetals are two large enterprise groups, China National Chemicals Import & Export Corporation and the China Five Metal Groups respectively.

13. The measure used comes from the Political Risk Services (PRS) group and comprises: 'economic expectations versus reality; economic planning failures; political leadership; external conflict; corruption in government; military in politics; organised religion in politics; law and order tradition; racial and nationality tensions; political terrorism; civil war; political party development; and quality of the bureaucracy' (PRS, 2000). The highest overall rating (100 points) indicates the lowest risk, and the lowest rating (0) indicates the highest risk. A rise in the index therefore refers to a reduction of the political risk.

14. This was an important motivating force prompting their entry to the Chinese market as expressed by foreign life insurers in Shanghai when they were interviewed in June 2000.

15. This framework is adapted from 'The Challenges facing China's financial services industry', ch.12 (written by Wu Qing) of Nolan (2001).

16. Along with their operations on the mainland, the three largest global firms, together with AIA, Prudential and Manulife are the key life insurance providers in Hong Kong.

17. It may be difficult for the big Chinese firms to become globally competitive firms, given the various institutional constraints in China and the global business revolution in recent years. For a full discussion, see Nolan (2001).

18. The average tariff for US agricultural products in soyabean, fruit and dairy products will be reduced from 31.5 per cent to 14.5 per cent. *China Daily*, WTO Special, 12 Nov. 2001, p.9.

19. 'WTO 2001 Special Report', *South China Morning Post*, 12 Nov. 2001, p.15.

20. 'China joins WTO', Business Weekly, *China Daily*, 13 Nov. 2001, p.8.

21. 'WTO 2001 Special Report', *South China Morning Post*, 12 Nov. 2001, p.14

22. The liberalization measures were based on the bilateral agreement reached between China and the United States in November 1999 and the one between China and EU in May 2000. *China Daily*, 23 Nov. 2001, p.1.

23. The USA abolished the Glass-Steagall Act that had separated the insurance, banking and securities business for 65 years in 1999.
24. The assets per employee for the AXA Group in 2000 were US$ 4.7 million.
25. Business Weekly, *China Daily*, 30 Oct. 2001, p.7.
26. The increase in demand for insurance services may be mitigated by the unemployment caused by the collapse and mergers of state-owned enterprises as a result of the current state-owned enterprise reforms in China.
27. An example of this is a CIRC regulation providing clarifications and guidelines for the operation and management of insurance companies, which became effective on 1 March 2000.
28. The Insurance Association of China was set up in Beijing in November 2000.
29. The number of retail investors was 67 million in July 2001. (China Securities Regulatory Commission website: http://www.csrc.gov.cn [8 November 2001]
30. 'China joins WTO', Business Weekly, *China Daily*, 13 Nov. 2001, p.6.
31. *Yearbook of China's Insurance*, 1999, 2000 and 2001.
32. It is reported that 80 per cent of the local staff working in foreign banks were formerly from Bank of China, a former specialized bank in foreign exchange. 'WTO Special', *China Daily*, 12 Nov. 2001, p.1.

REFERENCES

Allen, A., Leyssens, E. and Liu, P. (1999), *The Insurance Industry in China*. Hong Kong: Asia Information Associates Limited.
Caves, R.E. (1971), 'International Corporations: The Industrial Economics of Foreign Investment', *Economica*, 38, 149, pp.1–27.
Dorfman, M.S. (1998), *Introduction to Risk Management and Insurance*. New Jersey: Prentice Hall, 6th edn.
Dunning, J.H. (1977), 'Trade, Location of Economic Activity and the MNE: A Search for an Eclectic Approach' in B. Ohlin, P.O. Hesselborn and P.M. Wijkman (eds.), *The International Allocation of Economic Activity*. London: Macmillan.
Goldberg, L.G. and Saunders, A. (1981), 'The Determinants of Foreign Banking Activity in the United States', Journal *of Banking and Finance 5*, pp.17–32.
Hymer, S.H. (1976), *The International Operations of National Firms: A Study of Direct Foreign Investment*. Cambridge MA: The M.I.T. Press.
Kindleberger, C.P. (1969), *American Business Abroad*. New Haven: Yale University Press.
Kong, Q. (2000), 'China's WTO Accession: Commitments and Implications', *Journal of International Economic Law*, pp.655–90.
Langlois, J.D., Jr. (2001), 'The WTO and China's Financial System', *China Quarterly*, Vol.167, pp.610–29.
Lauffs, A. (1999), 'New Medical and Unemployment Insurance Regulations Complete PRC Social Security Reform, but Practice Will Be the Test', *China Law & Practice*, April, pp.17–21.
Leung, M.K. (2000), 'Foreign Banking in China', *Business Horizons*, 43, 6, Nov./Dec., pp.4–5.
Leung, M.K. and Young, T. (2002), 'China's Entry to the WTO: Managerial Implications for Foreign Banks', *Managerial and Decision Economics*, 23, pp.1–8.
Moshirian, F. (1997), 'Foreign Direct Investment in Insurance Services in the United States', *Journal of Multinational Financial Management*, 7(2), pp.159–73
Moshirian, F. (1999), 'Sources of Growth in International Insurance Services', *Journal of Multinational Financial Management*, 9(2), pp.177–94.
Nolan, P. (2001), *China and the Global Business Revolution*. Basingstoke: Palgrave.
OECD (2002), 'The Development of China's Insurance Industry', *China in The World Economy: the Domestic Policy Challenges*. Paris: OECD, ch.8, pp.269–97.
Sabi, M. (1988), 'An Application of the Theory of Foreign Direct Investment to Multinational Banking in LDCs', *Journal of International Business Studies*, 19, pp.433–47.

Conclusion:
The Future of Chinese Management

MALCOLM WARNER

The People's Republic of China (henceforth to be referred to as China) formally entered the World Trade Organization (WTO) in December 2001, after a long period of debate and negotiation (see Holbig and Ash, 2002; Magarinos *et al.*, 2002; Ostry *et al.*, 2002).[1] It was the culmination of a reform programme that had transformed its economy and its management starting at the end of the 1970s, not long after the deaths of the leading lights of the 'Long March' generation, former Prime Minister, Zhou Enlai in January 1976 and former Party Chairman, Mao Zedong in September of that year.

The nation had enjoyed two decades of economic growth – an average of around 10 per cent per annum, over the years since Deng Xiaoping launched the 'Open Door' and 'Four Modernizations' policies in 1978 (see Newton and Subbaraman, 2002). Deng successfully carried forward these reforms throughout the 1980s and part of the 1990s, remaining the guiding influence until his death in February 1997. From the onset of the reforms, dramatic changes have taken place in China's enterprise structure and its management, including the decentralization of planning and decision–making processes, the introduction of responsibility systems that enhanced individual accountability for performance, and the encouragement of private and foreign–invested enterprises. In place of the old Soviet–style command economy model (see Kaple, 1994), a pragmatic 'socialist market economy', as it was known in official usage, became *de rigueur* (see Naughton, 1995). Whether China's leaders had a clear strategy at the time is hard to know. Deng had long been accused of being a 'capitalist roader' but would have probably been decidedly surprised as to where the reforms had led even five years after his death! The description of 'Confucian Capitalism', often heard these days when referring to the business system found in the new China, may be apt but it is too soon to decide whether this description is accurate and the *definitive* future of Chinese management.

For decades under Mao's influence China had closed in on itself, but by officially joining the international economic community it entered another epoch even potentially one of globalization. Economies of scale and scope depend on globalizing markets, where multinational corporations (MNCs) endeavour to buy and sell as far and wide as they can. The WTO seeks to shape the rules of the game, in order to regulate and police this process and to make it more orderly. The intention is to extend global markets beyond goods to services and to parts of the world they did not reach because of the 'developmental state'. Critics of globalization do not endorse this strategy and think it is a form of neo–imperialism (see Warner, 2002).

Most of the Asian Pacific countries have arguably been statist in their development strategies (see Whitley, 1991; Wilkinson, 1994) with some exceptions like the Hong Kong Special Administrative Region (HKSAR).[2] Here, China is the most extreme case, with its own highly specific institutional framework 'with Chinese characteristics', a term we will explore at greater length shortly. At the present time, China's billion and a quarter population and vast labour force, the largest in the world (see Warner, 1995) puts human resources high on the agenda as far as WTO entry is concerned (see Warner, 2002).

Growing pressure in this domain comes from sister international governing bodies, such as the International Labour Organization (ILO), and international labour union bodies, such as the International Confederation of Free Trade Unions (ICFTU), over the issues of employment standards, labour law and the like, as well as more generally human rights, social protection and political reform in China. The role of trade unions, held together by the All–China Federation of Trade Unions (ACFTU), with over 100 million members, is a contentious one. Whilst union membership is optional in law, it has been mainly concentrated in SOEs, especially the larger ones, although much of the non–state sector is not unionized; today, the ACFTU has less and less chance of entering firms as the non–state sectors in the economy have been expanding, for examples Town and Village Enterprises (TVEs) and privately–owned firms (see Ding *et al.*, 2000). Union representation in the larger International Joint Ventures (IJVs) may be found where they are linked to SOEs but are less likely to be found in Wholly Owned Foreign Enterprises (WOFEs).

The topic of globalization, underlined by China joining the world trade body and how Chinese management will have to confront it *proactively*, we may argue more or less ties neatly together many of the strands of the various contributions to this collection of essays on *The*

Future of Chinese Management set out earlier. The participating authors covered a wide range of cutting–edge research topics, including Human Resource Management, Industrial Relations, Joint Ventures, WTO entry, highlighting the two decades or so of reforms consequent to Deng's major policy shift in 1978. Rather than speculate on open–ended future developments, the contributors have looked at empirically researched key topics in the management field that would illustrate state of the art practices in different ownership contexts that are likely to become *de rigueur* in the near future. If the 'future' is the focus of this symposium, the time horizon is perhaps the next decade rather than beyond. We are cautious in our assessment in the set of conclusions, drawing only tentative inferences from current research.

There are a number of major challenges implicit in the contributions to this collection that will face Chinese managers as they approach their daily tasks after WTO entry and provide clues to the future of Chinese management, the long-term impact of the SARS virus notwithstanding.

The first of these is likely to be changes in the external economic environment. For a start, with WTO entry, barriers against foreign imports will fall over the coming years. It is hoped that this will stimulate the already buoyant level of imports and exports and enhance the linkages between the external economic environment and the internal one. The second is likely to be major changes in the internal economic environment itself over the coming decade. An increase in internal competition will lead to fundamental changes in how enterprises respond to both demand and supply factors. The third is likely to be changes in business goals and how to achieve them, that is, mainly in the organizational strategy and structure of the enterprises themselves. The effect of external and internal economic changes will most likely lead to a decisive shift from a strategy that is reactive to one that is *proactive*, although this is not to say some firms and their managers do not already adopt the latter stance already. The fourth is the effects of the above on Chinese managers and the development of a managerial culture at an enterprise level that may be initially 'transitional' after the initial wave of economic reforms and only partly performance–based, evolving to one that is significantly performance–based.

These four factors may be seen to be connected in a diamond–shaped relationship and may have interactions with each other (see Figure 1), perhaps mostly one–way in that the economic environmental changes will tend to be the *independent* variables. In the background of the diamond, we have placed the key influences of Tradition, Society, Economy and Polity (State/Party). Although we emphasize economic environmental changes as the main drivers of organizational and managerial behaviour, we do not underestimate the role particularly of State/Party influence as the ultimate lever of macro–level policy, given the way China is still governed. The effects of changes in the respective main *dependent* variables in the diamond, such as organizational strategy and structure (we postulate the latter follows the former) as well as managerial culture, will not be felt immediately but may occur *over time*, often unevenly. Similarly, there may already have been influences in train that have been causing change for some time, say, in the period building up to formal WTO entry. The external economic environment was becoming more open in any event; the internal economic environment was already undergoing structural reform; the managerial culture had been evolving in order to adapt to the market forces that have been unleashed since 1978. We hope to explore these themes in greater detail below, in each of the following sections.

FIGURE 1
RELATIONSHIPS BETWEEN EXTERNAL AND INTERNAL ECONOMIC
ENVIRONMENTS, ORGANIZATIONAL STRATEGY, STRUCTURE AND
MANAGERIAL CULTURE

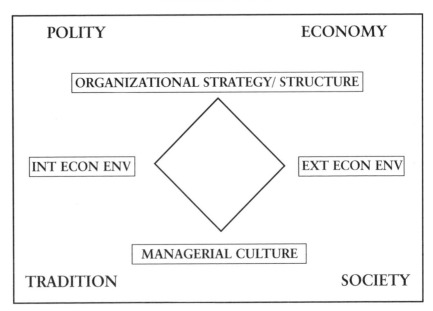

CHANGES IN THE EXTERNAL ECONOMIC ENVIRONMENT

The future of Chinese management will, we believe, most heavily depend on the changes in the external economic environment. The main effect of the latter will be to link China even further to the international economy and the processes of globalization, noted above, now sweeping the world (see Warner, 2002).

On the assumption that international trade will continue to grow, the consequences here for China are likely to be considerable. The Chinese leaders have taken a calculated gamble that the *net effect* on not only the Chinese economy but also the wider society and even its polity will be positive. If the original 'Open Door' policy was the major catalyst for change over almost all the last quarter-century, the new démarche will no doubt be at least as significant.

As the authors of a new study of WTO entry put it: 'This [policy] is a high–stakes game for all concerned. The major risk incurred by China is the potentially disruptive social implications of carrying out, within a decade or so, the wholesale adaptation of its economic, institutional and social structure to a still untested brand of market–led competition. China's trading partners risk significant shifts in relative competitive advantage.' (Magarinos *et al.*, 2002:1).

Amplifying what we set out in the introduction to this symposium, we see that China's economy grew apace in 2002 vis–à–vis both external as well as internal dimensions. According to official figures, US$50 billion of new investment was attracted from abroad; goods exported rose by over 20 per cent. Gross Domestic Product (GDP) rose by almost 8 per cent and retail sales by nearly 9 per cent (Becker, 2003:8). Deflation was endemic and consumer prices only rose by under one half of 1 per cent. By contrast, the growth in GDP in the US was only 3.2 per cent in 2002 and a mere 0.8 per cent in the Euro–area (see *The Economist*, 25 Jan. 2003, p.110). The savings ratio was the highest in East Asia at 43.5 per cent of GDP. But the indebtedness of the state–owned sector has not gone away and the financial health of the domestic banking sector cannot be viewed with complacency. Although Chinese official statistics may vary by 1 per cent or so in accuracy, according to the optimists, others, like the US economist, Rawski, are more sceptical of what they see reported (as noted in *The Economist*, 14 March 2002, p.64).

It is estimated that China's exports have grown fourfold over the 1990s, from US$ 62 billion to US$ 250 billion and may go up from a quarter of GDP to one half in the present decade. It is now the largest exporter to the US market. China's economy did not catch the 'Asian 'flu' during the 1997 crisis. By 2002, her foreign reserves exceeded US$ 200 billion. By 2005, with WTO entry bedded–down, it is predicted that import tariffs will fall to around 10 per cent, on a par with open neighbouring economies in Asia (see Becker, 2003, p.8). It is clear that this will have a major impact on the domestic economy.

THE INTERNAL ECONOMIC ENVIRONMENT

There are several changes in the internal economic environment that will affect Chinese management. One important strand, we would strongly argue, has been the 'marketization' of the Chinese economy. Most factors of production are now responsive to market forces to a degree unimaginable in the early days of the reforms. Broadly speaking, managers now have to respond to market signals. Second, the extent of structural reform in the Chinese economy has also been remarkable by any measure, although there still remain grey areas. Even so, much of the loss–making state sector has been reformed and pruned but there is a way to go yet on this point. By and large, since the late 1970s, China has pursued an industrial policy of phasing out its ailing state–owned enterprises (SOEs) (see Laaksonen, 1988; Lu and Perry, 1997; Lee *et al.*, 1999) and has attempted to build up competitive large firms (Nolan, 2001), by way of 'corporatization' (the word 'privatization' had been more or less taboo until recently) and able to hold their own in the global market. Third, the optimist would further point to the deepening and widening of the economic reforms in the last decade. Not only factor but also factor markets have been made responsive to market forces (see Korzec, 1992). Market efficiency must now take precedence over political considerations – the role of the Party has been reduced in enterprise–level decision making – but even here not a few managers in the state sector still live in a world of government support and state direction. To beat the system, 'bureaucratic entrepreneurs' have set up new businesses to find new sources of revenue (see Tang and Ward, 2003, pp.59–60). But structural reform will have to be qualitatively different in the coming years, less extensive and more focused, with more emphasis on the service sector in general and high–value added services, as well as products, in particular (see Magarinos *et al.*, 2002, pp.4–5).

Next, the *diversification of ownership* in the economic structure has made a critical impact on both enterprises and their managers, through their business strategy, structure as well as their managerial culture (see Tang and Ward, 2003, pp.132ff). The state sector underwent amalgamations in the 1990s holding on to big firms but letting go of small ones. This policy was directly bound up with changing ownership structure (*gaizhi*). As a result, there is now a variety of new, often 'hybrid', ownership forms in Chinese business (Tang and Ward,

2003, p.132). As we have seen in earlier contributions in this collection, for example, Human Resource Management (HRM) practices, as well as decision–making in joint ventures, are day by day becoming more like those in Western companies; equally, the changing level of 'trust' in firms may also depend on the nature of the firm's ownership. Last, the degree of competition in the internal economic environment was a major determinant not only of the firm's strategy and structure but also of managerial culture. More competition meant managers had greater challenges in both manufacturing sector firms, as well as in the service sector, as WTO entry as we have seen meant more foreign businesses entering their markets.

Formal accession to the trade body holds out the promise of enhanced economic growth and expanded exports; on the other hand, the threat to Chinese workers' jobs cannot be underestimated but at the same time cannot be accurately estimated either (see Solinger, 2001; 2002). According to official figures, 26 million SOEs employees were laid–off (*xiagang*) between 1998 and mid–2002 (*People's Daily*, overseas edition, 12 Nov. 2002). The number officially unemployed was 14 million in 2002. The official rate of urban unemployment reached 4.5 per cent but adding in those laid–off, it rises to around 7 per cent; unofficial estimates suggest a figure of over 10 per cent urban joblessness.[3] Vis-a-vis the increasing number of unemployed, the number of re–employed has not improved. For example, the official figures show that the rate of 're–employment' continued to fall from 50 per cent in 1998 to 42 per cent in 1999, and then further declined to 35 per cent in 2000 and 31 per cent in 2001.There are many who think the number losing their jobs will rise in future years.[4]

Wang Dongjin, Vice-Minister of Labour and Social Security, noted that the number of urban jobless would rise to more than 20 million over the next four years (O'Neill, 2002). The problem may be exacerbated by China's entry to the WTO, with even more peasants likely to flock to cities to find work, amid the increased commercial competition. China will therefore face serious structural imbalances, with an abundant supply of low–skilled workers mismatched with a greater demand for skilled professionals. On the assumption that there are probably more than 20 million surplus urban industrial workers yet to be dismissed, SOE restructuring and WTO entry may yet have further negative impacts (see Newton and Subbaraman, 2000, p.42). In the next few years, the Chinese economy needs to generate 8–10 million new jobs for the new entrants on the labour market and 5 million for the displaced SOE workers (see Asian Development Bank, 2002, p.28). At least 100 million new posts need to be created over the coming decade, according to another estimate (see Magarinos *et al.*, 2002:3).

CHANGES IN ORGANIZATIONAL STRATEGY AND STRUCTURE

The main effect of changes in the both external and internal economic environments on management will be on the latter's strategy, as well on its culture. As the new economic environments become more competitive, we can expect this to be mirrored in strategic responses at enterprise management level vis-à-vis the former SOE–based work unit (*danwei*) model (see Lu and Perry, 1997). As organizational strategy – and no doubt structure – shift, firms and their managers may be under greater pressures to better adapt to the new market forces and to improve their performance. 'Formalization' and a more systematic approach to transmitting and sharing information, as Jolly points out earlier in this volume, increasingly redefine the 'framework of managerial authority and responsibility' (see Tang and Ward, 2003, p.196). Western joint ventures and wholly–owned firms rely heavily on *formal* methods of authority and control; Japanese ones try to promote this by building strong *informal* corporate and managerial cultures.

In China, the 'iron rice bowl' system (see Warner, 1995; Walder, 1986; Lu and Perry, 1997; Ding *et al.*, 2000) is more or less being phased out, as it enters an era of greater openness in its product and factor markets, with the WTO entry and accompanying flood of foreign direct investment. As we have seen in the contributions preceding this concluding essay, performance–driven rewards systems are being more extensively adopted. Social security has also been diluted – with the demise of the 'iron rice bowl' – and is now dependent on individual workers' contributions added to by the employers, if available at all. Collective contracts offer the prospect of a nascent collective bargaining system in a number of contexts. More MNCs will establish their business operations in China and the more so–called 'international standardized HRM' policies and practices will be implemented in their Chinese ventures, albeit with certain modifications. On the other hand, organizational inertia may of course place a brake on a convincing degree of change in a fair number of enterprises, particularly SOEs, adapting as fast as others.

According to one piece of evidence, Jolly cites in this volume a specific empirical example, the distribution of roles for decision–making observable in Sino–foreign International Joint Ventures (IJVs) appears to be no different from the traditional pattern existing in the West: the board of directors deals with strategic decisions, company general managers with functional decisions and department heads with operational decisions. Interestingly, and contrary to his hypothesis (see the text presented earlier) strategic decisions, he argues, appear to be taken not jointly, but are dominated by the foreign partner. Examination of barriers and incentives to knowledge exchange showed that *exogamic* differences between Chinese and foreign partners act as barriers. These differences encompass cultural and language differences, different approaches to management as well as unwillingness to share technology. On the contrary, business perspectives may act more and more as incentives in the dynamic process of knowledge transfer.

Third–country nationals do not necessarily have superior cross–cultural skills compared with parent–country nationals, as another contribution makes clear. Selmer argues that the reverse may be true for regional third–country nationals in terms of work adjustment. Second, regional third–country nationals may not be better adjusted than their non–regional counterparts, or even parent–country nationals. In fact, regional third–country nationals may be even less well adjusted to their work than both other groups of expatriates. Although primarily concerning foreign companies in China, he concludes that these insights may also comprise a powerful message to MNCs in general not to take anything for granted in future years when building up their international workforce.

Again, dealing with another important theme, Supervisory Boards should be increasingly important governance mechanisms in major firms in China, according to Xiao *et al.* in this collection; that is because of the contradiction between government direct intervention in corporate affairs and the spirit of economic reform, because of the need for balancing the power of insiders who control most listed companies, because of the lack of a market for corporate control, and because of the young audit profession which is perceived to lack independence. The authors propose that Supervisory Boards be given additional powers as well as granting greater independence by amending company law. The legal responsibilities of the Supervisory Board should be clearly prescribed. They also argue that further economic and political reforms are needed to reduce government control over corporate affairs. In addition, China may consider replacing the two–tier board with a unitary board or incorporate some of its elements into the two–tier board structure in future years.

As we have seen in the preceding essays here, managers will have to maintain a harmonious working relationship between expatriates and locals, and between overseas Chinese and mainland Chinese, and to retain the motivation and loyalty of the existing managers to prevent them from being headhunted by competitors. They will also have to strike a balance between fulfilling international standards and maintaining product competitiveness, as we have seen in the

FIGURE 2
PROACTIVE AND REACTIVE STRATEGY IN CHINESE FIRMS

		OWNERSHIP	
		State–owned	*Non–State–owned*
STRATEGY	Reactive	(+)	(–)
	Proactive	(–)	(+)

contributions on WTO entry. Apart from the high costs of implementing international standards, some importing countries may use the latter as non–trade barriers to protect their local industries. The transaction costs for managers to comply with all these national standards are even higher than for the international standards involved in the process.

The post–WTO strategy of enterprises will be more proactive than in the pre–reform ones but this may vary according to the ownership dimension (see Figure 2). Strategy, structure and managerial culture in Chinese business organizations may also be mutually interactive, in that a change in the former may affect the latter and even vice–versa.

CHANGES IN MANAGERIAL CULTURE

The main effect of changes in the both external and internal economic environments on management will be a recognizable shift from a culture that was not individually performance–based, to one that is ostensibly decidedly so. But this change may have already started earlier as we suggested above. We believe that there will be a spectrum of change over time, such that there will be the pre–reform model at one extreme and the post–WTO one at the other, with one or more transitional stages in between (see Figure 3). The number of firms to be found in each category will depend on the rate of change and also the degree of *organizational inertia*.

Deng had explicitly promoted the building of market socialism 'with Chinese characteristics', an economic leap forward but within recognizable, older (often traditional) cultural parameters (see Kim, 1994; Sklair, 1994; Yao, 2002). It was a further step towards China's 'search for modernity' (see He, 2002) but still holding onto 'Chineseness'. In embarking on this, China has to evolve new *institutional norms* in its economy and management (see Scott, 2002).

Chinese society today is the result of a long process of adaptation to changes in its cultural environment. Its core–structures have perhaps persisted as the 'bed–rock' of the Chinese system on the Mainland, as well as among the Overseas Chinese (*nanyang*), but had been arguably submerged for many decades by post–1949 layers of institutional change as the People's Republic built up its infra–structure and super–structure. The core of the aforementioned characteristics was actively suppressed for many years under Mao but was, we would argue, so strong it prevailed as an under–current in many important ways and re–surfaced in recent decades as the system became more 'open' under the post–1978 reforms.

A good example which might come to mind here is 'relational networking' based on inter–personal connections (referred to in Chinese as *guanxi*) as a 'co–ordination' mechanism that we can find in both socialist and capitalist Chinese organizations. This cultural practice is basically East Asian; it is very much ascriptive, communitarian, and particularistic and hence akin to the closer–knit *Gemeinschaft*, as distinct from the looser–knit societal *Gesellschaft* type of integration in the West, as sociologists often characterize it. It shows up the persistence of Chinese societal patterns, in spite of changes from Imperial rule to Republican, from Revolutionary to Reformist. Indeed, such is the *continuity* that the regime under Mao was seen as 'Confucian Leninism' (Pye, cited in Warner, 1995, p.147), as we find 'Confucian Capitalism' (see Yao, 2002) referred to earlier, as a possible descriptor for today's system.

A number of characteristics that are ostensibly 'Chinese' come mind here – but may be also found elsewhere in East Asia – in the management context. Key characteristics such as *collectivism, hierarchy, harmony, loyalty,* and *strategic thinking* can, for instance, be found in management systems in China as well as in the Overseas Chinese business community or Korea and Japan. These characteristics are reflected, for example, in culturally-based practices such as group-oriented production activities (teamwork), group-based performance evaluation and incentives, relatively close salary differentials between management and employees, co-operative and harmonized labour–management relations, and seniority-based wage systems (in particular during the pre-reform systems). In addition, strategic thinking and management policies have to deal proactively with such changes, in particular during the period of economic transition.

The 'pre–reform' managerial culture associated with 'Confucian-Leninism' and its command economy (Kaple, 1994; Naughton, 1995; Warner, 1999) is already withering away. The pre–reform model had embodied the 'three old irons' (see Warner, 2000): the 'iron rice bowl' which refers to life–time employment, 'iron wages' which refer to the fixed rewards system, and the 'iron chair' which refers to the inflexible positions of cadres and managers. It was related to institutional norms that characterized labour management in a particular historical setting (see Warner, 1995, 1999, 2000). Breaking the 'three old irons' was important because the economic reform process called for greater efficiency in factor allocation, with labour flexibility a priority.[5] In recent years, both increasing global competition and the recent financial crises have forced enterprises to adopt more flexible policies and management systems.

The 'post–WTO' managerial culture associated with the market economy is likely to become more characteristic of Chinese business. Xin *et al.* found that organizational cultures in Chinese SOEs had differences from those developed in the West as well as some similar features (Xin *et al.*, 2002). It has evolved within a new institutional context of contracts, incentives and rewards. It may not be as individual–based in its values as in the Western paradigm it often seeks to emulate but may blend both individualist and collectivist ones (as in Taiwan). In doing so, it will probably however still retain a high degree of 'Chineseness'.

FIGURE 3
CHANGES IN CHINESE MANAGERIAL CULTURE OVER TIME

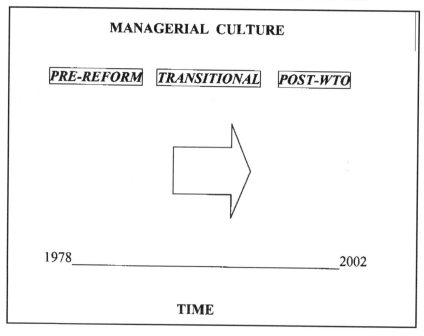

Domestic and privately owned firms, joint ventures and foreign wholly owned–enterprises will constitute the *avant–garde* of Chinese business. Some SOEs will also be pioneers of 'cutting–edge' practice. However, a residual number of enterprises will continue to have 'transitional' characteristics, partly due to organizational inertia and partly due to ownership. The less reformed, older state–owned enterprises will probably fall into this category where reform has sometimes been 'more cosmetic rather than real' (Tang and Ward, 2003, p.63); firms in the non–state sector may be less likely to be found described so. New hybrid ownership forms now abound, with town and village enterprises (TVEs) and privately owned ones (PEs) burgeoning. Sometimes the ownership forms are blurred, with a firm registered in collective ownership but in effect being privately owned – the so–called 'red hat' phenomenon of a private capitalist boss in effect running the company and pretending officially to be a local government cadre manager (Tang and Ward, 2003, p.107ff).

Managerial culture and specific manager values may also vary between the regions and cities of China (see Ralston *et al.*, 1996; 1999a; 1999b). The north–east (*dongbei*), where the SOEs were more dominant, produced industrial bureaucrats; whereas eastern coastal cities and the south–east ones brought forth more entrepreneurial types. We can thus say that the managerial culture in cities like Shanghai and even more so in Guangzhou will probably be more likely to be more individualistic and ready to take risks, than those from inland in say, Chengdu or Lanzhou (see Ralston *et al.*, 1996), let alone Shenyang in the northern 'rust belt'.[6]

DISCUSSION AND EVALUATION

On the one hand, we cannot assume that there will be explicit 'convergence' between Chinese and Western management models, but on the other we must not assume that very distinct often tradition–based cultural differences will be effaced. There may be well a significant degree of 'relative convergence', or even 'cross–vergence' (that is, values overlapping between cultures) involved here (see Ralston *et al.*, 1996, for example).

The changing political environment, reformed legal frameworks and economic pressure have added new dimensions of HRM (see Poole, 1997; Pange, 1999). However, there is overwhelming evidence that shows traditional Chinese culture (see Warner, 2000) having a profound influence on HRM policies and practices, as well as political, economic and historical factors. The argument from the weight of tradition and the pervasiveness of 'culture' would point to greater 'family resemblances' between mainland China and its Taiwanese neighbour, for example. The SOE sector would drastically shrink in number and importance; IJVs or foreign–owned firms would be prominent; private firms would become more predominant. Chinese management may evolve into something akin to the overseas Chinese model – which itself is also evolving; this may well become the path for the future. Yet Nolan's (2001) magisterial work on Chinese big business concludes with a number of possible scenarios (pp.897–933) emanating from WTO entry ranging from the most to the least benign. He points to 'high–quality, ambitious Chinese large enterprise managers seeking to build a powerful 'national team' of large corporations (p.926) and concludes that is at least conceivable (p.933), whilst nonetheless reserving judgement.

As Child and the present author have noted elsewhere (see Child and Warner, 2003) Chinese managers and employees who are exposed to 'Western' values possibly through their work role, or as consumers, may keep open the option to segment their cultural outlook and switch between them. For example, if fitting–in to certain Western norms and practices offers material attractions, such as larger pay–packets in return for taking on individual responsibility for performance, then Chinese managers and employees may decide to go along with them within the constraints of their workplace roles. They may also be encouraged to accept norms and practices imported from another culture if these are perceived to be part of a more comprehensive policy, justified as 'best international practice', offering other benefits such as equitable treatment, comprehensive training, and good prospects for advancement. This may be why Chinese managers prize jobs with a joint venture or a subsidiary. Simultaneously, as they possibly switch social identities in 'converting' to their non–work roles in the family and community, they could well revert back to a more traditional Chinese culture–based outlook (see Child and Warner, 2003).

Broadly speaking, Chinese managers have become both more professional and more reactive. Training and development, in larger firms at least, has improved considerably. Recruitment from both domestic and foreign business schools has grown impressively, particularly in the 'cutting–edge' former state owned joint stock companies, as well as in large IJVs and wholly–owned foreign enterprises (WOFEs), in the past decade.

Managers have to use their human resources more professionally in Chinese firms. A good example of this is the deployment of performance evaluation and performance–based rewards systems. Many Chinese managers may also be involved in tripartite industrial relations more often in some instances, although grass–roots union influence is on the wane. Management knowledge–sharing and decision–making have become more sophisticated, at respectively strategic, functional and operational levels. Expatriate third country managers have become more common in mainland firms. Corporate governance in major Chinese corporations has taken the form of the Supervisory Board but they now should be given more independence and a unitary board might be considered preferable to a two–tier one. Greater employee and managerial trust may be built up as more private firms become the norm. With WTO entry, managers in the manufacturing sector will have to strike a balance between fulfilling domestic and international standards and retaining competitiveness. In the service sector, managers will have fewer restraints from home market and institutional factors but more from foreign competition.

IMPLICATIONS

The main implications for managers and policy–makers from the findings in this collection of essays related to expecting a set of new opportunities as well new challenges. The new opportunities relate to more open and competitive markets on the demand side, as well as greater flexibility in factor markets on the supply side. As far as management and managers (or even just employees) are concerned, the demand for better–qualified people will battle against the limited but expanding supply of highly skilled human resources.

There are still too few Chinese managers with appropriate managerial skills, especially in functional areas like accounting, auditing, finance, HRM, marketing, operations and so on. Management (as opposed to 'cadre') education in China has come a long way from being a novelty, as it was in the 1980s (see Warner, 1992). Most major Chinese universities now sport MBA–awarding business schools; many other lesser institutions produce tens of thousands of business graduates a year but of lesser quality. Even so, Shanghai's high–flying China–Europe International Business School (CEIBS) is rated as one of the best in Asia. Some but not all the Chinese students sent abroad to study management now return home. But as Nolan (2001: 920) argues, the prospects for Chinese global corporate champions appearing are uncertain in the least benign scenario. 'Privatization', he continues, may lead to takeovers of domestic firms by foreign competitors or bankruptcy.

While WTO entry has many implications for managers and policy makers, the main thrust of the economic reforms had already transformed ways of doing business in China, even prior to the formal signing in late 2001. The external and internal economic environmental changes had already created factor and product markets. Key 'red chip' firms, even former SOEs, now joint stock companies like *Haier* (domestic appliances), *Founder* (publishing software), *Legend* (computers), *SINOPEC* (petrochemicals) and so on, had introduced competitive strategic and structural changes in many instances. Not a few of these more entrepreneurial, former SOEs have seen their shares quoted on domestic and sometimes overseas stock markets. Managerial culture in the new wave of competitive corporations had become more attuned to the new economic ethos. The contributions to this symposium have borne adequate witness to this *status quo ex post*.

The WTO entry scenario is not wholly a 'paradigm shift' in any absolute sense, however. Here, both indigenous, as well as Western and East Asian managers in China and outside, have to come to terms with the new state of play. Asian, especially overseas Chinese *nanyang*, firms are rushing in to set up even more manufacturing plants on the mainland; Japanese corporations are signing mutual marketing arrangements with Chinese firms; Taiwan. for instance, has become more economically enmeshed with China and now over 400,000 of its citizens are reported to be working in the Shanghai area alone. The economic models that have worked in East and South East Asia for decades are now being increasingly discarded, as investors, entrepreneurs and managers are drawn into the post–WTO China syndrome.

CONCLUDING REMARKS

To sum up, management in China has changed significantly since the 'Open Door' and 'Four Modernization' reforms were introduced in 1978, despite any caveats to the contrary, referring to lags in the system and not infrequent organizational inertia. Much of this evolution has directly resulted from changes in both the internal and external economic environments, as we have seen above, culminating in the WTO entry in December 2001, perhaps the culminating achievement of the now formally outgoing Prime Minister, Zhu Rongji and retired President, Jiang Zemin.

The resulting impact on businesses, particularly on their strategy and structure, as well as managerial culture, has been considerable by any criteria, compared with the days of the command economy and the *danwei* enterprise model, described earlier in this contribution. Western and Japanese inward investment, techniques and practices have launched a 'second industrial revolution'. 'Hardware' technology transfer has been accompanied by 'software equivalents'. What the Chinese refer to as 'modern management' has been implanted. Clearly, much has been learnt from 'best practice' abroad.

How far Chinese management will 'converge' with its Western (or for that matter, Japanese) counterparts in future years is still moot (see Child, 2002a and 2002b; Warner, 2002). The path Chinese management takes may be no straightforward projection of present trends. Extrapolation of what is happening currently is often problematic. But present 'cutting–edge' practices may provide pointers and the future trajectory may very well lay in the direction of 'relative convergence', or even 'cross–vergence', although a recognizable degree of 'Chineseness', emanating from the rich cultural heritage of past times (see Warner, 2003), may remain.

NOTES

1. Its WTO entry on 11 December 2001was a key event in modern Chinese tradition; it was the 143rd member to join. Such a move would have been hard to imagine two decades ago.
2. The former British colony was 'handed–over' to the PRC in July 1997, becoming a 'Special Administrative Region' (SAR). Five years have passed and it remains essentially a lightly regulated 'capitalist' enclave. Its economic growth has been muted in recent years mainly due to the backwash of the Asian financial crisis of 1997 and subsequent fluctuations in international trade in the region.
3. For a recent account of unemployment in China and Hong Kong, see Lee and Warner, 2001.
4. Attempts at re–employment of *xiagang* workers have met with mixed success; in Shanghai, around a third of displaced workers were helped to find new jobs. The attempts to diffuse this system across other parts of China have yielded even less encouraging results. Nonetheless, the state agencies have adopted an 'active' labour market policy.
5. The demise of the 'iron rice bowl' is explored empirically in a recent paper (Ding *et al.*, 2000).
6. We may also note that there will probably be differences between the coastal provinces and the interior ones, as well as on the north–south axis (see Warner, 1995; Ding *et al.*, 2000).

REFERENCES

Asian Development Bank (2002), *Asian Development Outlook 2002*. Oxford: OUP.

Becker, J. (2003), 'Foreign Investment Spurs China's Economic Miracle', *The Business* (London), 5 Jan. p.8.

Child, J. (1994), *Management in China During the Age of Reform*. Cambridge: Cambridge University Press.

Child, J. (2002a), 'Theorizing About Organization Cross–Nationally: Part I An Introduction' in M. Warner and P. Joynt (eds.), *Managing Across Cultures: Issues and Perspectives*. London: Thomson Learning, pp.26–39.

Child, J. (2002a), 'Theorizing about Organization Cross–Nationally: Part II Towards a Synthesis' in M. Warner and P. Joynt (eds.), *Managing Across Cultures: Issues and Perspectives*. London: Thomson Learning, pp.40–56.

Child, J. and Warner, M. (2003), 'Culture and Management in China' in M. Warner (ed.) *Culture and Management in Asia*. London: RoutledgeCurzon.

Ding, D.Z., Goodall, K. and Warner, M. (2000), 'Beyond the Iron Rice Bowl: Whither Chinese HRM?', *International Journal of Human Resource Management*, Vol.11, No.2, pp.217–36.

Economist, The (various).

He P. (2002), *China's Search for Modernity: Cultural Discourse in the late 20th Century*. London: Palgrave and New York: St Martin's Press.

Holbig, H. and Ash, R. (2002), *China's Accession to the World Trade Organization: National and International Perspectives*. London: RoutledgeCurzon.

Kaple, D. (1994), *Dream of a Red Factory: The Legacy of High Stalinism in China*. (Oxford, Oxford University Press).

Kim, K–D. (1994), 'Confucianism and Capitalist Development in East Asia' in L. Sklair (ed.), *Capitalism and Development*. London: Routledge, pp87–106.

Korzec, M. (1992), *Labour and the Failure of Reform in China*. (London: Macmillan and New York: St Martin's Press).

Laaksonen, O. (1988), *Management in China During and After Mao* (Berlin: de Gruyter).

Lee, G.O.M., Wong, L. and Mok, K. (1999), *The Decline of State-Owned Enterprises in China: Extent and Causes*. Occasional Paper, no.2. Hong Kong: City University, December, 79pp.

Lee, G.O.M. and Warner, M. (2001), 'Labour Markets in "Communist" China and "Capitalist" Hong Kong: Convergence Revisited', *Asia Pacific Business Review*, Vol.8, No.1, pp.172–3.

Lu, X. and Perry, E.J. (1997), *Danwei: The Changing Chinese Workplace in Historical and Comparative Perspective*. Armonk: New York and London, M.E. Sharpe).

Magarinos, C.A., Long, Y. and Sercovich, F.C. (2002), *China in the WTO: The Birth of a New Catching-Up Strategy*. London: Palgrave and New York: St Martin's Press.

Naughton, B. (1995), *Growing out of the Plan: Chinese Economic Reform 1978–93*. Cambridge: Cambridge University Press.

Newton, A. and Subbaraman, R. (2002), *China: Gigantic Possibilities, Present Realities*. London: Lehman Brothers.

Nolan, P. (2001), *China and the Global Business Revolution*. London: Palgrave and New York: St Martin's Press.

O'Neill, Mark (2002), 'China warns of 20 million urban jobless', *South China Morning Post*, 30 April 2002, p.1.

Ostry, S., Alexandroff, A.S. and Gomez, R. (2002), *China and the Long March to Global Trade: The Accession of China to the World Trade Organization*. London: RoutledgeCurzon.

Pange, L. (1999), 'Human Resistance or Human Remains? How HR Management in China must Change', *China Staff: The Human Resources Journal for China and Hong Kong*, V, 8, July/Aug., pp.8–11.

Poole, M. (1997), 'Industrial and Labour Relations' in M.Warner (ed.), *IEBM Concise Encyclopedia of Business and Management*. London: International Thomson Business Press, pp.264–82.

People's Daily Overseas Edition, Nov. 12, p.1.

Ralston, D.A., Yu K., Wang X., Terpstra, R.H. and He W. (1996), 'The Cosmopolitan Chinese Manager: Findings of a Study of Managerial Values Across the Six Regions of China', *Journal of International Management*, Vol.2, No.1, pp.79–109.

Ralston, D.A., Van Thang, N. and Napier, N.K. (1999a), 'A Comparative Study of the Work Values of North and South Vietnamese Managers', *Journal of International Business Studies*, Vol.30, No.4, pp.655–72.

Ralston, D.A., Egri, C.P., Stewart, S., Terpstra, R.H. and Yu Kaicheng (1999b), 'Doing Business in the 21st Century with the New Generation of Chinese Managers: A Study of Generational Shifts', *Journal of the International Business Studies*, Vol.30, No.2, pp.415–28.

Scott, W.R. (2002), 'The Changing World of Chinese Enterprise: An Institutional Perspective' in A.S. Tsui and C–M. Lau (eds.), *The Management of Enterprises in the People's Republic of China*. Boston, Dordrecht and London: Kluwer Academic, pp.59–78.

Sklair, L. (1994), (ed.) *Capitalism and Development*. London: Routledge.

Solinger, D.J. (2001), 'Why We Cannot Count the "Unemployed"', *The China Quarterly*, No.167, p.683.

Solinger, D.J. (2002), 'Labour Market Reform and the Plight of the Laid-off Proletariat', *The China Quarterly*, No.170 p.304.

Tang, J. and Ward, A. (2003), *The Changing Face of Chinese Management*. London: Routledge.

Walder, A.G. (1986), *Communist Neo-Traditionalism: Work and Authority in Chinese Industry*. (Berkeley CA: University of California Press).

Warner, M. (1992), *How Chinese Managers Learn*. (London: Macmillan and New York: St Martins Press).

Warner, M. (1995), *The Management of Human Resources in Chinese Industry*. London: Macmillan and New York: St Martin's Press.

Warner, M. (ed.) (1999), *China's Managerial Revolution*. London: Frank Cass.

Warner, M. (ed.) (2000), *Changing Workplace Relations in the Chinese Economy*. London, Macmillan and New York: St Martin's Press.

Warner, M. (2002), 'Globalization, Labour Markets and Human Resources' in 'Asia-Pacific Economies: An Overview', *International Journal of Human Resource Management*, Vol.13, No.3, pp.384–98.

Warner, (ed.) M. (2003), *Culture and Management in Asia*, London: RoutledgeCurzon.

Whitley, R. (1991), 'The Social Construction of Business Systems in East Asia', *Organization Studies*, 12, 1, pp.1–28.

Wilkinson, B. (1994), *Labour and Industry in the Asia Pacific: Lessons from the Newly Industrialised Countries*. Berlin: de Gruyter.

Xin, K.R., Tsui, A., Wang, H., Zhang, Z.–X. and Chen, W.–Z. (2002), 'Corporate Culture in State-Owned Enterprises: An Inductive Analysis of Dimensions and Influences' in A. S. Tsui and C.-M. Lau (eds.), *The Management of Enterprises in the People's Republic of China*, Boston, Dordrecht and London: Kluwer Academic, pp.416–43.

Yao, S. (2002), *Confucian Capitalism: Discourse, Practice and Myth of Chinese Enterprise*. London: RoutledgeCurzon.

Abstracts

Introduction: Chinese Management in Perspective *by Malcolm Warner*
This introduction attempts to put Chinese management in perspective by surveying past and present developments and then looking forward. In it, the author focuses on the extent to which management in the People's Republic of China (PRC) has changed since the economic reforms were launched by Deng Xiaoping in 1978, how it has developed over the last two decades or so, and where its future lies as China enters the World Trade Organization (WTO). It covers a wide range of topics including human resource management, industrial relations, joint ventures, corporate governance, WTO entry and so on, highlighting the past two decades of change.

Human Resource Management 'with Chinese Characteristics': A Comparative Study of the People's Republic of China and Taiwan *by Malcolm Warner and Ying Zhu*
This study examines the management of human resources in two Chinese cultural settings, namely mainland China and Taiwan. It compares and contrasts the similarities and differences of human resource management (HRM) policies and practices in the two economies. The main conclusions assess the impact of changing cultural, political and economic norms on HRM in the respective settings and their likely future developments.

The Diffusion of Human Resource Management Practices among Chinese Firms: The Role of Western Multinational Corporations *by Ingmar Björkman*
Research has shown that Western multinational corporations tend to implement human resource management (HRM) practices in their Chinese units that are rather similar to those of the parent company. However, there is a paucity of research on the effects of the Western-style HRM introduced by foreign-owned firms on the diffusion of HRM practices among local Chinese organizations. This essay develops a range of testable propositions concerning factors impacting on the HRM practices used in Chinese organizations, both present and future.

The Significance of a System of Tripartite Consultation in China *by Simon Clarke and Chang-Hee Lee*
This contribution, based on interviews at national and municipal levels in May and June 2002, reviews the first stages of the implementation of the new system of tripartite consultation introduced in China in August 2001. The hypothesis to be

explored in the paper is that China is developing industrial relations institutions similar to those of developed capitalist societies. The conclusion is that it is premature to characterize tripartite consultation as a developed system of social dialogue and the main barrier to the achievement of such a system in future is identified as the dependence of the trade union on management in the workplace.

Sharing Knowledge and Decision Power in Sino-Foreign Joint Ventures *by Dominique Jolly*
Sino–foreign joint ventures are exogamic partnerships where allies combine resources of different kinds. This implies a sharing of decision power and induces possible sharing of knowledge. Strategic, functional and operational decisions were analysed. Empirical data were drawn from face-to-face interviews in 67 equity joint ventures. The investigation shows that the more the decision is important for the venture's future, the less it is shared; foreigners tend to exert an overwhelming influence on decision processes. Several factors interplay in the knowledge transfer dynamic: it is hampered by exogamic barriers (such as cultural differences and language obstacles) but stimulated by business perspectives.

Adjustment of Third Country National Expatriates in China *by Jan Selmer*
Despite claims of superior cross-cultural effectiveness of third country nationals, such assertions have never been corroborated by rigorous academic research. To test these claims empirically, data on the adjustment of Asian and Western third country nationals as well as Western parent country nationals were extracted from mail surveys directed to business expatriates assigned to China. It was found that Asian third country nationals were not better adjusted socioculturally compared with Western third-country nationals, nor were they better adjusted in this respect than the Western parent-country nationals. In fact, the reverse was true in terms of work adjustment, where the Asian third-country nationals were less well adjusted than both groups of Western expatriates. Implications of these fundamental and surprising findings for globalizing firms and future research are discussed in detail.

The Supervisory Board in Chinese Listed Companies: Problems, Causes, Consequences and Remedies *by Jay Dahya, Yusuf Karbhari, and Jason Zezong Xiao*
This study examines the function of the Supervisory Board in Chinese listed companies. The focus is on the main problems facing the Supervisory Board. The main hypothesis is that the transitional nature of the Chinese economy creates problems and obstacles that inhibit the effectiveness of the Supervisory Board. Data was collected by means of interviews with directors, supervisors, and senior executives in 16 listed companies and four panel discussions in China. Consistent with the hypothesis, the study finds that lack of legal power, lack of independence, lack of technical expertise, perceived low status, information shortage, and lack of incentives are the major problems facing Chinese supervisory boards. It proposes that supervisory boards be given additional powers as well as greater independence by amending the Company Law. It also argues that further economic and political reforms are needed to reduce government control over corporate affairs and improve the future effectiveness of the supervisory board.

Which Managers Trust Employees? Ownership Variation in China's Transitional Economy *by Yuan Wang*
Based on investigation of managers drawn from Northern China, this research contributes empirical evidence to support the proposition that the trust placed by

management in employees varies in divergent ownership models. These include collectively owned, privately owned and international joint venture forms in China. The managers in private forms have the highest trust in employee predictability and good faith. Managers in collective enterprises develop the lowest trust in employees. The managerial values of power distance and collectivism are also found to have an effect on the present and future development of trust by management in these forms of enterprises.

WTO Accession and the Managerial Challenges for Manufacturing Sectors in China *by Godfrey Yeung and Vincent Mok*

Based on 31 case studies, this study tests the validity of four major managerial hypotheses for manufacturers in China after WTO accession. It is argued that the skills of managers will be severely tested in four specific areas after China accedes to the WTO: (1) preparing for trade disputes with their overseas competitors, (2) developing newer and higher value-added products and diversifying their markets, (3) selecting the appropriate localization strategy, and (4) upgrading manufacturing processes and work practices to comply with international (and regional) standards, as well as being aware of overseas competitors using these standards as non-trade barriers. Managers also have to strike a delicate balance to deal with these interrelated challenges under the constraints of time and available resources.

China's Entry to the WTO: Prospects and Managerial Implications for Foreign Life Insurance Companies *by Man-Kwong Leung and Trevor Young*

The availability of business opportunities and the improving political environment of the Chinese economy are important factors determining the entry of foreign life insurance companies. The paper further argues that a foreign life insurer with certain attributes, viz. large assets and special links to Hong Kong, is more likely to enter the Chinese market. Although the impact of WTO entry on the Chinese life insurance industry will be mixed, the prospects for foreign life insurers are promising. A foreign life insurer is more likely to be profitable if it is able to make sound managerial decisions, based on the attributes facilitating its entry, in its choice of market niche and Chinese partner, its long-term planning, and its product and personnel management. Investment expertise will become a critical determinant of profitability only when there is full access to capital markets.

Conclusion: The Future of Chinese Management *by Malcolm Warner*

There are a number of challenges facing Chinese managers as they approach their daily tasks after WTO entry, and these provide clues to the future of Chinese management. They relate to both the external and internal economic environments, organizational strategy and structure, as well as the managerial culture. The future trajectory may lie in the direction of 'relative convergence' or even 'cross-vergence'.

Index

Other Titles in the Series

Work and Employment in a Globalized Era
An Asia-Pacific Focus

Yaw A Debrah and Ian G Smith,
both at Cardiff University Business School (Eds)

The book explores the multiple impacts of global competitive pressures brought about largely by globalization on employment relations in Pacific Asia. In particular, it examines the diverse ways through which global competitive pressures are systematically transforming workplace relations and impacting on the strategies of managers, and the responses and behaviours of trade unions and employees.

The volume brings together research from Australia, China, Japan, Malaysia, New Zealand and Singapore to illuminate our understanding of what is actually happening to organizations, workforces, employee groupings and individual employees as a result of globalization and the intensification of global competition in Pacific Asia.

272 pages 2001
0 7146 5135 4 cloth
0 7146 8162 8 paper
Studies in Asia Pacific Business Volume 10

FRANK CASS PUBLISHERS
Crown House, 47 Chase Side, Southgate, London N14 5BP
Tel: +44 (0)20 8920 2100 Fax: +44 (0)20 8447 8548 E-mail: info@frankcass.com
NORTH AMERICA
920 NE 58th Avenue Suite 300, Portland, OR 97213-3786 USA
Tel: 800 944 6190 Fax: 503 280 8832 E-mail: cass@isbs.com
Website: www.frankcass.com

Managed in Hong Kong

Adaptive Systems, Entrepreneurship and Human Resources

Chris Rowley, *City University Business School, London* and
Robert Fitzgerald, *Royal Holloway, University of London* (Eds)

Hong Kong achieved remarkable rates of growth and improvements in living
standards, yet, the interpretation of this at the level of politics, culture, human
capital, and business organization is less obvious. As the contributors make clear,
Hong Kong faced a new (and renewed in some instances) set of challenges
linked to the up-grading of human resources, shifts in industrial structure, and
emerging market demands. The authors examine and analyze aspects of business
and management in Hong Kong including systemic 'adaptability' and
entrepreneurship, education and training, cross-cultural variations in the
generation and meanings of organizational commitment and contrasting
international human resource management practices and ways of managing
people in the retail sector.

144 pages 2000
0 7146 5026 9 cloth
0 7146 8082 6 paper
Studies in Asia Pacific Business Volume 8

FRANK CASS PUBLISHERS
Crown House, 47 Chase Side, Southgate, London N14 5BP
Tel: +44 (0)20 8920 2100 Fax: +44 (0)20 8447 8548 E-mail: info@frankcass.com
NORTH AMERICA
920 NE 58th Avenue Suite 300, Portland, OR 97213-3786 USA
Tel: 800 944 6190 Fax: 503 280 8832 E-mail: cass@isbs.com
Website: www.frankcass.com

Human Resource Management in the Asia Pacific Region

Convergence Questioned

Chris Rowley,
City University Business School, London (Ed)

As a new millennium approaches, many politicians, commentators, academics, management gurus and business people have been increasingly casting their gaze towards Asia in the belief that the 'Pacific Age' is also beckoning.

The region's dynamism is seen as rooted in particular managerial practices, such as kaizen and Total Quality Management; in state intervention; or in cultural factors, notably Confucianism. An integral ingredient to all these factors is the management of 'human resources', with the 'human touch' seen to proffer key advantages in an era of globalization, market flux, competition by quality and service, and rapid transference of technologies.

Within the fashionable icon of human resource management, several debatable assumptions are sometimes made and often more heat than light has been shed. HRM often suffers from a selectivity tendency and ad hoc approach, which misses the historical, paradoxical and often incoherent, incompatible and inconsistent nature of the subject. This volume reduces this myopia by adding to our knowledge of HRM and the rich milieu within which it operates.

216 pages   1998
0 7146 4849 3 cloth
0 7146 4407 2 paper
Studies in Asia Pacific Business Volume 4
A special issue of the journal Asia Pacific Business Review

FRANK CASS PUBLISHERS
Crown House, 47 Chase Side, Southgate, London N14 5BP
Tel: +44 (0)20 8920 2100 Fax: +44 (0)20 8447 8548 E-mail: info@frankcass.com
NORTH AMERICA
920 NE 58th Avenue Suite 300, Portland, OR 97213-3786 USA
Tel: 800 944 6190 Fax: 503 280 8832 E-mail: cass@isbs.com
Website: www.frankcass.com